The Inimitable Qurʾān

Texts and Studies on the Qur'ān

VOLUME 15

The titles published in this series are listed at *brill.com/tsq*

The Inimitable Qur'ān

Some Problems in English Translations of the Qur'ān with Reference to Rhetorical Features

By

Khalid Yahya Blankinship

BRILL

LEIDEN | BOSTON

Cover illustration: Khaled Al-Saai, Master Calligrapher

Library of Congress Cataloging-in-Publication Data

Names: Blankinship, Khalid Yahya, author.
Title: The inimitable Qur'ān : some problems in English translations of the Qur'ān with reference to rhetorical features / by Khalid Yahya Blankinship.
Description: Boston : Brill, 2019. | Series: Texts and studies on the Qur'ān, 1567-2808 ; 15 | Includes bibliographical references and index.
Identifiers: LCCN 2019040943 (print) | LCCN 2019040944 (ebook) | ISBN 9789004412521 (hardback) | ISBN 9789004417441 (ebook)
Subjects: LCSH: Qur'an–Translating–Criticism, interpretation, etc. | Qur'an–Language, style.
Classification: LCC BP131.13 .B56 2019 (print) | LCC BP131.13 (ebook) | DDC 297.1/22521–dc23
LC record available at https://lccn.loc.gov/2019040943
LC ebook record available at https://lccn.loc.gov/2019040944

Typeface for the Latin, Greek, and Cyrillic scripts: "Brill". See and download: brill.com/brill-typeface.

ISSN 1567-2808
ISBN 978-90-04-41252-1 (hardback)
ISBN 978-90-04-41744-1 (e-book)

This book is printed on acid-free paper and produced in a sustainable manner.

Contents

Preface vii
Note on Transliteration xv

Introduction 1

1 Inversion of Word Order 41

2 *Iltifāt* 48

3 Indicative in Place of Imperative or Jussive 62

4 Indefinite Nouns 67

5 Non-Consequential Exception 72

6 Pleonasm and Redundancy 79

7 Repetition for Emphasis 83

8 Parallelism 94

9 Juxtaposition of Contrasting Conditional Sentences 111

10 Coordination 114

11 Lack of Conjunctive (Asyndeton) 124

12 Parenthesis (*iʿtirāḍ*) 133

13 Succinctness, or *ījāz al-qiṣar* 143

14 Ellipsis, or *ījāz al-ḥadhf* 152

Preface

The last five decades or so have seen a great reversal of fortune across the world as far as rhetoric is concerned. Before that time, rhetoric had indeed been neglected by Western scholars, except for a few, and most of the latter worked in languages other than English. Now, not only has rhetoric been rehabilitated in its own immediate province of language and literature, but it has also achieved a new relevance, if not dominance, in all the various fields of the humanities and social sciences, with some reference being made to it in the criticism of the natural sciences as well. This spectacular reversal has largely come about because of the development and spread of what may be loosely described as the postmodernist critique of modernist thought. Postmodernist critics have taken more notice of the effects that linguistic structures have on the content of what is conveyed in text. Furthermore, they have observed that language is full of ambiguities, so that a given narrative is unlikely to have a single undisputed, obvious, or correct interpretation. Because of such multiple possible interpretations or polysemy of texts, how the reader receives or interprets a text needs to be considered as well as the supposed original intention of the text or its author. This has usefully refocused attention on the problems of interpretation of texts, problems which are often related to underlying rhetorical structures that have been hitherto neglected.

While a great deal of work has been accomplished in Western rhetorical studies in the last fifty years, and a considerable number of modern Arabic-language rhetorical studies also continue to emerge, studies on the rhetoric of the Qurʾān, though increasing in number, remain comparatively sparse.[1] This is despite the importance that the Qurʾān has for Muslims, and despite the fact that Christians and Jews have produced a large literature of rhetorical analysis of various parts of the Bible. Partly, this relative lack of recent Muslim attention to the rhetorical structures of the Qurʾān may owe to the traditional form of the Qurʾānic exegesis or *tafsīr*, which tends to survey the Qurʾānic text verse by verse and to concentrate on the judicial implications of the individual verses.[2]

---

1 Philip Halldén, "What Is Arab Islamic Rhetoric? Rethinking the History of Muslim Oratory Art and Homiletics," *International Journal of Middle East Studies* 37, (2005), 19.

2 This classsical method of exegesis has started to be supplemented by new perspectives in recent times, however, for example, with the work *Fī ẓilāl al-Qurʾān* by the Egyptian literary critic Sayyid Quṭb (1324–1386/1906–1966), Beirut: Dār ash-Shurūq, 1394/1974, 6 vols. Larger structures of the Qurʾān have also been examined by Amīn Aḥsan Iṣlāḥī in his Urdu-language

The dearth of attention to rhetorical structures becomes even greater when our focus moves from the Arabic Qur'ān to the English translations of its meaning, for little analysis has been made of the various translations, and most of what has been done concentrates on "mistakes" in translation or ideological questions of interpretation rather than on the rhetorical structures themselves.[3] Thus, a work such as I have undertaken here is, I hope, now more timely than ever before.

My interest in the subject began with my first master's thesis, which I wrote at the American University in Cairo over forty-three years ago. However, the work before you, though incorporating some of that earlier effort, is a greatly expanded and more developed one. First, I now have more to say on the subject, both because of what I have learnt from new developments in rhetoric and because of my having had the opportunity to pursue a deeper and longer study of the Qur'ān and the English translations of its meaning. I have included many additional Arabic sources, including Ḍiyā' ad-Dīn Ibn al-Athīr's *al-Mathal as-sā'ir fī adab al-kātib wa-sh-shā'ir*, as-Sakkākī's *Miftāḥ al-'ulūm*, Najm ad-Dīn aṭ-Ṭūfī's *al-Iksīr fī 'ilm at-tafsīr*, al-Khaṭīb al-Qazwīnī's *al-Īḍāḥ fī 'ulūm al-balāghah*, and az-Zarkashī's *al-Burhān fī 'ulūm al-Qur'ān*, among others, all of which I was unaware of when I first wrote. Each of these is quite original and important. Furthermore, I have added references to parallel rhetorical features in Greek and Latin from ancient Greek and Roman rhetoricians where relevant. I have also updated my use of modern rhetorical studies, including more in Arabic than I previously used.

Beside rhetorical criticism, I have also now taken into account recent developments in translation theory, a field which has also mostly come into its own

commentary, *Tadabbur-i Qur'ān*, which is described in Mustansir Mir, *Coherence in the Qur'ān: A Study of Iṣlāḥī's Concept of Naẓm in Tadabbur-i Qur'ān*, Indianapolis: American Trust Publications, 1406/1986, and other examples could be cited in Arabic, English, and other languages as well.

3 For a fairly recent listing of Qur'ān translations in English, see Bruce Lawrence, *The Koran in English: A Biography*, Princeton: Princeton University Press, 2017, pp. 177–188. Lawrence also includes considerable commentary on and review of many of these translations, pp. 36–100 and *passim*. A similarly detailed but more selective description of such translations is found in Paula Youngman Skreslet and Rebecca Skreslet, *The Literature of Islam: A Guide to the Primary Sources in English Translation*, Lanham, MD: The Scarecrow Press, Inc. and American Theological Library Association, 2006, pp. 3–23. For a Muslim evaluation of Qur'ān translations to the present, see A.R. Kidwai, *Translating the Untranslatable: A Critical Guide to 60 English Translations of the Quran*. 1st ed. New Delhi: Sarup Book Publishers Pvt., 2011, and A.R. Kidwai, *God's Word, Man's Interpretations: A Critical Study of the 21st Century English Translations of the Quran*. New Delhi: Viva Books, 2018.

since I first wrote. In this effort, my work has been considerably informed and greatly helped by the work of Lawrence Venuti, a leading theorist on translation who is also my colleague at Temple University. I have particularly benefitted from his book *The Translator's Invisibility*, in which he shows that translation has always been a process strongly informed by ideology and a tendency to domesticate the foreign text for purposes that always have to do with the receiving society, even while those purposes can be quite varied.[4] Clearly, the work of every translator has to be considered in its historical and societal context.

Also, when I began to revise, I realized that it would have been better to deal with other translations of the Qurʾān beside those of Pickthall, Arberry, and Bell, the three that I almost exclusively concentrated on in my earlier work. The choice of these three may have been influenced by my mentor Dr. Mohammed al-Nowaihi, but ultimately also may derive from the original introduction to Arberry's translation of 1955, in which Arberry singles out Pickthall and Bell as important translations preceding his.[5] Although Pickthall has retained his importance considerably over the years, despite his archaic English, Bell is almost completely forgotten today, and even Arberry, despite his remaining in print and his continuing popularity as "the best translation" among many erudite non-Muslims, now has somewhat faded in popularity as well. While it has been possible to remedy this deficiency of coverage to some extent by adding further examples from some of the translations in wider use among the Muslims and in the world, especially those of ʿAbd Allāh Yūsuf ʿAlī and N.J. Dawood, and to a lesser extent those of Muhammad Ali and Muhammad Asad, it has been beyond my ability in this revision to deal with each of these translations fully or to add others that are likely to be equally or even more deserving of attention, such as those more recent ones by M.A.S. Abdel Haleem (2004), Thomas Cleary (2004), Ahmad Zaki Hammad (2007), Tarif Khalidi (2008), and the group under the chief editorship of Seyyed Hossein Nasr which produced *The Study Qurʾān* (2017).

Some parts of my work remain as originally written. The coverage of the original was limited mainly to features of Arabic rhetoric that are generally considered part of the rhetorical subdivision called *ʿilm al-maʿānī*, and that remains true of this revised version. Thus, I have dealt exclusively with syn-

4 Lawrence Venuti, *The Translator's Invisibility: A History of Translation*, 2nd ed. reissued with a new introduction, Abingdon, UK: Routledge, 2018, pp. xii–xiii.

5 Arthur J. Arberry, *The Koran Interpreted*, London: George Allen & Unwin, Ltd., 1955, Vol. I, pp. 20–24, Vol. II, pp. 11–12.

tactical structural features and have not included metaphor, simile, etc., which are considered to constitute *ʿilm al-bayān*. Out of the structural features of *ʿilm al-maʿānī*, I have selected some which seem particularly illustrative of the problems of translation into English. Through an analysis of these features using examples, I endeavor to show that not all the distaste of some English-speaking readers for the translated Qurʾān is attributable merely to dislike of the content, translation "mistakes," mechanical problems of grammar, or subjective differences of taste, but that much of it is because of substantial if sometimes subtle differences between the rhetorical systems of Arabic and English. Such a conclusion has implications far beyond mere academic linguistic matters. Indeed, it brings up the whole question of translation.

The art of translation has long been neglected and disparaged.[6] This has to a large extent owed to the demand for precision and fidelity of a translation to its original source text, to the exclusion of the translation being viewed as an independent work on its own. Thus, the best translator has been the self-effacing one who made himself or herself as absent and invisible as possible. Sometimes, the names of translators do not even appear anywhere in the books they have translated.[7] In this way, it has continued to be possible to believe one could read the "great books" of other languages in translation while feeling that one was reading the originals, a general belief that overlooks the fact that a translation can never be the same as an original, nor can it convey exactly the same meanings as the original, nor does it produce the same ethos as the original.[8] Conversely, free translations, unless they could achieve status as works of art in their own right, were frequently condemned for deviating from their originals.[9]

Today this situation has been partially reversed. Postmodern criticism has brought the process of translation to the very center of its concern, owing to the

6 Although this situation has been somewhat remedied recently by the recent emergence of the field of Translation Studies championed by Lawrence Venuti and others.

7 A recent example of an originally-anonymous Qurʾān translation is *The Qurʾān: Arabic Text with Corresponding English Meanings*, revised and edited by Saheeh International, Jeddah: Abul-Qasim Publishing House, 1997. This work contains no attribution at all to its translator or her assistants, except on a green sheet of errata stuck in the book, where it is disclosed that, in response to reader inquiries, the translator is an American woman named Umm Muḥammad living in Jiddah. Later editions are attributed anonymously to "three American women."

8 Venuti, *Invisibility*, 1, 6, 16, 47.

9 Willis Barnstone, *The Poetics of Translation: History, Theory, Practice*, New Haven: Yale University Press, 1993, pp. 89–95; Douglas Robinson, *The Translator's Turn*, Baltimore: The Johns Hopkins University Press, 1991, p. xiii.

realization that every reading of a text is a translation. That being the case, the process of translation no longer appears remote, foreign, or marginal to other literary concerns. Rather, literary translation from one language to another may now offer a paradigm of how we understand texts in general, even inside the same language. This has been observed and summed up most aptly and succinctly by the critic George Steiner (b. 1929) in his *magnum opus*, *After Babel*, where he states, "In short: *inside or between languages, human communication equals translation.* A study of translation is a study of language."[10] The usefulness of such a paradigm may be enhanced both by the vast historical record of literary translation going back nearly to the dawn of literate civilization and by the fact that the process of literary translation breaks down the processes of understanding and reproducing text into a long series of identifiable steps that can be examined in detail to show us how we read and comprehend. Thus, trying to understand how literary devices translate or fail to translate from one language to another may help us to understand the importance of rhetorical structures in language in general.

Such research also has considerable interest for Muslims and the field of Qur'ānic studies. Unlike the Christians with respect to the Bible, Muslims have always had an established principle, which continues to this day, never to accept translations of the meaning of the Qur'ān as scripture.[11] Thus, in Muslim religious practice as defined by the law, the readings from the Qur'ān recited in worship must be done in the original Arabic.[12] Attempts to promote the use of a translated Qur'ān as a valid liturgical scripture, such as that made by the

---

10 George Steiner, *After Babel: Aspects of Language and Translation*, 3nd ed., Oxford: Oxford University Press, 1998, p. 49. The italics are Steiner's.

11 Already mentioned by Abū Muḥammad ʿAbd Allāh b. Muslim Ibn Qutaybah, *Taʾwīl mushkil al-Qurʾān*, ed. by as-Sayyid Aḥmad Ṣaqr, Cairo: Dār at-Turāth, 1393/1973, p. 21. This point is also extensively discussed by Abū Isḥāq Ibrāhīm b. Mūsā al-Lakhmī ash-Shāṭibī, *al-Muwāfaqāt fī uṣūl al-aḥkām*, ed. Muḥammad al-Khiḍr Ḥusayn at-Tūnisī, Cairo: Dār Iḥyāʾ al-Kutub al-ʿArabiyyah (Fayṣal ʿĪsā al-Bābī al-Ḥalabī), [1969–1970], Vol. II, pp. 42–46. In modern times, it has been amply defended by Muḥammad Sulaymān in his *Ḥadath al-aḥdāth fī l-Islām: al-iqdām ʿalā tarjamat al-Qurʾān*, Cairo: al-Maṭbaʿah as-Salafiyyah, 1355/1936, a whole book by a traditional fourteenth/twentieth-century Egyptian *ʿālim* who marshals every text and every argument against translation, though he admits he can understand why speakers of other vernaculars than Arabic might like translations in their own tongues (pp. *sīn-ʿayn*). See also A.L. Tibawi, "Is the Qurʾān Translatable? Early Muslim Opinion," *The Muslim World* 52 (1962), 4–16.

12 Wahbah az-Zuḥaylī, *al-Fiqh al-islāmī wa-adillatuhu: ash-shāmil li-l-adillah ash-sharʿiyyah wa-l-ārāʾ al-madhhabiyyah wa-ahamm an-naẓariyyāt al-fiqhiyyah wa-taḥqīq al-aḥādīth an-nabawiyyah wa-takhrījihā*, 3rd ed., Damascus: Dār al-Fikr, 1409/1989, Vol. I, pp. 634, 655, 671; Vol. II, pp. 284–286, 289.

regime of Kamāl in Turkey in the 1930s, were not accepted and in fact completely defeated.[13] Indeed, written translations of the meaning of the Qur'ān in other languages generally were discouraged before the eighteenth century, although these were allowed in the form of interlinear translations for nobles who did not know Arabic. After that, a few translations began to appear in Persian and Urdu,[14] and by the twentieth century, with the advent of cheap printing and mass vernacular education, the trickle of translations became a flood. Today, with the rise of mass literacy and the worldwide reach of Qur'ān translations in the vernacular languages, however, the use of translations for private as opposed to liturgical reading has become widespread. In such a situation, it is surely relevant that postmodern literary theory, by placing so much emphasis on the subjectivity of the text and its reading, calls deeply into question the possibility of the fidelity of a translation to an original. If this is so, then the Muslims' unwillingness to accept a translated Qur'ān as scripture continues to make sense, for, however much our own reading of the Arabic text may distance us from the its original pronouncement and reception, there can be no question that our reading of a translator's reading puts us much farther away still. My study, by questioning the exact translatability of certain rhetorical features and effects from Arabic to English, likewise emphasizes the need for caution and reserve in taking a translation as a close representation of the original.

The idea for my exploration into such a neglected area as relative rhetorical structures began originally with my perusal of Robert Kaplan's attempt to classify systems of rhetoric, particularly his comments on parallelism in Arabic and the likelihood that these comments were based on the Qur'ān.[15] The problem of why the Qur'ān, thought so effective in Arabic precisely because of its *iʿjāz* or miraculous style, should be considered to make such a poor impression in English translation also always intrigued me both as a student of language and of the Qur'ān. Later, reading ʿAbd al-Qāhir al-Jurjānī's ideas about the science of

---

13 M. Brett Wilson, "The First Translations of the Qur'an in Modern Turkey (1924–1938)," *The International Journal of Middle Eastern Studies* 41 (2009), 419–435, especially p. 431.

14 A partial Urdu translation appeared in print as early as 1731. Shāh Walī Allāh ad-Dihlawī's influential Persian translation was completed in 1738. This was translated by his son Shāh Rafīʿ ad-Dīn into Urdu and has been plentifully published. Meanwhile, Shāh Walī Allāh's other son Shāh ʿAbd al-Qādir produced another Urdu translation. The first complete Muslim translation to be published was in Urdu, appearing in 1828. Ekmeleddin Ihsanoglu, ed., *World Bibliography of Translations of the Meanings of the Holy Qur'an: Printed Translations, 1515–1980*, Istanbul: O.I.C. Research Centre for Islamic History, Art and Culture, 1406/1986, pp. xxxviii, xlii, 356–364, 527–533, 574–582.

15 Robert B. Kaplan, *The Anatomy of Rhetoric: Prolegomena to a Functional Theory of Rhetoric*, Philadelphia, PA: The Center for Curriculum Development, Inc., 1972, pp. 34–35.

rhetoric further increased my interest, especially considering the relative lack of attention given to al-Jurjānī so far in publications in the English language.[16]

I wish to express my deep debt of gratitude to those who helped me in this work, and without whose assistance it would not have been possible to execute. Above all, I desire to commemorate, remember, and reiterate my gratitude to my late mentor, Dr. Mohammed al-Nowaihi (1917–1980) of the American University in Cairo, whose profound knowledge of the Qur'ān and invaluable assistance in the Arabic enabled me to complete my original work in 1975. Dr. al-Nowaihi's knowledge of both the Arabic and English languages and their respective literatures was truly unique. His expertise extended to the field of rhetoric in both languages, including the writings of ʿAbd al-Qāhir al-Jurjānī, to which he was the first to introduce me. I can well recall his refined and impeccable taste in weighing various constructions and phrasings during my original project, even though it was a mere MA thesis, and I am honored that he gave me so unstintingly many, many hours of his time, even though I was not a student in his department. Many of the suggestions and ideas contained herein are ultimately traceable to him. Also, I extend my warm thanks to the project's supervisor, Dr. Yehia al-Ezabi, for his kind encouragement and helpful suggestions. Further, I want to thank the late Dr. Richard Schmidt (1941–2017) of the University of Hawaii, whose encouragement at AUC from the first was decisive in making a beginning, and whose sensible review of my text greatly facilitated the clarity of my project. More recently, I want to thank my Temple University colleague of the English Department, Professor Lawrence Venuti, a leading world expert on translation theory, who has greatly helped to mentor me in bringing my points in this book up to date and who gave quite generously of his time to comment on various aspects of my work. I also wish to thank the College of Liberal Arts at Temple University for my two study leaves that enabled me to work on the updating, editing, and revising of this book. I also extend my thanks to the team at Brill for all the work they have done for the publication of this work, and particularly to the unnamed reviewer who provided me with many helpful suggestions for improving the text. I would furthermore like to express my gratitude to the master calligrapher Khaled Al-Saai, who kindly contributed the beautiful art for the cover of this book. Above all, I want to thank my wife Manar Darwish of Bryn Mawr College, who encouraged me to persist in revising this work and bore with my need to concentrate on it to get it done. Not only did she show exemplary patience with me while I was con-

16 An important exception is Margaret Larkin's *The Theology of Meaning: ʿAbd al-Qāhir al-Jurjānī's Theory of Discourse*, New Haven: American Oriental Society, 1995.

centrating on finishing this work, but she also contributed considerably to the work by discussing it with me and helping on various points.

Finally, any shortcomings in the work are mine alone.

References are to editions used in the bibliography. However, for Greek and Roman classics, the traditional system of chapter and section numbering has been used. I have generally not footnoted the Qur'ānic verses I cite either from the Arabic text or the English translations because the verse numbers should suffice for anyone wishing to look them up in the original texts.

Khalid ʿAbdulhadi Yahya Blankinship

Note on Transliteration

ا	a or u or i or ā	ض	ḍ
ب	b	ط	ṭ
ت	t	ظ	ẓ
ث	th	ع	ʿ
ج	j	غ	gh
ح	ḥ	ف	f
خ	kh	ق	q
د	d	ك	k
ذ	dh	ل	l
ر	r	م	m
ز	z	ن	n
س	s	ه	h
ش	sh	و	w or ū or aw
ص	ṣ	ي	y or ī or ay

Note

The glottal stop (ء) is represented by ʾ except at the beginning of a word, where it is omitted.

The definite article is rendered according to actual pronunciation.

The tāʾ marbūṭah (ة) is represented by a final "h," except where it is the last letter of a *muḍāf* in an *iḍāfah* construction, where it is represented by "t."

Introduction

1 The Question of Translation

Before discussing how rhetoric relates to translation of the Qurʾān, it is necessary first of all to discuss the question of translation itself, a question which the rise of the field of translation studies has brought into some focus and made a central concern in all matters related to language and linguistic studies. A continuous and ubiquitous practice attested in writing since well over 4,000 years ago,[1] interlingual translation is normally considered to be the rendering of words, discourses, or texts in one language into another language in a way that is accurate and can be understood, as clearly and completely as possible, in the receiving language.[2] Because the direction of translation is from the language of the original into the receiving language, it is clearly the receiving language which must dominate the process and the result, for, after all, the translated text is in it, not in the source language, and the expected audience too consists of speakers and readers of the receiving language, with all of their linguistic, rhetorical, and cultural expectations. Most often, the translator as well is a native speaker of the receiving language, or if not, has an almost-native competence in it. Owing to these facts, translation has usually raised some qualms, because it is quite clear that a translation can never be exactly equivalent to the original text it is based on, as is amply demonstrated by the fact that while an original text may have a single, absolutely fixed, and therefore canonical form (if its people choose to canonize it, as in the case of the Arabic Qurʾān), translations of that text may be countless, and no precise scientific standard exists or can exist to determine that one of the translations is exactly correct and all the others deviant. Nevertheless, sometimes such determinations have been made, even leading to canonizations of particular translations as authoritative. Such secondary canonizations of translations occur in particular when a religious

1 The very earliest translations attested are bilingual texts in Sumerian and Eblaite from Ebla, followed shortly by bilingual monumental inscriptions in Sumerian and Akkadian from the reigns of Sargon of Akkad and his son Rimush, all dating from approximately the period 2500–2250 BCE. William W. Hallo. "Bilingualism and the Beginnings of Translation," in *Texts, Temples, and Traditions: A Tribute to Menahem Haran*, ed. by Michael V. Fox et al., Winona Lake, IN: Eisenbrauns, 1996, pp. 348–350.

2 For an alternative definition and elaboration, see Bernard Dupriez, *A Dictionary of Literary Devices: Gradus, A–Z*, tr. & adapted by Albert W. Halsall, Toronto: University of Toronto Press, 1991, pp. 460–462.

 | DOI:10.1163/9789004417441_002

sect adopts a particular translation of its scripture as its only accepted liturgical text, forsaking all others, as happened with the early Christian canonization of the Greek Septuagint translation of the Hebrew scriptures or with certain contemporary Protestants who adopt the English King James Bible as revealed scripture. But such adoption and canonization of a translation is an ideological position which other groups may and usually do reject, offering their own versions instead.

The plethora of possible translations of a text and the many determining factors that influence the creation of each one has even raised the question of whether translation is possible at all, a question that has been considered for a long time but has come back to the fore recently in some works of translation studies.[3] Possibly, this has arisen partly as a reaction against what Lawrence Venuti and others have criticized as "transparent translation," the idea that a translation can transparently convey the meaning of the original author. Of course, as stated by Large et al., "the term 'untranslatable' is usually an exaggeration," meaning that it is not intended that a unique term in a source language cannot be rendered understandable at all in the target language, but rather that it requires some circumlocution or explanation to convey it.[4] Nevertheless, numerous limitations of translation in representing an original text have been extensively elaborated in translation studies. Even apart from strictly lexical or grammatical reservations that are important, Antoine Berman, for example, has identified twelve "deforming tendencies" which affect and undermine translation and include a very wide range of factors.[5]

However, while exact reproduction of an original text in translation is not possible, one must own that communication through translation undoubtedly occurs, however messy it may be. If we examine the process of communication within a language, it is not possible either to say that an utterance or a text is completely unambiguous, which is the position of the ultraliteralist medieval Muslim scholar Ibn Ḥazm (994–1064),[6] nor that it is completely ambiguous,

3 See for example Duncan Large, Motoko Akashi, Wanda Józwikowska, and Emily Rose, eds., *Untranslatability: Interdisciplinary Perspectives*, New York: Routledge, 2019, and Suzanne Jill Levine and Katie Lateef-Jan, eds., *Untranslatability Goes Global*, New York: Routledge, 2018.

4 Large et al., 2.

5 Antoine Berman, "Translation and the Trials of the Foreign," tr. by Lawrence Venuti, in *The Translation Studies Reader*, ed. by Lawrence Venuti, 3rd ed., New York: Routledge, 2012, pp. 244–252.

6 Because he states that the entire Qur'ān is unambiguous except for the oaths and the mysterious separated letters (*al-ḥurūf al-muqaṭṭaʿāt*), both of which appear at the beginnings of certain of the surahs. Abū Muḥammad ʿAlī b. Aḥmad Ibn Ḥazm, *al-Iḥkām fī uṣūl al-aḥkām*, ed. by Aḥmad Muḥammad Shākir, Beirut: Dār al-Āfāq al-Jadīdah, n. d., Vol. 1, p. 48.

depending entirely on the interpretation of the recipient, without any input at all from the speaker or writer.

First, in responding to the ultraliteralist position, which still might be found among some textualist-literalist religious believers who insist on the complete transparency of their sacred books, one might imagine the following: If I give you a paragraph and ask you to provide the meaning of it in your own words, in effect translating the original, but you can do no more than parrot back the original words without the least alteration, then you have understood nothing. Since the basis of language is obviously communication rather than parrot-like repetition, if you cannot explain the text in your own words, then communication has not occurred. Thus, interpretation is essential in all language.

But what if the assertion is rather that interpretation is not possible for the opposite reason, that all interpretations are equally valid, so that the meaning is only created by the receiver without any input whatever from the speaker or writer? In this case also, communication does not take place; therefore, such a linguistic theory is an inadequate one, because of course communication actually does happen. We are forced rather to conclude that communication must inhabit the gray area between these two puristic extremes; that is, language is not perspicacious and transparent, because the receiver does indeed bring all of his or her own abilities and baggages to the interpretation of the text she or he is receiving, and also because all kinds of misunderstandings take place, some consisting of real errors, but others partial misunderstandings owing to subtle shifts, nuances, and ambiguities that are also common in languages. But also communication does take place, sometimes with considerable precision, so that utterances and texts, while not transparent, are also not completely opaque. This is the position adopted by Hans-Georg Gadamer in his *Truth and Method*, where he considers the reader to encounter and experience the text in a middle ground, and he explicitly relates this process to translation.[7] And in fact, as with understanding and communication within a single language, translation between languages clearly occupies this same gray middle ground as well, the original text contributing meaning to the translated text in the receiving language, but not ever in a way that reproduces the original text either exactly or approximately, because of the numerous factors that interfere.

But we can elaborate still a little more on the possibilities of representation of the original in the receiving language, even though the result is still a matter of dispute, because of doubts raised about the possibilities of communication

7 Hans-Georg Gadamer, *Truth and Method*, tr. originally by W. Glen-Doepel, 2nd rev. ed. by Joel Weinsheimer and Douglas G. Marshall, New York: Continuum, 1993, pp. 384–389.

of meaning and understanding across times, places, cultures, and languages. It is quite clear that what can be mostly conveyed is semantic meaning. It is from this that ancient and medieval civilizations, societies, and conditions can be known at all. Semantic meaning may be conveyed in literalist or word-for-word translations, where the translated text is bound as closely as possible to the original. With the possible exception of some scientific treatises, even word-for-word translation cannot convey some of the meaning of an original, because the words of each language contain many different shades of meaning and are thus often ambiguous. And most commentators on translation have also lambasted the tendency of word-for-word translations to deflate or even render ugly or repulsive the source text,[8] a tendency that certainly will alter the reception of the meaning with the reader.

2 Question of Cultural Effects on Rhetoric and Translation

For a large part of the last century, linguists of various schools, including the audio-lingual, structuralist, and generative-transformational, among others, primarily concentrated their efforts on defined linguistic units the size of a single sentence or smaller, avoiding the consideration of optional features and stylistic factors as functional parts of language. These latter were relegated to the domain of taste, rhetoric, or style, skills to be developed as arts no doubt, but not fundamental in judging the correctness of a given passage, which was rather confined to the consideration of grammaticality. Yet, if language is looked at as a continuous whole, it seems likely that these other factors have semantic value as well and thus shade meaning, as do extralinguistic factors of culture,[9] in so far as they affect the reader's expectations.

This observation is hardly a fresh one, nor is it restricted to linguistics. For example, E.M. Forster wrote in *A Passage to India*:

> The Indians were bewildered. The line of thought was not alien to them, but the words were too definite and bleak. Unless a sentence paid a few compliments to Justice and Morality in passing, its grammar wounded their ears and paralyzed their minds. What they said and what they felt

8 See, for example, Jerome's "Letter to Pammachius" of 395 CE, translated by Kathleen Davis, in Lawrence Venuti, ed., *The Translation Studies Reader*, 3rd ed., New York, Routledge, 2012, pp. 23–24, with quotations from Cicero and Horace.

9 As noted, for example, in Edward T. Hall, *The Silent Language*, Garden City, NY: Doubleday & Co., Inc., 1959.

> were (except in the case of affection) seldom the same. They had numerous mental conventions, and when these were flouted they found it difficult to function.[10]

Of course, Forster was a colonial-era British writer who lived in India and who, despite his expressed sympathy for the Indians, which he tries to show here, was after all a European and thus subject to the disposition of Europeans summed up in the term "orientalism." Nevertheless, his description here repeats a common theme and raises the question of cultural and therefore also of rhetorical content in particular languages. The line of thinking, the underlying semantic content, is familiar to these Indians. But the way it is put fazes them completely; it upsets their linguistic stylistic expectations so much that they cannot react normally to the content. Thus, language has failed, the speaker's intended message has not been communicated, correct understanding has not occurred, all because rhetorical conventions were violated.

The idea that language is more than a mere instrument of communication actualized in an objective material reality has long been debated, resulting, for example, in the Whorf Hypothesis and the controversies over linguistic relativism that continue down to this day, questioning whether language influences human perception, thought, and behavior or not, and if so, in what ways. On the one hand, the idea that language may influence perception, thought, and behavior has been severely criticized since the 1950s by universalists who believe in an objective scientific reality that is available to everyone, while linguistic differences are to be explained as trivial epiphenomena. Such universalists have also, perhaps, been alarmed at the potential for racist nationalists to derive support for their ethnic or national chauvinism from the idea that human differences result from their languages. Sometimes, the idea has been traced back to Johann Gottfried Herder (1744–1803), Wilhelm von Humboldt (1767–1835), and the German romantics and is thus taken to run counter to the prevailing trends of pluralistic universalism. On the other hand, more recently, linguistic relativists have also counterattacked, trying to avoid overgeneralizations suggesting that language determines everything for humans, but pointing out that it nevertheless has significant effects on human society and culture.[11] This view also seems dominant in translation studies, where it is emphasized that language is constitutive of meaning and that meaning does not come in an unmediated manner from physical facts or realities of the world. Rather,

---

10 E.M. Forster, *A Passage to India*. London: Penguin Books, 1961, pp. 108–109.

11 Caleb Everett, *Linguistic Relativity: Evidence Across Languages and Cognitive Domains*, Berlin: De Gruyter Mouton, 2013, pp. 10–32.

language is constitutive of reality.[12] This being so, differences across languages really matter, and translation cannot be carried on according to some kind of absolute formula.

This question can also be illuminated from the field of second language teaching. In that area, the composition teacher might often feel that the production of what is grammatically correct by the students is of most importance; if there are stylistic errors or weaknesses, these can be corrected in time by experience. Perhaps he or she should not stifle the individualism and creativity represented by novel elements of style in the students' papers. Nevertheless, such a teacher will encounter expressions which are unnatural in the target language although not outright grammatical errors. Teachers who mark these wrong under some vague rubric such as "usage error," are likely to find their students asking questions only answerable by, "We don't say it that way," or, "It doesn't sound right." The bewildered students may come away with a sense of discouragement, feeling that a second language is much more difficult and mysterious to learn than they had supposed.

If this is the case with second language learning, then how much more clearly the area of "usage errors" should create difficulties in translation. Now, translation is certainly possible at least to a degree, for one can give an approximately equivalent meaning for a passage through translation, although the literary beauty may be partly or wholly lost. But is it really possible to convey even an apparent literal meaning without reference to the style?[13] Granted, cultural effects may make it difficult for the uninitiated to understand anyway, but does not the taste of the readers create certain expectations likely to be disappointed if the wrong signals are given? Indeed, the attitude of the readers must be taken into account as well as the text itself, among other factors. The translation must extend beyond the written word, and thus cannot be made as a set object for all time. That this is so is shown by the rapidity with which translations go out of fashion, as new ones supplant the old.

Clearly, the key to understanding why some translations are seen to be more effective than others lies at least partly in the common semantic elements shared by languages. But while semantic concepts may be somewhat similar across different languages, cultural attitudes toward them may differ. This must

---

12 Venuti, *Invisibility*, 13, 32, 92–93, 127; Lawrence Venuti, ed., *The Translation Studies Reader*, 3rd ed. London: Routledge, 2012, pp. 6, 71, 395.

13 Venuti, *Invisibility*, 13, citing Derrida, observes, "Because meaning is an effect of relations and differences among signifiers along a potentially endless chain (polysemous, intertextual, subject to infinite linkages), it is always differential and deferred, never present as an original unity."

extend to rhetoric also. So an unnecessary amount of error is then introduced when the rhetorical forms and devices of one language are introduced directly into another to which they are alien, perhaps creating misunderstanding or disdain. On the other hand, deliberately domesticating translations also create distance from the original source text, and however beloved by readers they might become, they are never that text itself.

The origin of these cultural-linguistic or rhetorical differences lies in past literary traditions and present usage as taught in the various linguistic regions. To take up Kaplan's example of English and Arabic, we find that the English-speaking native is reminded constantly in school to use more modifying (subordinate) clauses for variety so his writing will not be boring. Likewise, he or she is admonished for the same reason to break up the monotony of a long passage with paragraphs and to avoid beginning sentences with an article whenever possible. On the other hand, the Arab is taught that balance and equilibrium is important in writing; thus, two words are often used where one will suffice (which is 'wordy' to the English teacher). A Syrian from Aleppo was annoyed enough by the Arabic usage in one of my letters to him to send corrections in his reply. In beginning a letter in Arabic, a flowery formal greeting is preferred. Thus, *taḥiyyah ṭayyibah* (a sweet greeting) is too short, especially to a person who is not a close friend of the writer. But, that which I had actually written, *taḥiyyah ṭayyibah wa salāmāt* (a sweet greeting and salutations), was yet worse, requiring a correction because the second noun *salāmāt* needed an adjective as well for balance and did not sound right without one. The Syrian correspondent suggested *ḥārrah* (warm) or *akhawiyyah* (brotherly). This confirms what Kaplan says about the Arab preference for parallelism,[14] a feature also widespread in the Hebrew of the Bible. There is an inexhaustible supply of examples of this. Thus, on the whole, balance has been more important than brevity to Arab writer and their reading publics.

As hinted above, part of the problem is historical. Expectations of language, like other things conditioned by culture, are always in a state of flux. Kaplan points out that there was a time when elaborate parallelism was in vogue in English,[15] as well as other rhetorical flourishes. Thus, a direct translation of Arabic might be liable to conjure up the English of 400 years ago, with all its attendant connotations, and so is likely to be regarded as archaic. Arabic style continues to be influenced by the Qur'ān as a model of perfection down to the present day,[16] owing to the effect of at least tacit religious belief and the resulting cul-

14 Kaplan, 38–46.

15 Kaplan, 35–36.

16 Badawī Ṭabānah, *al-Bayān al-ʿarabī: dirāsah fī taṭawwur al-fikrah al-balāghiyyah ʿinda l-*

tural preference that attempts to minimize foreign influences emanating from a predominant Western material culture. This results in misinterpretation in both languages. What the American considers "corny" may so move the Arab that the former, forgetting temporarily any similar susceptibilities of his own, will dismiss the latter as too subject to emotions, too sentimental.

In general, English, as taught in books on writing and style, strongly favors clarity, brevity, and concision, to the extent of visiting criticism on previous forms of English style. Indeed, the writers of a very popular, standard manual of style cannot restrain themselves from revising passages from the likes of James Fenimore Cooper and George Orwell in the interests of clarity, brevity, and concision to demonstrate these writing virtues for students.[17] The same book has a chapter on concision, and two of its four parts are called "Clarity" and "Clarity of Form."[18] A recent prescriptive handbook on rhetorical features in English states, "Clarity—writing so that your reader has an accurate understanding of your ideas—is at the heart of good writing."[19] Another venerable style manual also emphasizes the need for brevity.[20] Directness is also a prescribed virtue, embodied particularly in a studied avoidance of using the passive voice[21] and negatives, as well as the requirement for "definite, specific, concrete language."[22] Of course, clarity is certainly regarded as a virtue in many languages, including Arabic; indeed, the Qur'ān frequently proclaims itself to be a clear or clarifying book (5:15; 12:1; 15:1; 26:2; 27:1; 28:2; 36:69) in a clear Arabic language (16:103; 26:195). But classical Arabic rhetoric lacks the same overall emphasis on concision,[23] even though concision is one of its features (see Chapter 13, below), and the Qur'ān strives neither to avoid negatives nor the passive voice.

ʿArab wa-manāhijuhā wa-maṣādiruhā l-kubrā, 4th ed., Cairo: Maktabat al-Anjlū al-Miṣriyyah, 1388/1968, pp. 18–40. See also Kaplan, 34–35.

17 Joseph M. Williams and Gregory G. Colomb, *Style: Lessons in Clarity and Grace*, 10th ed., New York: Longman, 2010, pp. 3–5.

18 Williams & Colomb, 27, 100, 163.

19 Robert A. Harris, *Writing with Clarity and Style: A Guide to Rhetorical Devices for Contemporary Writers*, 2nd ed., New York: Routledge, 2018, p. 49.

20 William Strunk, Jr., and E.B. White, *The Elements of Style*, 4th ed., New York: Pearson Education, Inc., 2009, pp. 23–26, 72–75.

21 Cleanth Brooks & Robert Penn Warren. *Modern Rhetoric*, New York: Harcourt, Brace & World, 1970, 375.

22 Strunk & White, 18–23. While Williams & Colomb, 53–59, note the preference for avoiding the passive voice, they also cite exceptions where its use is preferable.

23 Avigail Noy, "The Emergence of ʿIlm al-Bayān: Classical Arabic Literary Theory in the Arabic East in the 7th/13th Century," Ph.D. dissertation, Harvard University, 2016, p. 17, incl. n. 51, mentions the views of medieval Arabic rhetoric towards concision and prolixity is a topic for future investigation.

Of course, change continues and it may be that contemporary Arabic style is becoming closer to English through time. There have been some deliberate attempts to hasten this, which have provoked an opposition trying to prevent it. Each group has its own axes to grind.[24] Nevertheless, no one will deny that distinct stylistic differences remain and will continue, owing to the mere exigencies of linguistic difference if nothing else. Even if a major amount of Western influence were admitted, the result would still remain a synthesis of the new and traditional influences. And, as long as they exist, Arabic will never be just like English, neither in grammar, nor rhetoric, nor cultural expectations.

As already implied, the field of rhetoric exists between the grammar examined by linguists and taught by teachers and the literary evaluation done by the critics. Hence it has been somewhat a neglected area, as mentioned by Roderick Jacobs,[25] and linguists especially might profit from its examination.

3 Inimitability of the Qurʾān

The Qurʾān poses an interesting problem and holds a unique and immeasurable position of importance among Muslims which is rarely understood by others. Mainly, the Qurʾān's unique importance owes to its status as the primary scripture of Islam, universally acknowledged among Muslims as being the veritable word of God. A major traditional proof offered by Muslims of its divine origin is the challenge the Qurʾān itself lays down to any doubters to produce speech like it, which it says they can never do (Qurʾān 2:23–24; 10:38; 11:13–14; 17:88; 52:34), so that it therefore is an inimitable text. Whatever their original context, these Qurʾānic passages present an interesting comment from the book itself on the impossibility of true and accurate translation.

Early Muslims, reflecting on these verses, arrived at more than one theory. While it was widely thought from the earliest times that the inimitability of the Qurʾān must have a considerable connection with language, a large body opined that the reason it was impossible to imitate the Qurʾān in any way was not in the Qurʾān itself but owed to the *ṣarfah*, or "preventing," namely God's continuous intervention to prevent any human from succeeding in imitating the Qurʾān, even though it was theoretically possible. This view was

24 See, for example, Muḥammad Muḥammad Ḥusayn, *Ittijāhāt haddāmah fī l-fikr al-ʿarabī al-muʿāṣir*, 2nd ed., Beirut: Dār al-Irshād, 1391/1971, for a conservative view opposing westernization.

25 Roderick A. Jacobs, *Studies in Language: Introductory Readings in Transformational Linguistics*, Lexington, MA: Xerox College Publishing, 1979, pp. 87–88.

embraced by the Muʿtazilīs, but rejected by many others who instead attributed this impossibility of imitation to the Qurʾān's "miraculous style" or *iʿjāz*, which in Arabic literally means, "rendering incapable."[26] Thus, the Qurʾān's language itself became the basis for the doctrine of "the inimitability of the Quʾrān." Although the term *iʿjāz* never occurs in the Qurʾān or hadith themselves, it is clear that this interpretation of the Qurʾānic challenge goes back to the earliest commentators. It is already found greatly elaborated in the commentary of aṭ-Ṭabarī (225–310/839–923), who cites the earlier commentators Mujāhid and Qatādah on this point.[27] Slightly earlier, Ibn Qutaybah (213–276/828–889) emphasized the impossibility of translating the Qurʾān precisely because of its figurative language (*majāz*), which no other language can equal in degree.[28]

Muslim linguists of the Middle Ages wrote many books on its *iʿjāz* or "miraculous style,"[29] but it will be more interesting for us to study this quality with our own contemporary methods and perceptions in order to identify some of the rhetorical factors that may be thought to make such a book uniquely eloquent in Arabic but ordinary or even sometimes incomprehensible in English translation. The Qurʾān certainly continues to have an effect on Arabic rhetoric to this day, and knowing some of the structural differences that are really rhetorical could also be of assistance in promoting better crosscultural understanding. On the other hand one must beware of describing something as untranslat-

---

26 For a discussion of the history of this idea, see Jane Dammen McAuliffe, ed., *Encyclopaedia of the Qurʾān*, Leiden: E.J. Brill, 2001–2006, s. v. Richard C. Martin, "Inimitability," Vol. II, pp. 526–536; Margaret Larkin, "The Inimitability of the Qur'an: Two Perspectives," *Religion and Literature* 20, No. 1 (Spring, 1988) 31–47; Lara Harb, "Form, Content, and the Inimitability of the Qurʾān in ʿAbd al-Qāhir al-Jurjānī's Works." *Middle Eastern Literatures* 18 (2015), 301–321; Rebecca Gould, "Inimitability versus Translatability: The Structure of Literary Meaning in Arabo-Persian Poetics," *The Translator*, 19 (2013), 81–104; Alford T. Welch, "The Translatability of the Qurʾān: Literary and Theological Implications of What the Qurʾān Says about Itself," in David M. Goldenberg, ed., *Translation of Scripture: Proceedings of a Conference at the Annenberg Research Institute, May 15–16, 1989*, Philadelphia: Annenberg Research Institute, 1990, pp. 249–285. For other coverage of it, see Hussein Abdul-Raof, *Arabic Rhetoric: A Pragmatic Analysis*, London: Routledge, 2006, pp. 16–18, 21, 57–60; Safaruk Z. Chowdhury, *Introducing Arabic Rhetoric*, new rev. & expanded [4th] ed., London: Dar al-Nicosia Publishing House, 2015, pp. 47–84.

27 Abū Jaʿfar Muḥammad b. Jarīr aṭ-Ṭabarī, *Jāmiʿ al-bayān fī tafsīr al-Qurʾān*, Būlāq: al-Maṭbaʿah al-Kubrā al-Amīriyyah, 1323–1329, Vol. I, pp. 128–129.

28 Ibn Qutaybah, 21.

29 Possibly the best known of these is Abū Bakr Muḥammad b. aṭ-Ṭayyib al-Bāqillānī, *Iʿjāz al-Qurʾān*, Cairo: Dār al-Maʿārif, 1977, but there are many others, including much recent literature on this in Arabic, including, for example, Muṣṭafā Ṣādiq ar-Rāfiʿī, *Iʿjāz al-Qurʾān wa-l-balāghah an-nabawiyyah*, Beirut: al-Maktabah al-ʿAṣriyyah, 1424/2003 (originally published in 1926).

able simply because of the shortcomings of the existing renditions, so it is also essential to know when the problem is simply a translation error rather than attributable to differing rhetorical concepts. It is hoped this study will throw some light on Arabic and English rhetorical differences as revealed in translations and lead to a further examination of Arabic and English rhetoric, and will provide a useful departure point for future research in this field.

4 Special Problems in Translating the Meaning the Qur'ān

As a sacred scripture of considerable antiquity, originally revealed c. 609–632, the Qur'ān presents the reader as well as the translator with special problems. Unlike most modern literature, it comes from a context that is very remote and whose historical character is quite contested. As the foundational document of Arabic literature, it stands in splendid isolation from contemporary texts with which it might relate, much like the *Iliad* and the *Odyssey* of Homer in Greek literature. On the other hand, it also occasioned the rise of a long-lasting Muslim interpretive tradition with an enormous exegetical literature containing more than one thousand commentaries in Arabic that continues to be added to at present more than ever. While this interpretive tradition naturally has limited the potential interpretations of the text in various ways, it has also from very early on recognized its multivocality by recording and transmitting an expansive quantity of various and often contradictory interpretations. Some of these differences of interpretation resulted from sectarian developments inside of Islam, but many represented differences in reception and recollection within groups. Nevertheless, one will have to own that overall the way in which Muslims look at the Qur'ān has been profoundly influenced by its exegetical tradition, and at the popular level, certain interpretations are more commonly encountered than others. In interpreting and translating the Qur'ān, this exegetical tradition cannot be ignored, because it represents the ways in which the Qur'ān has been understood over the centuries by the Muslims, and thus constitutes an important part of the signification of that text. Translations that simply ignore the commentary tradition thus fail to convey how most Muslims actually construe the text, and surely how Muslims construe the text is often an important consideration for non-Muslims too, because in many or most cases, they will be interested not just in a supposed underlying essential meaning of the text, but also in how Muslims have traditionally understood it and understand it now.

Today, the effects of modernism, including mass education and mass literacy everywhere, have significantly altered the reception of the Qur'ān and its translations among Muslims. On the one hand, the decline of the monopoly of the religious scholars (*ʿulamāʾ*) on interpretation has led to a wider variety of understandings of the text.[30] In translation, there has been the additional factor of the great explosion in the number of different translations, now exceeding one hundred in English alone.[31] On the other hand, modern mass vernacular literacy, which created the demand for vernacular Qurʾān translations in the first place, has also contributed to a certain demand among modern-educated Muslims for a single best or correct translation to rely on, which can quickly descend into conflicting sectarian preferences, something which does not exist with the Arabic Qurʾān, which is a single, agreed-upon text.[32]

An especially notable example of this is from a small four-page brochure advertising *The Noble Qur'an* translated by Muhammad Taqi-ud-Din Al-Hilali and Muhammad Muhsin Khan and published by Dar-us-Salam Publications of Riyadh, Saudi Arabia.[33] This brochure includes the words:

> "It is for the first time that the distinguished interpretation of the meanings of the Noble Qur'ân along with Arabic text is presented in English language in its real and pristine form, clear and pure—as understood by the early Muslims of this nation without the least going away from it or deviating from the original interpretation.
>
> "The exact and precise meaning of the Qur'ânic verses are taken from the most authentic books ..."

30 Amply examined, described and criticized by Kidwai, *Translating*, throughout his work.

31 Lawrence, 177–187, lists 109 complete English translations as of 2017. By my own count, currently there are at least 137 complete, different translations, and I am certain I have missed some.

32 This is notwithstanding the different *qirāʾāt* or "readings" of the text, which mostly concern different vowelling. Even here, in the interests of unity and standardization, the reading of Ḥafṣ ʿan ʿĀṣim has tended to drive out the other readings everywhere except in North and West Africa, where Ḥafṣ now nevertheless also competes with the dominant reading of Warsh ʿan Nāfiʿ. See *Encyclopaedia of Islam*, 2nd ed., s. v. "Ḳirāʾa" by Rudi Paret. For a comprehensive cataloguing of variants in the Qurʾān, see Aḥmad Mukhtār ʿUmar and ʿAbd al-ʿĀl Sālim Makram, *Muʿjam al-qirāʾāt al-qurʾāniyyah, maʿa muqaddimah fī l-qirāʾāt wa-ashhar al-qurrāʾ*, 2nd ed., Kuwait: Maṭbūʿāt Jāmiʿat al-Kuwayt, 1408/1988, 8 vols.

33 Muhammad Taqi-ud-Din Al-Hilali and Muhammad Muhsin Khan, *Interpretation of the Meanings of the Noble Qur'an in the English Language: A Summarized Version of Al-Tabarî, Al-Qurtubî, and Ibn Kathîr with Comment from Sahîh-Al-Bukhârî, Summarized in One Volume*, 12th ed., Riyadh: Maktaba Dar-us-Salam, 1995. The brochure evidently came with the purchase of that edition of the book.

This text contains an astonishing and unprecedented deviation from the classical Muslim tradition about the Qur'ān. Instead of the Qur'ān being inimitable, here Al-Hilali and Khan are stated to have exactly reproduced the original text in English without the least deviation from its meaning. That such a claim can be made and pass muster in supposedly ultraconservative Saudi Arabia illustrates how unstable such claims to "orthodoxy" often are, as this one would seem to contradict a major orthodox doctrine in order to assert a literal, univocal truth for its own position. Such a view has never been the classical stance of the Muslim religious scholars, even while they argued fiercely at times for their own interpretations of particular verses. Nor is it correct that the Al-Hilali and Khan translation represents a new type of translation, as it is highly derivative, mostly consisting of borrowing from Yūsuf 'Alī with some substitutions from Pickthall, both of whom I have dealt with extensively below.

5 Methodology of This Work

In order to carry out the purpose of this study, I will examine some verses of the Qur'ān which demonstrate particular rhetorical features, and then look at the attempts of several translators to render them into English. To help understand how the Arabic of the Qur'ānic verses has been traditionally received by Arabic speakers, I have chosen to rely on several well-known exegeses of the Qur'ān by aṭ-Ṭabarī, az-Zamakhsharī, al-Qurṭubī, al-Bayḍāwī, and Ibn Kathīr. The first of these, aṭ-Ṭabarī (d. 310/923), compiled the earliest surviving major *tafsīr*, and it remains arguably the most important. Aṭ-Ṭabarī not only frequently gives his own view on the correct interpretation of the verses but most significantly has amassed the earliest huge collection of interpretive traditions from a large variety of sources.

Next, the commentary of az-Zamakhsharī (d. 538/1144) is particularly useful for this study, as it includes detailed rhetorical and grammatical explanations of many verses. That az-Zamakhsharī has enjoyed lasting popularity among Sunni Muslims despite his pronounced Mu'tazilī views, which are amply exposited in his work, demonstrates how his work has become accepted as a standard text on the subject. It is also of relevance that even the very early translators of the Qur'ān Luigi Marracci and George Sale made much use of az-Zamakhsharī, so that his influence entered strongly into the tradition of Qur'ān translation in English, and later translators have consulted his commentary as well. Furthermore, he alone among the classical *mufassirūn* is cited as being particularly concerned with *balāghah*, i.e., eloquence or rhetoric, by Bint ash-Shāṭi' in her short rhetorical exegesis of some surahs of the Qur'ān,[34] and Muḥammad Muḥammad Abū Mūsā's large volume on rhetoric in al-Zamakhsharī's commentary and its later effect on the development of Arabic rhetorical studies also attests to his lasting importance in this realm.[35] Owing to his usefulness on the points I am considering and his frequent references to and explanations of rhetorical features, I have relied on az-Zamakhsharī by far the most among the commentaries I have cited.

Among later commentators, al-Qurṭubī (d. 671/1273) brings in a variety of viewpoints in his monumental work, although he is not particularly concerned with rhetoric. Al-Bayḍāwī (d. 716/1316) often repeats or summarizes what az-Zamakhsharī has said, but sometimes in his own way, and he occasionally has a different view. Finally, Ibn Kathīr (d. 774/1373) is mainly concerned with adducing hadiths to demonstrate the meaning of the verses rather than attending to the rhetorical aspect. His exegesis cannot be neglected, however, for it is possibly the most popular classical one with both scholars and laymen among Arabic-speaking Muslims today and thus often represents the most widely-received interpretation.

My method in the text below will be as follows. First, I will separately take up each of the fourteen or so rhetorical features I am going to deal with. After a discussion of each feature in general, including what mention of it can be found in classical Greek, Roman, Arabic, and modern works on rhetoric, I will cite examples from the Qur'ān. I will then discuss the meaning of the each verse when that presents any difficulties. Then, I will move on to examine one or more of the versions of the translators I have chosen, namely those of M.M. Pickthall, 'Abd Allāh Yūsuf 'Alī, Richard Bell, A.J. Arberry, and N.J. Dawood, about whom more below. I will also make occasional reference to the translations of Muhammad Ali of Lahore and Muhammad Asad. For each verse or set of verses I cite, I will only use enough translations to illustrate the point, citing additional ones only when they illustrate some difference. I shall endeavor to determine the probable effect of the verses in the English translations, whether this effect is because of rhetorical or other causes, and, if the former, why. In this way it should be possible to isolate which, if any, difficulties in conveying the Arabic into English arise from rhetorical factors.

34 'Ā'ishah 'Abd ar-Raḥmān, "Bint ash-Shāṭi'," *at-Tafsīr al-bayānī li-l-Qur'ān al-karīm*, Cairo: Dār al-Ma'ārif, 1990, Vol. 1, pp. 12–13.

35 Muḥammad Muḥammad Abū Mūsā, *al-Balāghah al-qur'āniyyah fī tafsīr az-Zamakhsharī wa-atharuhā fī d-dirāsāt al-balāghiyyah*, Cairo: Maktabat Wahbah, 1408/1988.

6 The Qur'ānic Text, Translations, and Reader Response

Before proceeding to our main discussion, however, we must examine three important factors that must enter into our consideration. First, the Qur'ān itself and its actual character and genre in Arabic must be briefly examined to give a basis for comparing how English speakers react to the translations. Then, we must turn to the translations themselves, to show the different purposes and audiences they were written for, so the reader may fairly consider the examples we will bring from the pages of these attempts and understand why they contain certain features that characterize each of them. Finally, we must make a few remarks about the character of the different expected audiences themselves, and how there may be both various reactions to the same passage and a certain general reaction to the nature of a certain type of writing or a certain feature, this last of which is of most importance for our consideration.

Turning our attention to the text of the Qur'ān itself then, we note several important points to be borne in mind. First of all, this is, as the book itself plainly states, a prophetic revelation. Whatever one's opinion of the original source of it may be, it can be readily acknowledged that this notion of direct revelation is a concept that permeates the Old and New Testaments of the Bible. This is particularly true of the prophetic biblical books of Isaiah, Jeremiah, Ezekiel, the twelve minor prophets, and Revelation, each of which self-referentially proclaims itself to be a revelation from God. While other prophetic books outside the Bible exist, these are not familiar to most readers, but a very large reading public is at least somewhat familiar with the Bible.[36] Now, I am not here concerned with the general attitude of the audience to books of a scriptural nature such as the Qur'ān and the Bible, as that is a matter of religious belief or perhaps taste, not of rhetoric. But I do note that the reaction of readers to a close rendition of the meaning of the Qur'ān is likely to be associated with their experience with the most parallel book in English, the Bible, and the "biblical English" associated with its translations. Second, we must remember that, like many of the prophetic books of the Hebrew Bible, the Qur'ān was revealed orally and is fundamentally an oral text to be heard, not a written one to be read. Indeed, the very words *qara'a, yaqra'u*, sometimes translated as "to read" and commonly used in modern Arabic in that

---

36 Works identifying themselves as prophetic revelations at a later date, such as *The Book of Mormon*, however they may be possessed of a certain degree of popularity, do not enjoy so wide a circulation among the general public. Furthermore, they tend to follow the expected style of "biblical English," and thus tend not to change the rhetorical expectations originally formed by knowledge of the English Bible.

sense, really originally mean "to recite," as reading the Qur'ān (*qirā'at al-Qur'ān*) means to recite it aloud, with or without the help of a written text. The Qur'ān was revealed at a time when written Arabic was little developed, though the tradition of oral poetry was highly refined and constituted an important aspect of the cultural life of the Jāhiliyyah, perhaps the most important aspect. We can then account for some features like the frequency of repetition of certain kinds, as being because of the oral nature of the Qur'ān rather than necessarily rhetorical features in Arabic fundamentally different from English.[37] Thirdly, the Qur'ān was revealed in a kind of rhymed prose having rhymed endings at the end of verses of various length. Whatever effect this may have in Arabic is obviously not going to be reproduced in English, and in general English translations have not tried to reproduce or imitate any of the rhymes. Naturally, this does not detract from the Qur'ān's position of importance in Arabic rhetoric. In *Dalā'il al-i'jaz*, for example, al-Jurjānī relies heavily on the Qur'ān and poetry for his examples of rhetoric but rarely cites any other prose source.[38] And the Qur'ān has remained important to this day in this respect.[39]

As for the English translations of the Qur'ān, it is not possible to evaluate them individually without first understanding the history of English Qur'ān translation, in order to elucidate the relationship of the various versions to one another. This is all the more important because almost all Qur'ān translations to date belong to *a single tradition of English-language translation of the meaning of the Qur'ān* and are thus closely interrelated. This means that each translator usually depended on those who went before him, relying mainly on their wording rather than attempting a totally fresh rendering directly from the Arabic. As a result, most, if not all, Muslim translations are clearly indebted to the translations of the non-Muslim English-speakers who first translated the Qur'ān's meanings, going right back to the first anonymous translation formerly but wrongly[40] attributed to Alexander Ross (1059/1649) and the second by George Sale (1147/1734). These early translations plainly influenced the first Muslim translations, such as that of the Ahmadi Muhammad Ali of Lahore, which first appeared complete in 1335/1917 and became in turn a major influence on most

---

37 On the oral/aural nature of the Qur'ān and its reception by the Muslims, see Neal Robinson, *Discovering the Qur'an: A Contemporary Approach to a Veiled Text*, 2nd ed., Washington, DC: Georgetown University Press, 2003, pp. 9–20.

38 Aḥmad Aḥmad Badawī, *'Abd al-Qāhir al-Jurjānī wa-juhūduhu fī l-balāghah al-'arabiyyah*, Cairo: al-Mu'assasah al-Miṣriyyah al-'Āmmah li-t-Ta'līf wa-t-Tarjamah wa-ṭ-Ṭibā'ah wa-n-Nashr, 2nd printing, [1962], p. 65.

39 Kaplan, 35–37.

40 Noel Malcolm, "The 1649 English Translation of the Koran: Its Origins & Significance," *Journal of the Warburg and Courtauld Institutes* 75 (2012), 261–295.

if not all subsequent Muslim translations. It is true that some translations, like those of Muhammad Ali and Muhammad Asad (1400/1980), were more independent of their predecessors, while others were more closely dependent, but all were influenced by earlier models. Thus, there exists no completely independent Muslim tradition of Qur'ān translation in English. Rather, the translation process went from English non-Muslims to marginal Muslims to mainstream Muslims, the exact opposite of the original process of Qur'ān revelation, which went from the original source to the later Muslims and from them to the world. One might add that the development of Qur'ān translation in English, from outside the religion to its margins to its inside, is also exactly the opposite of Bible translation, which always took place inside of Christianity. It is highly desirable that scholars undertake to study the history of Qur'ān translation just as the history of biblical translation has been dealt with in great detail, but such an effort is unfortunately far beyond the scope of the present work. Therefore, a few observations on each of the translations I am using in this book will have to suffice.

Going through the seven translations I have chosen according to the chronological order of their appearance, I will begin with that of Muhammad Ali of Lahore (1876–1951),[41] whose translation was begun in 1909 and published in its first edition in 1917,[42] followed by the third edition of 1951 on which all the further editions have been based. Although preceded by the translations of Mohammad Abdul Hakim Khan of Patiala (d. 1940) of 1905, Mirza Abu'l-Fadl (1865–1956) of 1911–1912, and Mirza Hairat Dihlawi (c. 1850–1928) of 1916, the work of Muhammad Ali of Lahore was the first Qur'ān translation by a Muslim to have a major impact and achieve a wide distribution among Muslims, and it certainly helped to motivate, inspire, and inform all subsequent translations, earning praise in particular from Pickthall and Daryābādī. This did not prevent Muhammad Ali's work from being severely criticized at the time by orthodox Muslims for being the work of an Ahmadi heretic, however, and such criticism increased through the twentieth century as Muslim sectarian criticism of the Ahmadiyyah grew greater. Thus, much of the influence of Muhammad Ali's translation, even though it is fairly widely distributed, has been indirect. Apart from his Ahmadiyyah views, which he certainly minimizes in the work, Muhammad Ali also displays a thoroughgoing modernism that is somewhat at odds with the rank and file of Muslims in the world. Like other early translators, Muhammad Ali uses the now archaic forms of the second person singular, thee,

41 Muhammad Ali, *The Holy Qur'ān; Arabic Text, English Translation and Commentary*, 7th ed., Chicago: Speciality Promotions Co., Inc., 1985.

42 Muhammad Ali, v.

thou, thy, and thine, to preserve the same distinctions that exist in the Arabic, which help to give his work a biblical flavor. However, his archaizing tendency is less than that of Pickthall, for example.

Our second translator is Muhammad Marmaduke Pickthall (1875–1936),[43] son of an Anglican priest and himself a novelist, who embraced Islam privately in 1914 and then publicly in 1917. Pickthall clearly identified with the Muslim world, was viewed with suspicion by the British during the First World War, and migrated to India in 1920 to work for an Indian nationalist newspaper. Pickthall accomplished his translation starting in 1928 under the patronage of the Nizam of Hyderabad, then the ruler of the world's largest Muslim polity, who was undoubtedly interested in such a presentation of Islam as an English Muslim could give to English-language readers, including the British colonial officials who were the Nizam's overlords. By the time it was published in 1349/1930, the work had been further revised in Egypt with the help of Muḥammad Aḥmad al-Ghamrāwī and approved by Shaykh Muḥammad Muṣṭafā al-Marāghī (d. 1364/1945), the Grand Shaykh of al-Azhar in 1928–1930 and 1935–1945.

Pickthall's own stated aim in his translation is "to present to English readers what Muslims the world over hold to be the meaning of the words of the Koran, and the nature of that Book, in not unworthy language and concisely, with a view to the requirements of English Muslims." Elsewhere he says, "It is only an attempt to present the meaning of the Koran—and peradventure something of the charm—in English."[44] Interestingly, Pickthall's statement clearly acknowledges the impossibility of preserving rhetorical excellence or charm except by accident, the meaning being the matter of first importance. This is not surprising for a religiously-motivated translator, who naturally might be expected to favor "meaning" at the expense of "charm." But Pickthall's own statement of aim must be measured against his obvious dependence on the 1917 translation of Muhammad Ali of Lahore.[45] Considering the close similarity of Pickthall's work to Muhammad Ali's, and considering that Muhammad Ali, being an Ahmadi, was considered a heretic by many Sunnis, Pickthall's translation seems to represent mainly the revision of Muhammad Ali's work into a form acceptable to and usable by Sunnis, and indeed Pickthall strove to have his translation approved by al-Azhar, the authoritative Sunni Muslim institution in Egypt, and, though he failed to obtain the imprimatur of the institution, he did obtain an

43 For a recent critique of Pickthall's translation, see Muhammad A.S. Abdel Haleem, *Exploring the Qur'an: Context and Impact*, London: I.B. Tauris, 2017, pp. 263–265.

44 Mohammed Marmaduke Pickthall, *The Meaning of the Glorious Koran*. London: George Allen & Unwin, 2nd impression, 1948, p. vii.

45 Muhammad Ali, vii–viii.

endorsement from the Azharī Shaykh al-Marāghī there, as mentioned above.[46] Pickthall's work also frequently harks back to the earlier translations of the British Christians Rodwell (1861, 1876) and Palmer (1880).

Generally, Pickthall's version differs from some others in having frequent parenthetical glosses to fill out all possible semantic lacunae in the English text, as his language differs in being more archaic in character, like the biblical language referred to above. Perhaps Pickthall as an English Muslim was seeking to produce something more parallel to the English Bible both to give the English Muslims something equivalent in their own language and to impress the Christians with something on a level similar to that of their own Holy Book. Despite Pickthall's promise to provide an almost literal rendering,[47] he seems to stray more often from the Arabic than his later competitor Arberry. Also, his translation suffers from some surprising errors.[48]

Third among the translations chosen for this study is *The Holy Qur'ān: Text, Translation, and Commentary* by 'Abd Allāh Yūsuf 'Alī (1872–1953).[49] This work, which appears still to be the most widely used among Muslims who use English, was originally published piecemeal starting in 1934 and revised in its final form in the translator's third edition of 1938. Thus, it is nearly contemporary with the work of Pickthall and Bell. In 1989 and 1990, two related but different revisions of Yūsuf 'Alī appeared, showing the continuing importance of the work. While Yūsuf 'Alī's translation contains exegetical expansions as well as somewhat ornate, archaic language, it is nevertheless frequently eloquent, and his lasting popularity has been further enhanced by his copious notes to the text, which constitute a nearly complete commentary. Though he was not a native speaker of English, that should not disqualify him from consideration, as many native speakers read, understand, quote, use, and are influenced by his text. In his introduction, Yūsuf 'Alī promises to stay free of the too literal renderings which he feels have marred the work of his predecessors, such as Pickthall.[50] Like Pickthall, Yūsuf 'Alī frequently depends on the earlier Muhammad Ali translation, and he must have been aware of Pickthall's work as well.

While Yūsuf 'Alī became well known among the modern-educated South Asian Muslims of his time, many of whom certainly appreciated his trans-

46 Pickthall, vii–viii; Ann Fremantle, *Loyal Enemy*, London: Hutchinson & Co., Ltd., 1938, pp. 405, 408–420.

47 Pickthall, vii.

48 See for example Pickthall, 101 (surah 4, v. 64), 131 (surah 5, v. 93).

49 'Abd Allāh Yūsuf 'Alī, *The Holy Qur'ān: Text, Translation, and Commentary*, 3rd ed. 1938, reprint Beirut: Dār al-'Arabiyyah, 1968.

50 Yūsuf 'Alī, xv.

lation, his intended audience was more likely the native English speakers of the British Empire, of which Yūsuf ʿAlī was a faithful servant. This can be surmised, perhaps, from his two unsuccessful marriages to English women and his estrangement from all five of his children from them, all of which transpired before he began work on the translation. It can also be seen from the tone of his commentary, which would appear constantly to have sought to harmonize the content of the Qurʾān with expectations of the British ruling classes by explaining, defending, and justifying the book against misconstruals by imagined uninformed questioners or opponents. While Yūsuf ʿAlī may have wished therefore to produce a comfortably domesticated version of the Qurʾān, the result is hardly that, as his English is florid and frequently overloaded, probably owing to his anxiety to produce a rendention that would cover all that he believed the book to contain, as well as to make its language as beautiful as possible. While his work seems never to have gained much approval from the non-Muslim English-language readers he may have been aiming at, it became very popular among Muslims using English.

The fourth translation used in this study, that of Richard Bell (1876–1952), was published in 1937–1939[51] and stands apart from the others owing to its apparent hostility to traditional Muslim interpretation explicitly stated in the introductory notes to the text and to the various individual surahs. His purpose, far from that of Arberry and Pickthall, is to produce "a new translation of the Qurʾān which would present the results of critical study."[52] Hence, Bell states, "I have not aimed at literary elegance, but have rather sought to keep as close to the Arabic as the difference in the structures of the two languages would allow."[53] Thus, we are promised by our fourth translator a literal rendition like those by Muhammad Ali and Pickthall, but with no attention to any conveyance of rhetorical beauty. Having studied all of the seven translations that I am using here thoroughly, I would have to opine that Bell has succeeded in making his the most literalist of all—most of the time. However, given his faithfulness to his literalist purpose, it is surprising how often he agrees with rather than differs from the other translations and how often his renditions differ little even in literary elegance from those other efforts, occasionally even producing renderings that appear more felicitous or accurate. Such similarities to other translations in many cases go back to a shared dependence on the tradition of English-language Qurʾān translation. In this case, Bell often follows

51 For a recent critique, see Abdel Haleem, *Exploring*, 265–267.

52 Richard Bell, *The Qurʾān Translated, with a Critical Re-arrangement of the Surahs*, Edinburgh: T. & T. Clark, 1937–1939, Vol. I, p. v.

53 Bell, I, viii.

Pickthall and may have occasional effects from Rodwell, even though on the whole his translation is rather more original than is usual in these translations.

As Bell has not sought to make his translation particulary readable, it is not surprising that it never gained any popularity. Most noticeably, he has literally torn the text to pieces[54] by grouping the verses in scattered sections, sometimes placed alongside each other in two or more columns, sometimes separated by confusing dotted lines in an attempt to show what a haphazard collection of scraps the Qur'ān is in his opinion.[55] Some verses have even been broken into two or more pieces, which are assigned different places in the text, sometimes evidently because Bell did not understand a certain point of Arabic rhetoric, as will be demonstrated below. Bell's version is also not free of certain errors, some of which we will note, as well as occasional distortion, and he openly expresses his tendentiousness.[56] We must beware of his attitude, bearing it in mind while concentrating on the rhetorical points in his rendition of the Qur'ān, as in the case of the others.

Because Bell appears to have somewhat perversely torn the text to pieces in his desire to show its disunity, he has produced a work widely regarded as unreadable. To some extent, this parallels the idea already well established among Europeans that the Qur'ān is a disordered and incomprehensible book, as Voltaire, for example, claimed.[57] But rather than let the text stand with its contents in the order of the received text, and rather than merely rearranging the chapters, as done by Rodwell and some others, Bell has considerably rearranged the verses as well, turning the book into a jumble of scraps. So who then was his translation intended for? It might have been meant as a refutation of Islam thrown into the faces of the Muslims to show them that their scripture was not what they had supposed it to be. But more likely it was for European scholars to use in order to help them to understand how the Qur'ān was composed, in Bell's view. Because of all this, Bell's work cannot be considered much of a domesticating translation, even if it was done for a domesticating purpose,

54 Warned against by the Qur'ān itself in 15:91.

55 Bell, I, vi. Bell's contention about the composition of the Qur'ān has never gained much support even among non-Muslim scholars.

56 Bell, II, 612. Here there is a plain denial that the Qur'ān was revealed and an attempt to prove that the Qur'ān itself called on the Prophet to invent it.

57 See Voltaire, *Oeuvres complètes*, Vol. VII, *Dictionnaire philosophique*, Paris: L'Imprimerie de Fain, 1817, pp. 156, 158, where Voltaire says, "... cet Alcoran dont nous parlons est un recueil de révélations ridicules et de prédications vagues et incohérentes ..." and "Le Koran est une rapsodie sans liaison, sans ordre, sans art ..." Voltaire mentions the translations of du Ryer (French, 1647), Marracci (Latin, 1698), and Sale (English, 1734), all of which he may have consulted.

in this case, a kind of distancing from and disparagement of an other. Thus, it is foreignizing, if at all, only in a polemical sense. Yet his actual renderings in detail often nonetheless bear comparison with other translations, and he seems to have influenced Arberry occasionally, which illustrates the ambiguity of the English-language Qur'ān translation tradition.

The fifth translation that I will use is *The Koran Interpreted* of the well-known English orientalist Arthur J. Arberry (1905–1969), first published in 1955.[58] The book is generally free of obvious anti-Muslim prejudice or distortion, the translator, though not a Muslim, even clearly acknowledging in his revised and final introduction that the Qur'ān could be a divine revelation.[59] He states it is his purpose "to produce something which might be accepted as echoing however faintly the sublime rhetoric of the Arabic Koran." He likewise claims to have attempted to reproduce something of the rhythm of the original.[60] Furthermore, he asserts that he has tried to compose "clear and unmannered English, avoiding the 'biblical' style favored by some of my predecessors." Concluding, he notes he has been forced to retain the antique usage of the distinction between second person singular and plural, i.e., "thou" and "you," different verb endings, etc., to avoid confusion and has refused to include notes and glosses which do not occur in the original.[61] Being in the Oxford World's Classics series, the work is plainly intended for an educated audience, but we must assume from Professor Arberry's own words that he intended the work for the widest audience possible and that he tried to put it into "clear and unmannered," i.e., unaffected English as much as possible. However, as will be seen, the tone often nevertheless seems archaic, and it is surprising how many actual mistakes occur, considering Arberry's qualifications for the task. In fact, Arberry's work draws heavily on both Bell and Pickthall, which suggests why it is often similar to them. A major structural difference is that in contrast to Bell's deliberate cutting up and rearrangement of the text, Arberry has endeavored to separate the verses into semantic blocks, while retaining precisely the original order. This sectioning helps to make reading the text more comfortable than either the systems of Bell or of Pickthall, who merely gives the verses in numbered order as though in a list, each following its number in each surah. One has to own, however, that Pickthall's system is closer to the received text of the Qur'ān, which likewise contains no sectioning but has each verse clearly numbered.

---

58 For recent criticism of Arberry's translation, see Abdel Haleem, *Exploring*, 267–270.

59 Arthur J. Arberry, *The Koran Interpreted*, London: Oxford University Press, 1964, pp. xii–xiii.

60 Arberry, 1955 ed., I, 25–26, 1964 ed., x.

61 Arberry, 1964 ed., xii.

The sixth translation I am citing is that of N.J. Dawood (1927–2014), *The Koran*, first published by Penguin Classics in 1956,[62] the year after Arberry. This translation is important for the volume of its sales and use, as it crows on the back of the 1990 and 2014 editions, both of which I use and refer to below, "Over a million copies sold worldwide." This comment and its appearing in the very popular Penguin Classics series suggests that a major motive for its publication was commercial. Its potential audience was probably anticipated as worldwide, as has in fact turned out to be the case, but, as it was viewed as a literary publication rather than a religious or liturgical one, it was clearly aimed primarily at the non-Muslim audience. Being a translation of a very alien text, and being in the Penguin Classics series, which has always striven to enlist academically-qualified translators, it was not aimed at just any non-Muslim audience, but one consisting of educated readers, including academics, who might adopt it as their textbook, and their students. That Dawood's work has well suited the intended audience is proven by its continuing durability over a very long time, over sixty years, during which it has never ceased to be in print. Dawood's success is also indicated by the many revised versions he undertook to produce, eventually reaching a total of ten separate editions, representing nine major revisions after his original text,[63] as well as many reprints of the same editions.

As for the quality of Dawood's translation, its excellence is extolled on the back cover of the 1990 edition in an excerpt from *The Times* saying, "Across the language barrier Dawood captures the thunder and poetry of the original in such passages as those dealing with the Day of Judgement and Heaven and Hell." This underlines Dawood's fluency and easy accessibility as well as the literary merit of the translation in its own right, making it worthy of inclusion in the Penguin Classics literary canon of English, a canon that at first consisted entirely of translated classics from other languages, an element that is still dominant in the series. As observed by Lawrence Venuti in other contexts, the domesticating translation gives the illusion that it constitutes the original work itself, even while it in reality clearly does not.[64] By creating this illusion for all the diverse books translated in the Penguin Classics series, Penguin is able to annex many of the most outstanding works of other languages and cultures

62 N.J. Dawood, *The Koran*, 5th revised ed., London: Penguin Books, 1990, and extensively revised ed., London: Penguin Books, 2014.

63 Different editions of 1956, 1959, 1966, 1968, 1974, 1990, 1993, 1997, 2006, and 2014, as shown in Dawood, 2014, iv, xii–xiii.

64 Venuti, *Invisibility*, viii, 1, 6.

and assimilate them into the English literary canon.[65] The choice of the Qur'ān as an outstanding document in Arabic is obvious, and Dawood's translation is certainly a worthy effort in this assimilationist project.

The seventh and final translation I am considering is that of Muhammad Asad (1900–1992),[66] who was born Leopold Weiss and became Muhammad Asad on embracing Islam in 1926. Asad lived an active religious and political life in the Middle East, South Asia, and Europe. He is accounted one of the founders of Pakistan and even represented Pakistan in the United Nations. His last and greatest project was his Qur'ān translation completed in 1980, for which he was at first supported by Saudi Arabia but from which the Saudis withdrew support because his work contained modernist views they deemed unacceptable. Well-equipped to do the translation by his excellent knowledge not only of Arabic but also of much classical Muslim religious literature, especially Qur'ān exegesis, Asad was able to frame a translation and commentary that has appealed strongly to more educated and upper or middle-class Muslims, especially those living in English-speaking countries. While it has never achieved the circulation of Pickthall, Yūsuf 'Alī, or Dawood, it is nevertheless widely used and influential. Asad's translation is also characterized, even to a greater extent than Yūsuf 'Alī's, by exegetical expansions inserted into the translated text itself, in addition to detailed notes which constitute an almost comprehensive commentary. Thus, Asad's is the wordiest of the translations we are considering here.

In comparing these translations generally, we should note that Bell, Arberry, and Dawood present the bare text with very few explanatory footnotes or parenthetical insertions. Pickthall likewise has very few explanatory footnotes and mostly barebones introductions to the surahs but numerous parenthetical insertions in the text. Muhammad Ali also has some parenthetical additions, but he has a full commentary in his footnotes, while Yūsuf 'Alī is similar but with more insertions in the text. Muhammad Asad, like Muhammad Ali and Yūsuf 'Alī, has a full commentary in his footnotes and also the longest and most parenthetical additions to the text. These considerations matter, because more meaning can be given in more words. In general, I have not considered the footnotes in analyzing the translations of these translators, but one ought to remember that they do have the additional input in the footnotes to help them define the text. Of course, it is unsurprising that the four Muslim translators

65 See Venuti, *Invisibility*, 25–29, for comments on the Penguin Classics series in the context of another work.

66 Muhammad Asad, *The Message of the Qur'ān: The Full Account of the Revealed Arabic Text Accompanied by Parallel Translation*, Bristol, England: The Book Foundation, 2003.

are the ones with more such aids in parentheses and footnotes inserted into their texts, because their coreligionists who constitute a large part or nearly all of their audiences welcome such additional details as may be thus obtained.

As for the third preliminary consideration, the audience, we have already touched on that subject above. As we have seen, both Arberry and Pickthall aimed their works at a general audience of contemporary English-language readers, i.e., the widest possible audience. It must have seemed likely to them, however, that this group would differ somewhat from the general public as a whole, perhaps in being a little more educated and well-read. Thus we can account for Arberry's attempt at an elegant, literary rendition in the Oxford Classics series as aimed at a group that might be interested in reading the foreign classics as literature or books of wisdom. Pickthall was rather more concerned with religious overtones, in effect trying to create the equivalent of the Bible in English. To understand that, we should recall that his translation was published in 1349/1930, when more archaic language, especially for religious purposes, was popular.

However these seven translations may have been aimed at particular audiences, there is no doubt that six of them at least have achieved lasting success by remaining in print since their first appearance and and going through multiple editions. The oldest two, Pickthall and Yūsuf ʿAlī, have, according to one count, numbered 148 and 204 editions respectively in the seven or so decades since their first publication down through 2002;[67] the same writer claimed over 160 and over 200 for each of them by 2017,[68] and it is probable that there are many more editions of each that have escaped the record. It is also significant for Pickthall's lasting importance that his translation has been updated and republished by two different editing projects, both meant for mass circulation,[69] and Yūsuf ʿAlī has likewise been issued in two major revisions, although in his case these affect his commentary more than his translation

67 Abdur Raheem Kidwai, *Bibliography of the Translations of the Meanings of the Glorious Qur'an into English, 1649–2002: A Critical Study*. Riyadh: King Fahd Printing Complex, 1428/2007, pp. 8–76, 276–326.

68 A.R. Kidwai, "Muhammad Marmaduke Pickthall's English Translation of the Quran (1930): An Assessment," in *Marmaduke Pickthall: Islam and the Modern World*, ed. Geoffrey P. Nash, Leiden: E.J. Brill, 2017, p. 235.

69 The first revision of Pickthall is: M.M. Pickthall, *The Meaning of the Glorious Qur'an: Explanatory Translation*, rev. and ed. by Arafat Kamil El-Ashi, Beltsville, MD: Amana Publications, 1417/1996, while the second is in Jane McAuliffe, ed., *The Qur'ān: A Revised Translation, Origins, Interpretations and Analysis, Sounds, Sights, and Remedies, The Qur'ān in America*, New York: W.W. Norton & Co., 2017, pp. 3–349.

itself.[70] Arberry has also had several editions and remained continuously in print, while Dawood appears to have at least ten distinct editions as well as a number of unaltered reprints of those editions. Furthermore, Penguin claims that Dawood has sold over a million copies worldwide, making it obviously a major factor in the market for Qur'ān translations. One would imagine that Pickthall, Yūsuf ʿAlī, and Dawood are among the most widely circulated translations of any works into English. Meanwhile, Muhammad Ali and Muhammad Asad have also remained continuously in print since their first publication, with a number of new editions for each. Only Bell, only once reissued in 1960,[71] seems largely to have fallen by the wayside.

Thus, one must admit that these translations and others like them have been received by a very general audience with some variety of particular rhetorical expectations. This does not mean that there is only one kind of rhetoric that is stylish or effective, but rather that various kinds of rhetoric will have various effects on the readers. Hence, it is highly probable that, religious prejudices aside, a person's attitude towards the Bible and its prominent "biblical" style of the King James or even the Revised Standard versions will determine his or her attitude toward "biblical" style generally. From this we must grant that personal taste along with those very present personal prejudices in a number of readers will be large factors in determining reactions of English-speaking readers to these translations. Our task, then, is to separate, if we can, the instances of structural rhetorical difference from the other factors which may be operative, while at the same time giving some attention to the reasons for the probable reaction of a contemporary literate audience. As we shall see, the points that cannot be rendered into English successfully while maintaining something close to the original are relatively few, but there are a number that cause some difficulty or other that gives rise to a deviation from "normal" twentieth-century literary English rhetoric while nevertheless producing a certain rhetorical effect, suitable or not to its place in the text, on the mind of the reader.

---

70 These, which are related to each other but different, are: ʿAbdullah Yūsuf ʿAlī, *The Meaning of the Holy Qur'ān: New Edition with Revised Translation and Commentary*, 4th revised ed., Brentwood, MD: Amana Corporation, 1409/1989, and *The Holy Qur-ān: English Translation of the Meanings and Commentary*, ed. by the Presidency of Islamic Researches, Ifta, Call and Guidance, al-Madīnah: King Fahd Holy Qur-ân Printing Complex, 1410/1990.

71 As mentioned by Abdel Haleem, *Exploring*, 267, and verified in Worldcat.

7 The Development of Classical Arabic Rhetoric

In discussing rhetoric, I would first like to note that while the term "rhetoric" in English may have a pejorative sense, no such sense is intended here by me. By "rhetoric" I mean only the art of using language effectively,[72] with nothing of the connotation of empty talk, insincerity, or exaggeration often ascribed to this word. The Arabic term *balāghah*, usually translated as "rhetoric" or sometimes "eloquence" likewise contains no pejorative meaning. It is an expression relating to arrival, finishing, or reaching a goal and refers to the relation of words to each other, not the words themselves.[73] Regarding the speaker, it means he or she can originate speech most suitable to the requirement of the moment on any subject she or he desires.[74] If we ponder these attempts at defining rhetoric, we see that they are non-self-contradictory and fundamentally the same, all connected with the ideas of appropriateness and effectiveness of speech, and, of course, writing. Whether something is strictly grammatical or not, then, does not directly enter into consideration. In literature it is possible to make ungrammatical sentences and get away with them successfully, perhaps because other rhetorical features influence the point in question, rendering an effective and appropriate expression in its place. Nevertheless, we must concede generally that actually ungrammatical phrasing without artistic motive is likely to have an uneducated or else a foreign ring to it, and so affect the reader according to his attitude toward an alien style of expression. The reader will do well to bear in mind this definition of ours with its reservations in the following discussion, especially to enlighten himself or herself as to what we mean by rhetoric.

In the Muslim world, rhetoric has a long history of development.[75] Because Arabic was always the language of Muslim religious studies and has remained so to a large extent even down to the present, there has been a special focus on rhetoric of the Arabic language and the Qur'ān. The history of the develop-

---

72 Brooks & Warren, p. 6.

73 Muḥammad [ʿAlī] al-Basyūnī al-Bībānī, *Ḥusn aṣ-ṣanīʿ fī ʿilm al-maʿānī wa-l-bayān wa-l-badīʿ*, [Cairo]: Maṭbaʿat Dīwān ʿUmūm al-Maʿārif, 1301[/1883], p. 10; Aḥmad [b. Ibrāhīm b. Muṣṭafā] al-Hāshimī, *Jawāhir al-balāghah fī l-maʿānī wa-l-bayān wa-l-badīʿ*, ed. by Yūsuf aṣ-Ṣumaylī. Beirut: al-Maktabah al-ʿAṣriyyah, [1999], 40–42.

74 Bībānī, 11; Hāshimī, 42.

75 For a general coverage of this history, see Iḥsān ʿAbbās, *Tārīkh an-naqd al-adabī ʿinda l-ʿarab: naqd ash-shiʿr min al-qarn ath-thānī ḥattā l-qarn ath-thāmin al-hijrī*, Beirut: Dār al-Amāna, 1391/1971; Shawqī Ḍayf, *al-Balāghah: taṭawwur wa-taʾrīkh*, Cairo: Dār al-Maʿārif, [1965]; Abdul-Raof, *Arabic Rhetoric*, 31–56.

ment of Arabic rhetoric still contains many aspects that remain to be studied, but it is nevertheless possible to give a brief overview here, with particular reference to the main works which I will be using and citing in this book. Although all people, of course, use rhetoric as a normal part of language, the systematic study of it in a particular language or culture takes time to develop. In Arabic, language was studied from very early in Islam, so that the famous grammar book of Sībawayh (c. 143–c. 180/c. 760–c. 796) is one of the oldest surviving Arabic books, dating from the second/eighth century, just like the oldest Arabic history, Qur'ān commentary, hadith collection, legal texts, and genealogical works. Rhetoric began to get a start with the poetical criticism by the 'Abbāsid prince Ibn al-Mu'tazz (247–296/861–908), further elaborated by Abū Hilāl al-'Askarī (d. c. 400/c. 1010),[76] and with the rise of the concept of the inimitability of the Qur'ān which I have dealt with above, because it was felt that the quality of inimitability lay in the language of the Qur'ān specifically. In particular, ar-Rummānī (296–386/909–996) already presented ten divisions of rhetoric, which, though they differ from some later categories, already include pleonasm, coordination, lack of conjunctive, succinctness, and ellipsis,[77] out of the features we are considering here.

But Muslim rhetorical studies really did not gain their stride until 'Abd al-Qāhir al-Jurjānī (d. 471/1079 or 474/1081), who built a new theory of meaning on the idea that one had to go beyond considering the words to holding that their strength lay in their arrangement (*naẓm*). He held that the literary success or failure of a passage may well depend on an appealing arrangement of the words, not simply on the beauty of the sounds, words, and phrases, nor on the grammaticality of the passage alone. Thus, one grammatically correct passage may well not have the effectiveness of another carrying the same meaning.[78] To demonstrate his thesis, he elaborated on many of the rhetorical features or devices we are considering here. He also brought together both Qur'ānic verses and poetry as examples, uniting these two diverse kinds of discourse in rhetorical criticism. Most significantly, he foreshadowed the later division of Arabic rhetoric into *'ilm al-ma'ānī* and *'ilm al-bayān* by authoring one work, *Dalā'il al-i'jāz*, that became the basis for the former and another, *Asrār al-balāghah*, that

76 *Encyclopaedia of Islam*, 3rd ed., s. v. "al-'Askarī, Abū Hilāl" by Beatrice Gruendler.

77 Abū al-Ḥasan 'Alī b. 'Īsā ar-Rummānī, "an-Nukat fī i'jāz al-Qur'ān," in *Thalāth rasā'il fī i'jāz al-Qur'ān li-r-Rummānī wa-l-Khattābī wa-'Abd al-Qāhir al-Jurjānī, fī d-dirāsāt al-qur'āniyyah wa-n-naqd al-adabī*, ed. by Muhammad Khalaf Allāh and Muhammad Zaghlūl Salām, 3rd ed., Cairo: Dār al-Ma'ārif, [1976], p. 76; copied closely by Bāqillānī, 262; *EI*², s. v. "al-Rummānī" by J. Flanagan.

78 Abū Bakr 'Abd al-Qāhir b. 'Abd ar-Raḥmān b. Muḥammad al-Jurjānī, *Dalā'il al-i'jāz*, ed. by Maḥmūd Muḥammad Shākir. 3rd ed. Cairo: Maṭba'at al-Madanī, 1413/1992, pp. 98–102.

formed the basis for the latter. Al-Jurjānī was followed and used by the Qur'ān commentator az-Zamakhsharī (467–538/1075–1144), who analyzed many of the rhetorical structures in the Qur'ān.

In the next century, as-Sakkākī (555–626/1160–1229) was a foundational figure in Arabic rhetoric, first dividing it explicitly into the categories of *ʿilm al-maʿānī* and *ʿilm al-bayān*.[79] His near contemporary Ḍiyā' ad-Dīn Ibn al-Athīr (558–637/1163–1239), even though he organized his large works under a different scheme, was also tremendously influential on later developments in rhetoric itself, and he seems to be cited with much greater frequency than as-Sakkākī. One reason for this is simply that Ibn al-Athīr's two works together are larger and more comprehensive than as-Sakkākī's one book. Ibn al-Athīr's work seems to contain considerable original thought and commentary, which is perhaps why it is so often cited and its very examples quoted by later authors.[80]

After Ibn al-Athīr, rhetorical studies gradually began to adopt a more fixed form. Very significant is Badr ad-Dīn Ibn Mālik (c. 641–686/c. 1243–1287), described by B. Reinert as the first to add *ʿilm al-badīʿ*, which as-Sakkākī dealt with only cursorily as a subordinate part of *ʿilm al-bayān*,[81] to Arabic rhetoric as a third, independent branch.[82] Indeed, Badr ad-Dīn Ibn Mālik's work seems to detail the whole tripartite rhetorical scheme in the way that became canonical, but his subclassifications and explanations often differ from later writers, and he uses relatively few of the later standard examples. Also, because his work did not become the focus of later commentaries, his contribution has been somewhat neglected. In addition to Badr ad-Dīn Ibn Mālik and also possibly important in this endeavor, but not widely quoted or even known today, are the rhetorical works of Ibn an-Naqīb al-Maqdisī (611–698/1214–1298) and Najm ad-Dīn aṭ-Ṭūfī (675–716/1276–1316), both of whom extensively use and quote Ibn al-Athīr but also seem to have their own systems of classification.

---

79 Abū Yaʿqūb Yūsuf b. Abī Bakr Muhammad b. ʿAlī as-Sakkākī, *Miftāh al-ʿulūm*, 2nd ed. by Naʿīm Zarzūr, Beirut: Dār al-Kutub al-ʿIlmiyyah, 1407/1987, pp. 163–328 on *ʿilm al-maʿānī* and 329–432 on *ʿilm al-bayān*. The history of the origin and further development of these categories is extensively covered in *Encyclopaedia of Islam*, 2nd ed., s. v. "al-Maʿānī wa'l-Bayān" by B[enedikt] Reinert.

80 Ibn al-Athīr's work is placed by Abdul-Raof, *Arabic Rhetoric*, 55, under a category called "Simplified Summaries," which appears to me to be a gross underestimation of the former's importance and influence, even though Abdul-Raof seems to allow Ibn al-Athīr somewhat more importance in his paragraph on him.

81 Sakkākī, 423–432.

82 *EI*², "Maʿānī;" Badr ad-Dīn Muḥammad b. Jamāl ad-Dīn Muḥammad b. ʿAbd Allāh Ibn Mālik, *al-Miṣbāḥ fī l-maʿānī wa-l-bayān wa-l-badīʿ*, ed. by Ḥusnī ʿAbd al-Jalīl Yūsuf, Cairo: Maktabat al-Ādāb, [1989], pp. 159–275.

Finally, it was al-Qazwīnī (666–739/1268–1338) who came to be credited with most thoroughly systematizing and classifying all the rhetorical features in a system that became fairly fixed henceforth, even down to citing the same examples. Al-Qazwīnī's smaller work, *Talkhīṣ al-miftāḥ*, was written as a brief abridgement of as-Sakkākī's book, while al-Qazwīnī's other work, *al-Īḍāḥ*, is an expansion of and a commentary on his own *Talkhīṣ*. A number of other commentaries on the *Talkhīṣ* probably helped to make al-Qazwīnī's scheme the standard one. Nevertheless, later writers too, in particular az-Zarkashī (745–794/1344–1392), continued to show occasional new connections, ideas, and examples, and az-Zarkashī in particular did not adopt the classificatory scheme of al-Qazwīnī, possibly because that scheme had not become standard yet. But the adoption of al-Qazwīnī's system is clear in standard traditionalist modern works such as those of al-Bībānī (d. 1310/1892–1893) and al-Hāshimī (1295–1362/1878–1943). All of these, and other works from between the fourteenth and nineteenth centuries which I have not consulted, need to be studied more thoroughly to be establish the relationships of each to the others.

8 Western and Modern Reception and Analysis of Classical Arabic Rhetoric

Modern scholars have also considerably elaborated on classical Arabic rhetoric, including research into the particular tendencies and schools upheld by various writers. August Ferdinand Mehren (1822–1907) made a survey of the works of Arabic rhetoric available to Western scholars in his *Die rhetorik der Araber nach den wichtigsten quellen dargestellt* published in 1853. Translations of original Arabic books relating to classical rhetoric include Issa J. Boullata's translation *Three Treatises on the Iʿjāz of the Qurʾān: Qurʾanic Studies and Literary Criticism.*[83] These treatises on inimitability of the Qurʾān, of obvious relevance to rhetorical studies, were chosen for translation by the publisher no doubt because they are relatively short, but their authors, Abū al-Ḥasan ʿAlī b. ʿĪsā ar-Rummānī, Abū Sulaymān Ḥamd b. Muḥammad al-Khaṭṭābī (319–388/931–998), and ʿAbd al-Qāhir al-Jurjānī, are all both quite early and important. Another classical Arabic rhetorical work, albeit a later one, which is now available in

83 Abū al-Ḥasan ʿAlī b. ʿĪsā ar-Rummānī, Abū Sulaymān Ḥamd b. Muḥammad al-Khaṭṭābī, and ʿAbd al-Qāhir al-Jurjānī. *Three Treatises on the Iʿjāz of the Qurʾān: Qurʾanic Studies and Literary Criticism.* Ed. by Muḥammad Khalaf-Allāh Aḥmad and Muḥammad Zaghlūl Sallām. Tr. by Issa J. Boullata. Reviewed by Terri L. DeYoung. Reading, England: Garnet Publishing, 2014.

an abridged English adaptation is Pierre Cachia's *The Arch Rhetorician: or The Schemer's Skimmer: A Handbook of Late Arabic Badīʿ drawn from ʿAbd al-Ghanī an-Nābulsī's Nafaḥāt al-azhār ʿala nasamāt al-asḥār*.[84] Important recent scholars of Arabic rhetoric have included Seeger Bonebakker (1923–2005), with his studies on rhetoric and literary criticism,[85] and Wolfhart Heinrichs (1941–2014), who has presented studies on *majāz* and related topics.[86] Quite important for the history of Arabic rhetoric is a study by William Smyth.[87] A work dealing with ideological ramifications around the discussion of rhetoric of the Qurʾān is Mohammad Salama's *The Qurʾān and Modern Arabic Literary Criticism from Ṭāhā to Naṣr*.[88] Recent dissertations of importance include Lara Harb's "Poetics of Wonder: Aesthetic Experience in Classical Arabic Literary Theory," done at New York University in 2014 and forthcoming as a book from Brill, and Avigail Noy's "The Emergence of ʿIlm al-Bayān: Classical Arabic Literary Theory in the Arabic East in the 7th/13th Century," defended at Harvard University in 2016.

Indeed, Noy's work appears to be particularly important, as she criticizes the received tradition about Arabic rhetoric. She states that before an orthodox doctrine of rhetoric was established by al-Qazwīnī, there were other varieties of rhetorical tradition, but the authority accorded to al-Qazwīnī marginalized the contributions of previous scholars who did not adhere to his views while canonizing those who appeared to be his precursors. Thus, while ʿAbd al-Qāhir al-Jurjānī and as-Sakkākī became honored as early formulaters of the mainstream, many others were marginalized in various ways, particularly Ḍiyāʾ ad-Dīn Ibn al-Athīr, who, as mentioned above, did not follow the tradition

---

84 ʿAbd al-Ghanī an-Nābulsī, *The Arch Rhetorician: or The Schemer's Skimmer: A Handbook of Late Arabic Badīʿ Drawn from ʿAbd al-Ghanī an-Nābulsī's Nafaḥāt al-azhār ʿala nasamāt al-asḥār*. Tr., abridged, and rearranged by Pierre Cachia. Wiesbaden: Harrassowitz, 1998.

85 E.g., Seeger A. Bonebakker, *Materials for the History of Arabic Rhetoric: from the Ḥilyat al-Muḥāḍara of Ḥātimī (Mss. 2934 and 590 of the Qarawiyyīn Mosque in Fez)*, Napoli: Istituto Orientale, 1975; Seeger A. Bonebakker, "Religious Prejudices against Poetry in Early Islam." *Medievalia et Humanistica: Studies in Medieval and Renaissance Culture* 7 (1976), 77–99.

86 Wolfhart P. Heinrichs, "Contacts between Scriptural Hermeneutics and Literary Theory in Islam: The Case of Majaz," *Zeitschrift für Geschichte der Arabisch-Islamischen Wissenschaften* 7 (1991), 253–284; Wolfhart P. Heinrichs, "On the Figurative (*Majāz*) in Muslim Interpretation and Legal Hermeneutics," in Wolfhart P. Heinrichs, Mordechai Z. Cohen, and Adele Berlin, eds., *Interpreting Scriptures in Judaism, Christianity, and Islam: Overlapping Inquiries*, 2016, pp. 249–265.

87 William Smyth, "Criticism in the Post-Classical Period: A Survey," in *Arabic Literature in the Post-Classical Period*, ed. by Roger Allen and D.S. Richards, Cambridge: Cambridge University Press, 2008, pp. 387–417.

88 Mohammad Salama, *The Qurʾān and Modern Arabic Literary Criticism from Ṭāhā to Naṣr*, London, Bloomsbury Academic, 2018.

that became finally authoritative with al-Qazwīnī. Furthermore, the tradition followed by Ibn al-Athīr and continued in various ways by Ibn al-Naqīb, aṭ-Ṭūfī, and az-Zarkashī actually maintained an early tradition of Arabic rhetoric started by Ibn al-Muʿtazz and Abū Hilāl al-ʿAskarī, a tradition originally based more on the poetics of Arabic verse than on Qurʾān exegesis. Noy also points out that quite a few modern studies of Arabic rhetoric, because informed by the mainstream classical tradition, have tended to favor the study of al-Qazwīnī and the works he draws from, to the detriment of those not perceived as being in that tradition. Thus, Noy's thesis seems quite revisionist and likely to provoke much further discussion and elaboration. Noy's work is also welcome because it presents a detailed and nuanced handling of the relationships of several of the most prominent rhetoricians with each other.[89]

With regard to the rhetoric of the Qurʾan in particular, important works include those of Hussein Abdul-Raof,[90] Muhammad Abdel Haleem,[91] and Mustansir Mir.[92] Devin J. Stewart has also written on certain aspects of translation, rhetoric, and Qurʾanic interpretation. Many modern Arabic rhetorical studies also exist on various features of rhetoric, including not a few on the Qurʾān. These include works by Muṣṭafā Ṣādiq ar-Rāfiʿī (1298–1356/1880–1937), Sayyid Quṭb (1324–1386/1906–1966), Shawqī Ḍayf (1328–1426/1910–2005), ʿĀʾishah ʿAbd ar-Raḥmān, "Bint ash-Shāṭiʾ" (1331–1419/1913–1998), Badawī Ṭabānah (1332-at least 1418/1914-at least 1997), Aḥmad Maṭlūb (1355–1439/1936–2018), Aḥmad Aḥmad Badawī, and Muḥammad Muḥammad Abū Mūsā, among many others. Particularly important is Sayyid Quṭb's *at-Taṣwīr al-fannī fī l-Qurān*, which has even given rise to articles on it by Issa J. Boullata and A.H. Johns.[93]

89 Avigail Noy, "The Emergence of ʿIlm al-Bayān: Classical Arabic Literary Theory in the Arabic East in the 7th/13th Century," Ph.D. dissertation, Harvard University, 2016, pp. 1–19.

90 Hussein Abdul-Raof, *New Horizons in Qurʾanic Linguistics: A Syntactic, Semantic and Stylistic Analysis*. London: Routledge, 2018; Hussein Abdul-Raof, *Qurʾan Translation: Discourse, Texture and Exegesis*. Richmond, UK: Curzon Press, 2001.

91 M.A.S. Abdel Haleem, *Understanding the Qurʾan: Themes and Style*. London: I.B. Tauris Publishers, 1999.

92 Mustansir Mir, *Understanding Islamic Scripture: A Study of Selected Passages from the Qurʾān*, New York: Longman, 2008; Mustansir Mir, *Coherence in the Qurʾān: A Study of Islāhī's Concept of Nazm in Tadabbur-i Qurʾān*, Indianapolis: American Trust Publications, 1406/1986; Mustansir Mir, "Between Grammar and Rhetoric (*Balaghah*): A Look at Qurʾan 2:217," *Islamic Studies* 29 (1990), 277–285; Mustansir Mir, "Irony in the Qurʾan: A Study of the Story of Joseph" in Issa J. Boullata, ed., *Literary Structures of Religious Meaning in the Qurʾan*. Richmond, Surrey, England: Curzon, 2000. Pp. 173–187.

93 Sayyid Quṭb, *at-Taṣwīr al-fannī fī l-Qurʾān*, Cairo: Dār ash-Shurūq, 1993; A.H. Johns, "A Humanistic Approach to *iʿjāz* in the Qurʾan: The Transfiguration of Language," *Journal of Qurʾanic Studies* 13 (2011), 79–99.

9 Categories of Mainstream Classical Arabic Rhetoric

As we have seen, classical scholars of Arabic rhetoric divided the field into various categories, which became subsumed under al-Qazwīnī's nearly final classification into three, *ʿilm al-maʿānī*, *ʿilm al-bayān*, and *ʿilm al-badīʿ*. In this study, we will concern ourselves mainly with the first of these, *ʿilm al-maʿānī*, although one of the features we will consider is primarily categorized as a part of *naḥw* = grammar, while others are sometimes put under *ʿilm al-badīʿ*. The first category, *ʿilm al-maʿānī*, covers semantic distinctions that are more or less derived from syntax, in which the use of peculiar syntactical variations produces different effects on the meanings conveyed.[94] According to Herbjørn Jenssen, the central idea of *ʿilm al-maʿānī* to the Arabic rhetoricians like al-Qazwīnī is, "Meaning is not produced by the mere relationship—whatever the nature of that relationship may be—of a word to a concept, but rather through the ordering of words into structural patterns, where the patterns themselves contribute as much as the individual units combined into them."[95] Because such structural patterns are peculiar to each language, these syntactical aspects of texts add another problem to translation that must be considered. In the case we are dealing with here of translating Arabic Qur'ānic verses into English, it seems that, as we have already discussed regarding the question of translation in general, the bare meaning of a given passage in Arabic can be conveyed in English, though some of the existing translations may have lost it. Even if the loss is made inescapable by linguistic inadequacy, whether from lack of appropriate vocabulary items or another cause, it can nevertheless generally be at least partly overcome by the discovery of suitable idiomatic expressions, periphrastic excurses, sufficient explanations added in notes, or, perhaps occasionally, the development of new terminology.

The second field of Arabic rhetoric, *ʿilm al-bayān* as delimited by al-Qazwīnī, concerns those features which carry the intended meaning most effectively through the use of the accurate, concrete details which are embodied in simile and metaphor.[96] This is a more elastic category than *ʿilm al-maʿānī*, which

94 Hāshimī, 46–51; for a definition of syntax, see John Lyons, *Linguistic Semantics: An Introduction*, Cambridge, UK: Cambridge University Press, 1995, p. 375.

95 Herbjørn Jenssen, *The Subtleties and Secrets of the Arabic Language: Preliminary Investigations into al-Qazwīnī's Talkhīṣ al-miftāḥ*, Bergen: Centre for Middle Eastern and Islamic Studies, University of Bergen, Norway, 1998, p. 96.

96 Hāshimī, 216 n. 3. A third category of rhetoric called *ʿilm al-badīʿ*, dealing with rhetorical ornamentation and covering optional features of discourse, is also sometimes added. See Hāshimī, 298–299.

is largely bound to the different registers of meaning conveyed by finite syntactic features. Indeed, the variety of metaphor is endless. Possibly, one could make a distinction between the meaning itself conveyed in *al-maʿānī,* and the effect, conveyed in *al-bayān.* Accordingly, a bad metaphor may be decipherable but ineffective.[97] Thus, the category of *al-bayān* still relates to the area of translation through the problem of the loss of effect. Even if effect is not the same as the meaning itself, it may nevertheless play a crucial role in conveying the original intent clearly and accurately, since both rhetorical effect and meaning register in the consciousness and understanding of the hearer or reader.[98] So failure of rhetorical devices like metaphors and similes as well as the more syntactical devices may will dim the reader's comprehension in addition to affecting his or her attitude toward what he or she is reading.

The third area of Arabic rhetoric is *ʿilm al-badīʿ,* which is said to include adornment and special effects (*al-muḥassināt*). These seem vague enough that it would seem to be less clearly defined than the first two areas, but in al-Qazwīnī's system, it seems largely to consist of aspects of parallelism and counterpoint. The modern description of it by Abdul-Raof, who calls *al-badīʿ* "embellishments," appears to be rather broader, however.[99]

Although the areas of metaphor and simile are undoubtedly important, my work here is confined to a study of certain rhetorical features mostly falling under *ʿilm al-maʿānī.* Nevertheless, the reader may find I have made some redistribution of material from the original twofold division in order to go from the concrete, grammatical, and essential to features which may be more abstract, stylistic, and optional, as no firm border exists between these domains. From another angle, I will try to direct the reader's attention here to classifying what can be represented in English, what can only be approximated in English, and what is necessarily lost, the last of these not being my main concern. Of two of the particular classifications I will focus on, it does appear that the translation of discrete, syntactically-marked features into English results in less loss than the translation of those that are closer to metaphorical language.

---

97 Not to mention trite.

98 Henceforth we will say 'reader,' since we are here mostly concerned with the effect of rhetoric on the English-speaking reader, while recognizing that in Arabic the Qurʾān is meant to be heard. See above for discussion of this point.

99 Abdul-Raof, *Arabic Rhetoric*, 239–243. See also Jenssen, 42–45.

10 Extra-Rhetorical Features

In order to limit my discussion of rhetorical differences, I will first exempt from it certain extra-rhetorical factors that no doubt enter into the processes of semantics and rhetoric because of their strong effect on readers. Obviously one of these areas is word choice, the very point mentioned by Jenssen above as *not* pertaining to *ʿilm al-maʿānī*. Yet, word choice is a real difficulty for the translator not merely as a choice between two possible synonyms in the target language, but mostly owing to the lack of precise equivalence or appropriateness between two terms similar in meaning in two languages. One word in one language might be more appropriate and therefore "better" in a particular situation than its synonym in another language, because the areas of meaning covered by different words rarely coincide, and furthermore each word is surrounded by variously loaded connotations that prevent the possibility of exact equivalence.[100] Qurʾān 2:256 and its English translations provide us with a concrete instance:

(1) qad tabayyana r-rushdu min al-ghayy.

Pickthall translates the meaning of this[101] as:

(2) The right direction is henceforth distinct from error.

Whereas Arberry has:

(3) Rectitude has become clear from error.

Despite the similarity of the two translations and their agreement in meaning, each produces a different feeling in the reader. The matter turns on word choice; perhaps rectitude is too pedantic a term. "Right direction" conveys the

100 Jurjānī, 44, etc., denies that individual words in themselves can be considered more or less eloquent, except in the degree of familiarity of a word and in the pleasantness or harshness of its sounds. Based on this, he suggests that synonyms in one language or across different languages can exactly agree in their meaning; differences in effect are produced rather by the appropriateness of a particular word in its relations with other words in a text. Perhaps al-Jurjānī here claims a little too much for the exact equivalence of different words, for, although their effect is surely strongly determined by their environment as he says, word meanings do not usually fully coincide, but more commonly partially overlap.

101 Henceforth I will say "translates this" for brevity, realizing that nothing can provide a perfect translation.

message more clearly, "rectitude" being an obscure and rather archaic word of low frequency, possibly conjuring up moral stuffiness or prudishness, which "right direction" does not. While the collocation "right direction" may also be of relatively low frequency, it is clearer than "rectitude," and more explicit because it is analyzable into contemporary morphemes. Another point here is the question of the consistency of the word choice in the remainder of the translations of the verse, i.e., horizontal co-occurrence. It may be that "right direction" would go better in (3) and "rectitude" in (2) where the other archaic word "henceforth" appears. It must be admitted that there is a certain amount of difference among the various English translations in the matter of word choice and that this matter results in various degrees of effectiveness. What it reduces to in grammatical terms, of course, is that both "right direction" and "rectitude" may be literally correct translations of the Arabic *rushd*, which may also be translated in other circumstances as "consciousness," "reason," or "maturity."[102] This can be represented schematically as shown in Figure 1 below.[103]

In this figure, the lined area of the overlapping circles representing *rushd*, "right direction," and "rectitude" covers at least part of the semantic point in question in 2:256 (1). Since neither "right direction" nor "rectitude" covers exactly the semantic area of *rushd*, neither can have precisely the same implication for or effect on the English-speaking reader as the Arabic term has on the Arabic speaker, though they might convey the basic semantic meaning of *rushd* found in the original verse. The point is that one word in English will rarely if ever be found to cover the exact semantic province of an Arabic word and vice versa, much less have the same rhetorical value. Thus word choice will be left to the skill and preference of the translator and judgement to the taste of the reader, and such word choice will always lead to differences among the various translations offered.

To emphasize this point, we might examine one further example related to verse 37:64:

(4) innahā shajaratun takhruju fī aṣli l-jaḥīm.

This refers to the horrible tree of Zaqqūm, food of the ingrates in Hell.

Arberry renders the verse:

102 Edward William Lane, *Arabic-English Lexicon*, London: Williams and Norgate, 1863–1893, Vol. III, p. 1080.

103 Barnstone, 38, attributes the idea of words as circles of meaning to Schopenhauer, but unfortunately without reference.

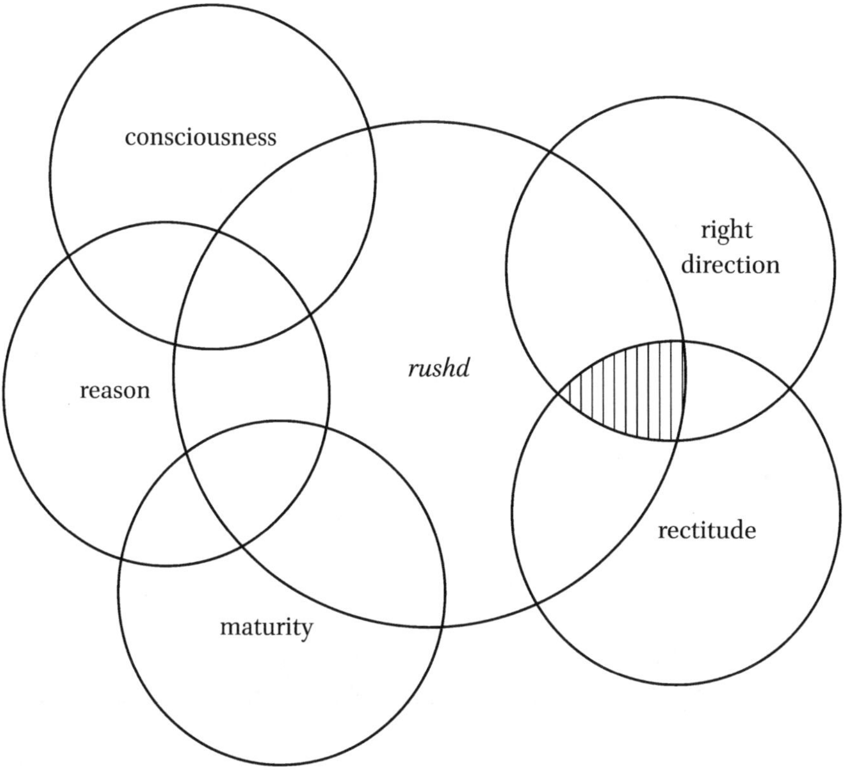

FIGURE 1 The overlapping meanings of *rushd* translated into English

(5) It is a tree that comes forth in the root of Hell;

He has adhered to as literal a translation as possible for all the words, conveying the meaning adequately enough except for the word "root," which has a narrower meaning in English than *aṣl* does in Arabic, and thus might seem slightly incongruous to the English-speaking reader, who also may mix up the images of "tree" and "root," a problem that does not occur in the Arabic because *aṣl* does not usually mean a tree root. However, the Arabic seems more exciting than Arberry's rendition would allow. The dull "It is …" hardly conveys the emphasis of *innahā* in the original. Pickthall, on the other hand, has attempted to capture the rhetorical effect of the original without literally translating the words, thus potentially running afoul of charges of disturbing the meaning:

(6) 64. Lo! it is a tree that springeth in the heart of hell

We might question the use of "springeth" for *takhruju* and "heart" for *aṣl*, although the latter conveys the notions of basicness[104] and origin implicit in *aṣl* better than "root" in this place. But, although both of these might work in this verse, Bell has:

(7) 62. It is a tree which cometh forth from the bottom of the Hot
Place, ...

Until the last two words, he has perhaps done better than Arberry, if we were to consider "bottom" preferable to "root." But, "Hot Place," while it may be literally a correct translation of *jaḥīm*, is inappropriate and unacceptable. "Hot Place" makes the seriousness of the Qurʾānic passage, which no one doubts in Arabic, evaporate into silliness in English. It is the kind of phrase that might be used in jokes about hell in English and hence conveys an unserious connotation, and it is also somewhat off from the literal meaning of *jaḥīm*, which involves blazing fire.[105] Since the Qurʾān presents itself as a serious book, the overall effect seems lacking in Bell's translation here.

Obviously, the nuances of the word choice and their effect on rhetoric deserve attention. Nevertheless, despite the numerous instances that could be cited, I must leave considering them out of the scope of the present study. I will try to avoid verses whose translations are unduly affected by word choice and other simple problems related to single words.

Aside from word choice, another major area outside of the structures of *ʿilm al-maʿānī* that doubtless strongly affects the understanding of the reader is that of cultural factors. Some imagery can only be discussed in a cultural context. An outstanding example is provided by verses 81:1–4:

(8) idhā sh-shamsu kuwwirat.
wa-idhā n-nujūmu nkadarat.
wa-idhā l-jibālu suyyirat.
wa-idhā l-ʿishāru ʿuṭṭilat.

As rendered by Bell, this becomes:

(9) 1. When the sun shall be veiled,
2. When the Stars shall become murky,

104 As in the expression, "the heart of the matter."

105 Lane, II, 384.

3. When the mountains shall be moved,
4. When the camels ten months gone with young shall be untended.

The surah goes on to paint the signs of the Day of Resurrection in similar colors until verse 14. Whatever the quality of Bell's translation, the English-speaking reader is bound to be struck by the incongruity of following the overthrow of the sun, stars, and mountains with the mention of camels. That aside, while the reader may or may not recognize the importance camels had to the original hearers of the Qur'ān, he is not at all likely to be able to distinguish this most valuable kind of camels (*ʿishār*) from other kinds,[106] at least not without the help of an expansion of the text or a footnote. Also, the incongruity of coming upon pregnant camels while reading a description of the eschatological cataclysm of Judgement Day is likely to spoil the effect for the westerner, even if he has some knowledge of the Middle East, for he will probably not find it dramatically appealing. In fact, he may find it laughable or rather bathetic, a fall from the sublime to the ridiculous, especially if reading Arberry's version of 81:4:

(10) … when the pregnant camels shall be neglected, …

While he has tried to preserve the brevity of the original, Arberry's use of the word "pregnant" in this context is even more likely to appear unserious, because of the gravity of the other events mentioned. Furthermore, the number of words necessary to render *ʿishār* into English is at least two; Bell employs six to convey the meaning more exactly. This causes the verses to appear unbalanced in English, whereas their Arabic ordering is rhythmically weighted and impeccable. There are naturally numerous passages of a like nature in the Qur'ān.[107] But these are more closely connected with culture than rhetoric.[108] As its effect on the reader will depend on his acculturation rather than on the structural features of *ʿilm al-maʿānī*, we will have to ignore them here.

Besides these two, word choice and cultural factors, there are other effects simply lost in translation. No attempt will reproduce the euphony of the Arabic sounds; one cannot make a translation and have an identical sound pattern at

106 Quṭb, *Fī ẓilāl*, VI, 3838, treats the Arabs' attitude toward camels and their various kinds.
107 See for example Qur'ān 88:17–20.
108 Verses dealing with the Last Judgement are related to the Arabian environment by Ibtisām Marhūn aṣ-Ṣaffār, *at-Taʿābīr al-qurʾāniyyah wa-l-bīʾah al-ʿarabiyyah fī mashāhid al-qiyāmah*, an-Najaf: Maṭbaʿat al-Adab, 1387/1967.

the same time. Likewise, the rhythm of Arabic can scarcely be reproduced,[109] though the jacket of Arberry's translation avers that he will attempt to do just that. Most noticeably, the "rhymed prose" endings of the Qur'ānic verses are lost. These and a host of other effects contained in *ʿilm al-badīʿ* of the Arabic rhetoricians, though rhetorical devices certainly affecting the hearer or reader, cannot, by the simple differences in language, be reproduced in English, and we will make no attempt to deal with them here.

Let us turn to the discussion, then, of the various rhetorical factors we are going to consider. These fall into a few broad categories, each of which contains several divisions which I will detail in turn. Going from the more concrete to the more abstract and from the smaller in scope to the larger generally, I begin with an examination of word order restraints and several other odd syntactic features in Arabic whose effect may be lost in English. There will follow the subjects of emphasis, long exposition (*iṭnāb*), and parallelism, coordination, separation or asyndeton (*faṣl*), and parenthetic insertions breaking the thread of the text (*iʿtirāḍ*), all of which are somewhat related. Then I will examine brevity or abridgement, omissions, and ellipsis. All these form an area of more or less mandatory Arabic rhetorical features that for one reason or another may sometimes raise problems in English.

109 The "destruction of rhythm" is singled out as a problem and limitation of translation by Berman, 248.

CHAPTER 1

Inversion of Word Order

To begin with, then, let us consider certain matters of word order. It must be realized that this area is exceedingly wide and includes many features and rhetorical conventions governing the use of these features in both Arabic and English. Many of these used in Arabic are catalogued by al-Jurjānī, Ḍiyāʾ ad-Dīn Ibn al-Athīr, Najm ad-Dīn aṭ-Ṭūfī, and others, who call this complex of features *at-taqdīm wa-t-taʾkhīr*, advancing and delaying.[1] In ancient rhetoric, the rhetorical feature of changing the word order for effect was known as *hyperbaton*,[2] which is still a technical term today.[3] This feature is also known as *hysteron proteron*.[4] We will look briefly at a few cases of varied treatment of placement of prepositional phrases in sentences in the two languages, what results, and how the Arabic might be rendered into English.[5]

---

1 Jurjānī, 106–145, 286–287, 338–339; Ḍiyāʾ ad-Dīn Naṣr Allāh b. Muhammad Ibn al-Athīr, *al-Mathal as-sāʾir fī adab al-kātib wa-sh-shāʿir*, ed. by Aḥmad al-Ḥawfī and Badawī Ṭabānah, Cairo: Dār Nahḍat Miṣr li-ṭ-Ṭibāʿah wa-n-Nashr wa-t-Tawzīʿ, 1379–1385/1959–1965, Vol. II, pp. 216–235; Najm ad-Dīn Sulaymān b. ʿAbd al-Qawī aṭ-Ṭūfī, *al-Iksīr fī ʿilm at-tafsīr*, ed. by ʿAbd al-Qādir Ḥusayn, Cairo: Maktabat al-Ādāb, 1397/1977, pp. 154–170, 216–218. See also Badawī Ṭabānah, *Muʿjam al-balāghah*, 3rd rev. ed., Jiddah: Dār al-Manārah, 1408/1988, p. 689; Jenssen, 90–94; Abdul-Raof, *New Horizons*, 141–142, 195.

2 Longinus, *On the Sublime*, ed. & tr. by W. Hamilton Fyfe, rev. by Donald Russell, Cambridge, MA: Harvard University Press (Loeb Classics 199), 1995, Ch. 22; Demetrius, *On Style*, tr. by Doreen C. Innes, Cambridge, MA: Harvard University Press (Loeb Classics 199), 1995, sections 139, 249. The examples of *hyperbaton* given in *Rhetorica ad Herrenium: Ad C. Herrenium: De Ratione Dicendi*, ed. & tr. by Harry Caplan, Cambridge, MA: Harvard University Press (Loeb Classics), 1954, Bk. 4:32:44 and Quintilian, *The Orator's Education*, ed. & tr. by Donald A. Russell. Cambridge, MA: Harvard University Press (Loeb Classics), 2001, Bk. 8:6:62–67; Bk. 9:4:26–32, do not seem so similar to the changes of word order we are discussing here, which reflects the very different structure of the Latin language and its rhetoric.

3 Dupriez, 214–215; Harris, 73–76, including also anastrophe; Theresa Enos, ed., *The Encyclopedia of Rhetoric and Composition: Communication from Ancient Times to the Information Age*, New York: Routledge, 1996, p. 334.

4 Mir, *Understanding*, 74.

5 This exact point in examined briefly in Abdullah S. Al-Sahli, "Non-canonical Word Order: Its Types and Rhetorical Purposes with Reference to Five English Translations of the Meanings of the Holy Qurʾan," Ph.D. dissertation, Durham University, 1996, pp. 158–160. For a longer comparison of *taqdīm wa-taʾkhīr* in Arabic and English, see Ahmed Saleh Elimam, *Marked Word Order in the Qurān and Its English Translations: Patterns and Motivations*, Newcastle upon Tyne: Cambridge Scholars Publishing, 2013, pp. 49–76.

 | DOI:10.1163/9789004417441_003

One instance requiring the precedence of a predicate before a subject in Arabic is *ḥaṣr*, limitation of a subject to its predicate only, as demonstrated by verse 109:6:[6]

(11) lakum dīnukum wa-liya dīn.

Here the Arabic clearly places the *khabar* (predicate) first to indicate that your religion is for you only, and my religion is for me. This feature is described by Arabic sources as a kind of narrowing specification, rendered variously by *ḥaṣr*, *takhṣīṣ*, or other terms.[7]

This verse is rendered by Arberry in a very literal manner, which does not sound like idiomatic English, borders on being incorrect usage, and appears ungraceful:

(12) To you your religion, and to me my religion!

Yūsuf ʿAlī, while likewise preserving the word order of the original, provides a verb to help the English:

(13) 6. To you be your Way,
And to me mine.

However, Bell takes a different approach, striving for a more lucid but less literal rendering:

(14) 6. Ye have your religion, and I have mine.

This latter rendition contains perhaps a slight variation of emphasis with a bit harsher tone than the first, because of the initial placement of "Ye" and "I." Neither contains the limitation of the meaning of the Arabic exactly, but Bell is closer. Striving further for the emphasis of the Arabic *ḥaṣr* (specification) here, Dawood translates:

---

6 Cited by Ibn Mālik, 38.

7 Sakkākī, 219, calls this feature in this verse a kind of *takhṣīṣ* = specification, while Ibn al-Athīr, *Mathal*, II, 216–218, followed by Ṭūfī, 158, calls it *ikhtiṣāṣ*, with the same meaning. Bībānī, 35, calls it *ḥaṣr*. Meanwhile Hāshimī, 136, being more specific, calls this *ifādatu qaṣr al-musnad ilayhi ʿalā l-musnad*, which also amounts to the same meaning or implication. See also Abdul-Raof, *Arabic Rhetoric*, 152, for a closely parallel example. See Abdul-Raof, *New Horizons*, 198–199, for what he calls "restriction tools" = *adawāt al-ḥaṣr*.

(15) You have your own religion, and I have mine.[8]

Here the word "own" added to Bell's translation further emphasizes the religious separation that the verse is speaking of, but at the cost of adding a word. That he nevertheless added that word shows that Dawood was perplexed by the problem of translating this Arabic rhetorical feature and was not satisfied with Bell's partial solution.

To further illustrate the difference in these translations, if we put the Arabic text in its normal, unmarked word order, we could say:

(16) dīnukum lakum wa-dīnī lī.

We might then be able to translate it:

(17) Your religion is for you, and mine is for me.

Both (16) and (17) imply in the idiom of each language that the other religion exists but that the persons mentioned each have their own religion already chosen. This differs from the preceding examples in that the feature of *ḥaṣr* implied by the advancement of the propositional phrase gives a more exclusive sense of possession, as indicated by Bell and Dawood with their use of "have" in (14) and (15). Thus in English the semantic change is achieved by a verbal change, from "yours is for you" to "you have yours," but in Arabic it is accomplished by placing the prepositional phrase of the predicate before the subject. A parallel semantic change is hence realized through variant surface structures. In the translations here, Arberry seems to give more the meaning of (16), while Bell and Dawood give the meaning of the quoted verse (11) more correctly. Arberry, by sticking to the Arabic word order as closely as possible has lost the nuance implicit semantically in the literal change from (16) to (11). But we must acknowledge that this is a problem that can at least be dealt with by the translator semantically.

A somewhat thornier problem arises in the matter of giving the verb its prepositional phrase before giving an object. An example of this occurs in 72:2:

(18) wa-lan nushrika bi-rabbinā aḥadā.

8 Dawood, 1990, 433. He has removed the word "own" by the 2014 edition. Dawood, 2014, 423.

Of course, there is nothing faulty or exceptional about the Qur'ānic Arabic of the verse. The direct object *aḥadā* being placed last creates a strong emphasis on that word, underlining in this case that the jinn who are speaking are truly faithful believers and would never worship anyone except Allāh.[9] However, the change of word order regarding the prepositional phrase *bi-rabbinā* as the object of *aḥadā* does not produce such a great semantic change here as in (16) to (11) above, though there may be a slight difference in emphasis:

(19) wa lan nushrika aḥadan bi-rabbinā.

But in English the same does not obtain. Bell has:

(20) ... and we shall not with our Lord associate any one;

This translation suffers from two weaknesses. First, the placement of the prepositional phrase complement "with our Lord" before the verb, not just before the object, represents a weakness not justified by any artistic effect derived from the change and is besides a license seldom used in Arabic that indeed does not occur in the Qur'ānic text here. A second problem is the ambiguity that arises should the reader take "with our Lord" as an addition to the subject "we," a potential reading of (21) given the text.[10] Arberry at least avoids these defects:

(21) ... and we will not associate with our Lord
anyone.

Pickthall, on the other hand, reverses the Arabic word order by placing the direct object immediately after the verb. But he also removes the negation from the verb to that object as "no partner":

(22) ... and we ascribe no partner unto our Lord.

Pickthall's translation possesses a more normal English word order, while both Bell and Arberry suffer from awkwardness in translating this verse. If Arberry's wording is changed to the more "normal" English word order, we get:

9 Placing a word last for emphasis is mentioned for Greek by Demetrius, 50–52.
10 For a similar kind of ambiguity, compare the critical comment of Quintilian, 8:2:14, on a line of Virgil.

(23) ... and we will not associate anyone with our Lord.

By "normal," we mean the ordinary word order of speech where no special motives for changing it exist. Thus (23) follows the word order given above in (19) rather than that of the verse (18). But while the Arabic can be written correctly either way, ordinary English prose heavily prefers (23), although English poetry has features of change of normal word order and even involutions of syntax that may be brought off successfully by an artist's skill. The principle involved in the acceptability of (23) as opposed to the awkwardness of, for example, (21) seems to rest on the idea of the heaviness of prepositional phrase in question. If we give (23), the normal, unmarked order and "associate X with Y," we find that changing this to "associate with Y X" is only acceptable if X is a heavy noun phrase. For example, if we have a sentence:

(24) And we will not associate with our Lord any of the prophets of religion who have been raised to divine status by some.

We will find that (24) is certainly acceptable and to many preferable to:

(25) And we will not associate any of the prophets of religion who have been raised to divine status by some with our Lord.

In this formulation (25), the prepositional phrase "with our Lord" is sundered from the verb "associate" with which it is necessarily tied in (24), introducing an element of ambiguity and confusion.

There are also other parallel examples. If we have:

(26) I gave it to him.

We find that the change of word order parallel to (21) is generally unacceptable in prose English, as in:

(27) I gave to him it.

However, as in the case of (24) and (25), by substituting a long noun phrase for the object, the order of (21) and (27) becomes acceptable if not actually preferable:

(28) I gave to him all the money which I'd been piling up in my savings account for years.

Yūsuf ʿAlī's translation of Qur'ān 72:2 manages to produce some of these wordy effects:

(29) We shall not join (in worship)
Any (gods) with our Lord.

Here, the effect of the original in placing the object last is lost, while the object is still separated from its verb by the parenthetical addition "(in worship)."

Returning to the translations, we notice that Pickthall's (22) represents the most usual English word order. But it might be objected, what about the changes of word order in literature? For example, we have in Henry IV, Pt. 2, Act 1, Sc. 1, v. 111:

(30) From whence with life he never more sprung up.

It is safe to assume that normal conversational or prose style using the same words would be:

(31) From whence he never more sprung up with life.

This too might seem a bit archaic because of the expression "whence," in addition to the clumsiness of "up with life." But the point is that Shakespeare brings (30) off successfully and similar changes are frequent in literature. What then is wrong with (21)? First, noting that the heaviness rule does not apply here, we must conclude the reader will recognize (21) as having a marked or unusual order. No discernable reason is present in the structure of the line to explain this change. There is no reason either in the context to suppose the reader can discern that Arberry has striven to place the English equivalent of the Arabic rhyme word at the end of each verse in Surah 72, as the rhyme is in Arabic, not English, and there is not any recognizable English artistic effect. Thus, the reader will be likely to suppose either that the translation is awkward or that it involves an "exotic" rhetorical device. That in turn may result in either a positive or negative judgement on the quality of the Qur'ān by English-language readers. To conclude, Bell and Arberry have evidently felt constrained to retain the Arabic rhyme word "any one" in its place, despite its ruining the rhetorical aspect of their treatment of this verse, just as Arberry's adherence to the surface appearance and order of the Arabic words in (12) produced a somewhat less natural-sounding result. From this, it appears there are cases when the English word order is under greater constraint than the Arabic.

Another example of similar nature from the same surah is found in 72:22:

(32) qul lan yujīranī min Allāhi aḥadun …

But here two of the translators have chosen to adopt a more unmarked English word order, abandoning the end placement of the English equivalent of *aḥadun*. This is probably because of *aḥadun* not being a rhyme word falling at the end of a verse as was *aḥadā* in (18) above, leaving them free to abandon attempts to keep it in its place. So Bell has, for example:

(33) 22. Say: "No one will protect me from Allah, …"

This is a fair rendering of the Arabic according to the English forms, as in (24) above. Pickthall and Yūsuf ʿAlī are similar in word order to Bell, but Arberry has:

(34) Say: 'From God shall protect me not anyone …'

Here, the translator completely reverses the normal English word order apparently only for the purpose of saving the position of the last word in the Arabic word order, similar to what we described above in the case of 72:2. Even so, he does not otherwise stick to the word order of the original (32). Again, line (34) represents a marked, heavy order which keeps the delayed positioning of the subject at the cost of opaqueness. It should perhaps be noted, however, that changing the normal Arabic word order is frequent in the Qurʾān, sometimes according with the rhyme pattern, but also often not for that purpose. And, of course, none of the Qurʾān's word order should be taken as accidental.

In my discussion of numbers (11) through (34), I have sought to draw the reader's attention to three points. First of all, it is clear that the order of Arabic in cases of the kind we have just examined, moving a prepositional phrase before object and/or subject, cannot be directly rendered into English retaining both word order and meaning. Second, the word order of English seems to be rather more fixed and Arabic more flexible, at least in these examples, especially verse 72:2. Lastly, we must state a reservation: The Qurʾān is a very special type of Arabic prose, and far wider word order shifts are certainly allowed to literature generally. Nevertheless, we can conclude this is an area that evidently offers some difficulty to translators.

CHAPTER 2

Iltifāt

Another area that may cause more difficulty to the translator is the feature known as *iltifāt*,[1] which means "turning attention." It is considered such a significant marker of Arabic rhetoric that the famous medieval rhetorician Ḍiyāʾ ad-Dīn Ibn al-Athīr (558–637/1163–1239) even asserts that it is a feature found only in Arabic and not in other languages,[2] though we shall see that this is not really the case. *Iltifāt* consists of three parts: 1) the use of pronominal terms or verbal inflections differing in person and number for the same referent in the same sentence or passage,[3] 2) using the imperative in place of the future or past, 3) using the future in place of the past or the past in place of the future. In this chapter, I will be dealing only with the first of these rather different features, though the second of these follows in Chapter Three below.

The relatively free changing in Arabic from one pronominal term or verbal inflection to another while still intending the same referent, is certainly one of the outstanding problems for translators of the Qurʾān, where is it quite common,[4] although the same feature occurs much less in both modern Arabic and English. Anciently, it was already recognized and mentioned by the famous Greek rhetorician called Longinus, who extends Greek technical term *polyptô-*

1 Abū al-ʿAbbās ʿAbd Allāh b. Muḥammad Ibn al-Muʿtazz, *Kitāb al-badīʿ*, ed. by ʿIrfān Maṭrajī, Beirut: Muʾassasat al-Kutub ath-Thiqāfiyyah, 1433/2012, pp. 73–74; Ibn al-Athīr, *Mathal*, II, 170–191; Muhammad b. Sulaymān al-Balkhī al-Maqdisī Ibn an-Naqīb, *Muqaddimat Tafsīr Ibn an-Naqīb fī ʿilm al-bayān wa-l-maʿānī wa-l-badīʿ wa-iʿjāz al-Qurʾān*, ed. by Zakariyyā Saʿīd ʿAlī, Cairo: Maktabat al-Khānjī, 1415/1995, pp. 202–209; Ṭūfī, 140–144; Jalāl ad-Dīn Muḥammad b. ʿAbd ar-Raḥmān al-Khaṭīb al-Qazwīnī. *al-Iḍāḥ fī ʿulūm al-balāghah: al-maʿānī wa-l-bayān wa-l-badīʿ*, ed. ʿAbd al-Qādir Ḥusayn, 1st ed., Cairo: Maktabat al-Ādāb, 1416/1996, pp. 102–107; Abū ʿAbd Allāh Badr ad-Dīn Muḥammad b. ʿAbd Allāh b. Bahādur az-Zarkashī, *Al-Burhān fī ʿulūm al-Qurʾān*, ed. Muḥammad Abū al-Faḍl Ibrāhīm, 1st ed., Cairo: Dār at-Turāth (ʿĪsā al-Bābī al-Ḥalabī), 1376/1957, Vol. III, pp. 314–337. For extensive coverage of Qurʾānic *iltifāt* written in English, see Abdel Haleem, *Understanding*, 184–210; Abdul-Raof, *New Horizons*, 142–167, 190–191; Mir, *Understanding*, 7, 26–27, 62, 73, 79–80, 132, 154. Abdel Haleem finds that the most extensive and penetrating coverage of *iltifāt* occurs in Ḍiyāʾ ad-Dīn Ibn al-Athīr and az-Zarkashī. For a modern overview, see Ṭabānah, *Muʿjam*, 626–629.

2 Ibn al-Athīr, *Mathal*, II, 171.

3 Abdel Haleem, *Understanding*, 186–187. Ibn an-Naqīb, pp. 209–213, names several other features *iltifāt* as well.

4 The hundreds of instances of *iltifāt* are extensively catalogued by Abdel Haleem, although he warns that his listing is not exhaustive. See Abdel Haleem, *Understanding*, 189–190, 198, 201, 203.

 | DOI:10.1163/9789004417441_004

ton, meaning "having multiple inflections," to cover the same area as the *iltifāt* of the Arabic rhetoricians.[5] This is not the same as the *polyptôton* described by Hussein Abdul-Raof, who places *iltifāt* in another category which he calls "shift" and calls "the most common feature in Qur'anic discourse."[6] Likewise, S.Z. Chowdhury calls *iltifāt* "shift" and identifies *polyptôton* as a different device he names morphological *jinās*.[7] However, it is clear that Longinus has exactly described a form of *iltifāt* equivalent to that used in the Qur'ān and in Arabic, and thus appears to be the first writer to note this rhetorical feature.

In modern English rhetoric, *iltifāt* overlaps considerably but not completely with the feature called apostrophe, meaning in ancient Greek "a turning away." First mentioned by ancient rhetoricians in the context of legal arguments,[8] it is defined in modern rhetoric as, "The orator breaks off suddenly to address someone or something."[9] Another definition of apostrophe in English rhetoric is "a direct address to someone, whether present or absent, and whether real, imaginary, or personified." Furthermore, "Its most common purpose is to permit the writer to turn away from the subject under discussion for a moment and give expression to built-up emotion."[10] While apostrophe would certainly qualify as a form of *iltifāt*, however, it is only a small part of the Arabic concept.

In Arabic, *iltifāt* is employed to bring something to the reader's immediate attention, owing to the necessity or suitability of meditating on its points, as well as being a means of introducing rhetorical variety so as not to bore the reader.[11] Thus it constitutes a device for emphasis, which we might perhaps describe as a rhetorical aside. This represents another area where English has a somewhat greater degree of constraint than Arabic, at least Qur'ānic Arabic. In English it might be likened, for example, to:

---

5 Longinus, 27. Arabic *iltifāt*, however, covers only a part of Longinus's examples of *polyptōton*.

6 Abdul-Raof, *Qur'an Translation*, 77–79, 96, 118; Abdul-Raof, *Arabic Rhetoric*, 258. Abdul-Raof also includes in "shift," beside "person and number shift," which is *iltifāt*, "word order shift" and "voice shift." Mir, *Understanding*, 7, etc., also refers to *iltifāt* as "shift." This usage of "shift" for *iltifāt* may have arisen from Abdel Haleem's earlier article, M.A.S. Abdel Haleem, "Grammatical Shift for Rhetorical Purposes: *Iltifat* and Related Features in the Qur'an," *Bulletin of the School of Oriental and African Studies* 55, no. 3 (1992), 407–432.

7 Chowdhury, 155–158, 165–166, 197.

8 Quintilian, 4:1:63–70, 9:2:38–39, 9:3:24–26; *Rhetorica*, 4:15:22.

9 Dupriez, 58–60; see also Enos, 14.

10 Harris, 117.

11 Bībānī, 78.

(35) You must do this. But do they ever listen?

This becomes immediately intelligible if we suppose this is said by a person speaking to a group who utters only the first sentence toward them. Then, realizing or, for enhanced rhetorical effect, pretending to realize the futility, he throws up his hands saying, "But do they ever listen?" Here we might say he is perhaps addressing another, imaginary audience, more objective than the first. But by this, we quickly can perceive the unusualness of this feature as exemplified in (35) to the English native speaker, especially when reading a book. Rather the feature is at once understandable as oral, performative, and dramatic or dramatizing.

The changes of Arabic *iltifāt* involve many of the different persons of speech and the pronominal forms used to represent them. We can cite six at least from the Qur'ān:

1st person singular to 2nd person plural
1st sing. to 3rd sing.
1st plural to 3rd sing.
2nd plural to 3rd pl.
3rd sing. to 1st pl.
3rd plural to 2nd sing.[12]

There may possibly be others besides these. As we shall see, English has at least one other than these, second singular to third singular, having some affinity to the fourth one above, so we will deal with them together. We shall examine each of these, beginning with those that appear most renderable into English and ending with the most difficult, while noting the varying degrees of comprehensibility or clarity.

One of the most well-known forms of *iltifāt* in a number of languages,[13] including Arabic and English, is that which occurs when the speaker changes

12 Abdel Haleem, *Understanding*, 188, likewise has a similar group of six arrived at independently. My list is in the same order as in my thesis of 1975. From my list, my first corresponds with his (v), my second and third to his (ii), my fourth to his (iv), my fifth to his (i), and my sixth to his (iii). His (vi) is an empty category not found in the Qur'ān. Bībānī, 78–79, also has six categories, my first corresponding with his 1, my second and third with his 3, my fourth with his 5, my fifth with his 4, and my sixth with his 6, for all of which he cites Qur'ānic verses; only his category 2 does not match any of mine, and for it he only finds examples in poetry. Longinus, 27, includes the 3rd to 1st, 2nd to 3rd, and 3rd to 2nd in his description.

13 See the very common use of this in Persian, both modern and classical, for example.

the person of self-reference, in this case from the first person plural to the third person singular. In the Qurʾān, there are many examples, as in 108:1–2:[14]

(36) innā aʿṭaynāka l-kawthar.
fa-ṣalli li-rabbika wa-nḥar.

Here we have *innā* in the first person plural and *rabbika* indicating the third person singular. Az-Zarkashī states that this is done to draw the attention of the addressee to the fact that God is his Lord.[15] This may be taken as odd by some readers in English because of the possibility one might imagine at first that the person or being of "we" (*innā*) differs from that of "your Lord" (*rabbika*). All seven of the translations are rather similar in rendering this point. For example, Bell offers:

(37) 1. Verily, We have given thee abundance;
2. So pray to thy Lord, and sacrifice.

Now at first glance, this change in reference to God, from first person plural ("We") to third person singular ("thy Lord," meaning "Him"), like other instances of *iltifāt* in English, may seem in opposition to the principle referred to in English rhetorical texts requiring an author's maintaining the consistency of the imagined audience which he is addressing. Likewise, it is important that the narrator's presentation of self be consistent, in order for the reader to be able to understand easily. This is connected with the importance of clarity in rhetorical presentation.

However, examples of the type of (37) are not uncommon in both speech and literature in English. It is quite possible to say, especially when emphasis is called for, in anger, for example, "I've done a lot for you, so don't get down on your benefactor!" or, "Talk to your wife civilly." Perhaps the instances of this are not so frequent, as with all emphatic statements and devices, for they would lose their effect with overuse or seem strange if used out of place.[16] But there are certain types of writing where the device at work in (37) is prominent, particularly the Old Testament. There are parallel examples of God speaking of Himself in the third person as well as the opposite, i.e., an inferior speaking to a superior by referring to himself in the third person, as in 1 Samuel 17:34–35:

14 Cited by Ibn Mālik, 33; Qazwīnī, 104, as an example of *iltifāt*.

15 Zarkashī, II, 493–494, III, 317.

16 Longinus, 23:4.

(38) But David said to Saul, "Your servant used to keep sheep for his father, and when there came a lion or a bear, and took a lamb from the flock, I went after him and smote him and delivered it out of his mouth; and if he arose against me, I caught him by his beard, and smote him and killed him. Your servant has killed both lions and bears …"

Here, David interchangeably uses "I" and "your servant" in referring to himself. The case is not isolated. It is also possible for the speaker to change the pronominal term used for the person being addressed. A striking example occurs while Polonius is addressing his daughter Ophelia in Hamlet, Act 1, Sc. III, vv. 6–7:

(39) You do not understand yourself so clearly
As it behoves my daughter and your honour.

In this case, not only does Polonius refer to his daughter in the third person, but Shakespeare deliberately pairs this with "your honour." It is a departure from normal English for effect, at once drawing special attention to her harming his interest as well as her own, as well as to her high station. It appears that the overall effect of this device as used in (36), (38), and (39) is somehow to emphasize the importance of the person or being referred to in the third person. Even the modesty of David in (38) must be taken in this way, as a kind of understatement to make his own actions seem larger by making himself appear less important. This would also be true of authors of scholarly writings who refer to themselves in the third person. Usually associated with the feature as we have discussed it so far is the sense of obligation or obligatory relationship between the two persons being considered in all the examples, Allah and Muhammad (36), Saul and David (38), and Polonius and Ophelia (39). In sum, even if this feature as represented in (36) might be considered uncommon or "biblical" in colloquial English—and that is far from established, as it is probably preferable to view it as oral—its presence in so many examples makes it doubtful that it would cause much difficulty to the reader, unless the pronominal references were really ambiguous, as we shall see below.

Next we have an example involving a number of changes, including from first person singular to third person singular and back again in verses 16:51–52:[17]

17 Chowdhury, 156, cites 16:51.

(40) wa-qāla allāhu lā tattakhidhū ilāhayni thnayni innamā huwa ilāhun wāḥidun fa-iyyāya fa-rhabūn.
wa-lahu mā fī l-samawāti wa-mā fī l-arḍi ...

These sentences contain some difficulty. Allah, the speaker, goes from the first person as speaker in his speech after *qāla* to the third person, then back to the first person. Then, in the succeeding verse, which constitutes a new sentence, the thread of speech goes back to the third person, constituting three shifts of person in a couple of sentences. Az-Zamakhsharī notices particularly the effect of the *iltifāt* shift from third person to first person between *wāhidun* and *fa-iyyāya*. He states specifically that this is more rhetorically effective (*ablagh*) than changing either of the two elements to accord in person with the other.[18]

Now, in English, in such a case as this, when going in and out of quoted speech, we change pronominal terms or points of reference rather often as well, but here the translators' efforts in seeking devices to make these rapid changes of person, in so short a space, seem appealing in English, without losing either the rhetorical effect or the original meaning, appear somewhat strained. Sticking to his literalist agenda, Bell writes:

(41) 53. Allah hath said: "Take not two gods;" "He is simply One God," "To Me then give reverence."
54. To Him belongs whatever is in the heavens and the earth ...

While he has avoided inserting explanatory words to smooth out the text, he has introduced quotation marks not found in the Arabic to explain the anomaly of the *iltifāt* here. This has a double effect, first of all amplifying the disjunctions of the shift in voice and thereby accentuating their strangeness, and second defining the text as the speech of different individual persons.[19] This further confuses the issue, as it is not at all clear that there is more than one voice speaking here, or that that is hard to grasp. The magnification of the disjunctions of the *iltifāt* here also serve Bell's agenda of trying to prove that the Qur'ān is a disjointed text, indeed a pile of separate pieces carelessly thrown together.

18 Abū al-Qāsim Jār Allāh Maḥmūd b. ʿUmar az-Zamakhsharī, *al-Kashshāf ʿan ḥaqāʾiq ghawāmiḍ at-tanzīl wa-ʿuyūn al-aqāwīl fi wujūh at-taʾwīl*, 3rd ed., Beirut: Dār al-Kitāb al-ʿArabī, 1407[/1986–1987], Vol. II, p. 610.

19 Philip E. Lewis, "The Measure of Translation Effects," in *The Translation Studies Reader*, Lawrence Venuti, ed., 3rd ed., London: Routledge, 2012, p. 229, specifies punctuation as a means by which distortion is introduced into translation.

Pickthall attempts a different solution by modifying the intrusive third-person sentence slightly:

(42) 51. Allah hath said: Choose not two gods. There is only One God. So of Me, Me only, be in awe.
52. Unto Him belongeth whatsoever is in the heavens and the earth …

By omitting all quotation marks, he has avoided the changes of speaker imposed by Bell. Nothing here is strange or sudden in the shifts from clause to clause except in the jump from the first person to the third person at the beginning of the second verse. This is much less sharp than the other shifts of person in (41), however, exactly because there is a transition to a new verse, allowing a possible pause. Otherwise, the pronoun shift in English here works perfectly. It also accords with the Arabic of (40) as the word *huwa* may be taken as an example of *ḍamīr ash-sha'n*, a feature similar to the use of the dummy "it" without antecedent in English. Thus, Pickthall's translation appears to be both correct in meaning and effective, but at the cost of altering the content of the Arabic text "He is only One God" slightly. Pickthall also has, instead of Bell's "To me then give reverence," the much more dramatic "So of Me, Me only, be in awe," highlighting the emphatic nature of the *iltifāt* in the Qur'ān's switch to the first person here. More emphasis is added by forwarding of the Arabic *fa-iyyāya*, a case of *hysteron proteron*, mentioned in Chapter One above, and this also makes the statement exclusive, as in Pickthall's "Me only."[20] Thus, the statement is rendered emphatic by the shift to the first person and exclusive by the forward placement of the object, a kind of double emphasis, or a combined use of two different rhetorical features in one place.

But are there any parallels to the *iltifāt* of the short sentences of English in Bell's translation in (41)? Certainly it could not be considered normal in colloquial English when one speaker is speaking, despite (38) and (39) above, perhaps because the third person in these examples as well as (36) does not involve a pronoun. However, we read in Isaiah 45:18, rendered in the Revised Standard Version:

20 Both az-Zamakhsharī and Ibn al-Athīr, referring to a different verse with the exact same construction, note that the placing of the direct object in *fa-iyyāya* first in the clause has the effect of limiting it to Allah alone, just as Pickthall has. Zamakhsharī, III, 461, Ibn al-Athīr, *Mathal*, II, 248; Abū al-Fatḥ Ḍiyā' ad-Dīn Naṣr Allāh b. Muhammad Ibn al-Athīr, *al-Jāmiʿ al-kabīr fī ṣināʿat al-manẓūm min al-kalām wa-l-manthūr*, ed. by Muṣṭafā Jawād. [Baghdad:] Maṭbaʿat al-Majmaʿ al-ʿIlmī, 1375[/1956], Vol. I, p. 133.

(43) For thus says the Lord, Who created the heavens (he is God!), who formed the earth and made it (he established it; he did not create it a chaos, he formed it to be inhabited!): "I am the Lord, and there is no other."

The translators of the Bible have been forced to employ a greater variety of punctuation devices here than Bell used in (41) to make the passage clear to their English speaking readers. At least this passage shows the possibility of finding parallel examples in biblical, particularly Old Testament, English, where the device of *iltifāt* is in frequent use.

Besides these changes in the pronominal term or point of reference used by the speaker in referring to himself or the one he is addressing (39), the *iltifāt* shift of attention from third person plural to second person plural, having in it an implied second person plural audience too, is also possible in English and is likewise not so difficult for the English speaker to follow, as in verses 19:88–89:

(44) wa-qālū ttakhadha r-raḥmānu waladā.
laqad ji'tum shay'an iddā.

Az-Zamakhsharī and az-Zarkashī specifically describe this as a case of *iltifāt*. Az-Zamakhsharī states that the purpose of the *iltifāt* here is to underline the enormity of the saying of those who say that God has adopted a son.[21] Az-Zarkashī notes that direct reproach to an audience who are present is more effective than indirectly reported blame, hence the shift to the second person plural.[22]

Pickthall, for example, renders:

(45) 88. And they say: The Beneficent hath taken unto Himself a son.
89. Assuredly ye utter a disastrous thing.

This example implies a greater change than those so far given. While the first sentence of the reported speech refers to persons not present, the second clearly addresses an audience which is the same as the absent persons of the first. The impact of this is to first let it be known that certain persons have ascribed a son to Allah. Then a certain audience is directly informed that they are the guilty party. Thus, attention is focused on them. It seems that examples of a similar, though not identical, usage can be found in English,

21 Zamakhsharī, III, 45.
22 Zarkashī, III, 322–323, 330.

such as saying, "Some people don't know when to stop talking. You'd better be quiet if you know what's good for you." Or, we could substitute another sort of English *iltifāt* device for the latter sentence to similar effect. "I'd be quiet if I were you." Still, there is a change in (45) of a sort not very common in English.

However, Bell has undermined the effect by adding quotation marks to show different speakers, perhaps in an attempt to imply the lack of connection between the two verses we are considering:

(46) 91. They have said: "The Merciful hath taken to Himself offspring."
"Ye have committed a thing monstrous, …"

Thus, he treats the verses as though the second is an immediate reply to their claim in the first verse, whereas Pickthall's version, accepting the *iltifāt*, is closer to the Arabic in that it avoids quotation marks and treats the second verse as more of a comment on their claim without any specific time reference. Bell seems also to increase the number of persons involved, making the first verse quoted by a narrator, the second a direct speech reply, really an unwarranted complication. Thus, the verses translated in (45) can conceivably present some problem in English as they constrain a rhetorical device of somewhat rarer usage in that language, but they are by no means incomprehensible nor necessarily ineffective. We might add that in the Arabic of the Qur'ān, the verses of (44) present no special problem or strangeness.

An example of *iltifāt* from the first person singular to the second person plural, also comprehensible but possibly ambiguous, is provided by verse 36:22:[23]

(47) wa-mā lī lā aʿbudu lladhī faṭaranī wa-ilayhi turjaʿūn.

The Arabic of the verse, with the *iltifāt*, presents no particular difficulty.[24] Bell translates:

(48) 21. And why should I not serve Him who created me, and to whom
ye will be caused to return?

---

23 Cited by Ibn al-Athīr, *Mathal*, II, 177; Ibn Mālik, 31; cf. Bībānī, 25.

24 Zamakhsharī, IV, 10. Sakkākī, 245, more or less copies az-Zamakhsharī. Zarkashī, III, 315–316, 328, notes specifically that this is a case of *iltifāt* turning from the first person singular to the second person plural to remind the hearers that they are included in the call to worship too.

Unambiguous modern English might be inclined to render the latter part of the sentence as "to whom I will be caused to return" for consistency of pronominal reference. The value of the *iltifāt* in carrying the message to the listeners is clear; first the speaker justifies his lonely service to Allah with a rhetorical question, quickly shifting the emphasis to the audience to remind them they too are returning to Allah. The possible ambiguity is that some might take the meaning as, "to whom you will be caused to return but I will not." The abrupt change of pronominal reference in a coordinate sentence like (48) might strike some readers as strange or rhetorically weak. Nevertheless, it seems not to be impossible as it consists really of two separate sentences connected only in that they share a reference to Allah.

So far, all the cases we have examined have been more or less renderable into English, despite the ambiguity of (45) and the obscurity of (41), which is only relieved by Pickthall's interpretation in (42). Certain other verses cause much more difficulty. For example, the reverse of (36) may be viewed in 35:9, where Allah goes from the third person singular to the first person singular in referring to himself:[25]

(49) wa-llāhu lladhī arsala r-riyāḥa fa-tuthīru saḥāban fa-suqnāhu ilā baladin mayyitin fa-aḥyaynā bihi l-arḍa baʿda mawtihā kadhālika n-nushūr.

This seems somewhat more sudden and incongruous in translation than any example we have yet come upon, perhaps because there is no clear benefit from any particular rhetorical effect in English. We may look at Pickthall:

(50) 9. And Allah it is who sendeth the winds and they raise a cloud; then We lead it unto a dead land and revive therewith the earth after its death.

This raises a thorny problem. Whereas in (36) the English speaking reader is likely to pick up on the synonymity of "We" and "your Lord," perhaps after a small initial hesitation or more likely not, there is no reason why she or he should be able to do so here. For anyone not knowing the context of Islam, why shouldn't he or she assume that the "Allah" and "We" of (50) represent different persons? After all, that is really what the grammar of the English conveys without the context.[26] The problem here is so serious it seems impossible to trans-

25 Cited in Ibn Mālik, 31; Abdul-Raof, *Arabic Rhetoric*, 258; Chowdhury, 158.

26 Indeed, based on my personal experience, non-Muslim American students reading the translated Qur'ān in class at the university level often *insist* that the plural "We" must refer to a plurality of gods or to deities other than Allah.

late the passage without changing the text or supplying footnotes or glosses in brackets. Why such difficulty? It was noted above that in English, third person to first person *iltifāt* changes seem to usually be associated with obligatory role relationships, while there is none particularly visible here, whereas the Arabic gives a greater degree of emphasis and particularization by the change.[27]

However, are there any instances when something of this kind occurs in English? We must answer that indeed there are, but that they are rare or particular cases. For example, if we consider "The human race is doomed to destruction unless we mend our ways," we find it may mean the same as "The race is doomed to destruction unless we humans mend our ways." But the first is more ambiguous than the second, because, similar to (50), it is possible to take "human race" and "we," the two subject nouns, as representing completely different groups. Another like example might be, "The presidency is in danger, but we've got to get on with the business of government." Again, the two subject nouns "presidency" and "we" are to be taken most probably as referring to the same person, the speaker, but they may be taken as separate persons. The difference we note from (50) is that these examples, although not involving obligatory role relationships, except perhaps the obligation of the speakers to themselves, do involve a contrast, but (50) involves coordination and conjunction, not contrast and subordination.

A further very complex and famously[28] difficult example is provided by verse 10:22, in which those addressed change from the second person plural to the third person plural:[29]

(51) huwa lladhī yusayyirukum fī l-barri wa-l-baḥri ḥattā idhā kuntum fī l-fulki wa-jarayna bihim bi-rīḥin ṭayyibatin wa-fariḥū bihā jā'athā rīḥun 'āṣifun wa-jā'ahum al-mawju min kulli makānin wa-ẓannū annahum uḥīṭa bihim da'aw Allāha mukhliṣīn lahu d-dīna la-in anjaytanā min hādhihi la-nakūnanna min ash-shākirīn.

Let us examine Arberry's translation:

(52) It is He who conveys you
  on the land and the sea;
and when you are in the ship—

27 Zamakhsharī, III, 601.
28 Abdel Haleem, *Understanding*, 198.
29 Cited already by Ibn al-Mu'tazz, 73; Ibn al-Athīr, *Mathal*, II, 181: Ibn Mālik, 34, and most later writers.

and the ships run with them
with a fair breeze,
and they rejoice in it,
there comes upon them a strong wind,
and waves come on them from every side,
and they think they are encompassed;
they call upon God,
making their religion his sincerely: …

There are compound problems here. "When you are in the ship" is a dependent adverbial clause or the condition clause of a conditional sentence, in either case relating grammatically to what follows, specifically, "there comes upon them …" This is not only in the third person instead of the second, but also apparently changes the number of what conveys them by linking the noun "ship" (*fulk*), a collective singular, to the feminine plural verb *jarayna*. As a collective noun for ships, *fulk* is often treated as a plural of inanimate objects and thus takes the feminine singular, as in Qur'ān 2:164. Here, however, it takes the feminine plural in order to emphasize the separateness and perhaps the fewness of the ships encompassed by the threatening, stormy sea. Neither Arberry's defensive hyphen, which serves to rather confuse the issue, nor Bell's explanation that the two parts of the passage were written at different times and hence are disjointed, is very illuminating. It is quite clear that all the parts of the passage are related in meaning to the same parable, and even if the clause preceding Arberry's hyphen were unconnected in meaning, there would then have to be a connective particle in the Arabic between *bihā* and *jā'athā*, which there is not. As az-Zamakhsharī says, this *jā'athā* is the result clause of the conditional clause which we are discussing. He takes the change in pronominal references to be a case of *iltifāt* for *mubālaghah* or emphasis, as it heightens the effect by making the hearers as though watchers of a drama.[30] This is done in order to distance the listeners from those on the ships, thereby heightening the repulsiveness of the latter's ingratitude.[31] In English, however, the change is merely confusing, producing no rhetorical effect. We might make an exception that, yes, this is an oral text, yes, a dramatic storyteller or preacher telling a parable might get away with something like this, but we still have to admit its strangeness and the insurmountability of the problem in written English. None of the translations satisfies. Attempting a different solution, 'Abdullah Yūsuf 'Alī has:

30 Zamakhsharī, II, 337–338; compare Ṭabarī, XI, 71.
31 Zuḥaylī, *Tafsīr*, XI, 142.

(53) 22. He it is who enableth you
To traverse through land
And sea; so that ye even board
Ships;—they sail with them
With a favourable wind,
And they rejoice thereat.
Then comes a stormy wind
And the waves come to them
From all sides, and they think
They are being overwhelmed:
They cry unto God, sincerely
Offering (their) duty to Him, …

In contrast to (52), Yūsuf ʿAlī's translation is in grammatically acceptable English, but this is at the expensive cost of altering the grammatical relationship in the Arabic, producing a semantic effect quite other than the intent of the original. "So that ye even board ships" is made independent, as if merely to emphasize what precedes or to say that the purpose of Allah's enabling them to travel on the sea is so that they may board ships. This explanation is categorically denied by az-Zamakhsharī, who regards it as senseless.[32] In the "so that" clause of (53), all connection with what follows is broken. With a similar addition, Yūsuf ʿAlī has supplied a "then" to separate the clause of the stormy wind from that of the favorable wind. If this "then" is taken as part of his translation of *ḥattā idhā*, it has been postponed in such a way as to alter the intent of the original; otherwise, it is extraneous. No such article appears in (52), where "there comes upon them a strong wind" provides the reply and complement to "when you are in the ship." Here we perceive that there is a case where semantic correctness cannot even be conveyed together with the meaning of the original in English, much less the rhetorical effectiveness of the original.

Concluding this chapter of changes in person without change in referent, we observe that there are various degrees of translatability and complexity as represented approximately by numbers (36), (40), (44), (47), (49), and (51) in ascending order of difficulty. Despite the possible permissibility of some cases in English, usually limited to peculiar usages as we have seen, it appears that Arabic generally, and especially Qurʾānic Arabic, has a greater freedom from constraint than English in this respect. This, as mentioned above, causes a major difficulty in some cases like (49) and (51) between the rhetorical sys-

32 Zamakhsharī, II, 338.

tems of the two languages. While it may be argued that this phenomenon of Qur'ānic Arabic is not common in modern standard prose Arabic, it must be acknowledged that some reflection of this freedom exists even there potentially, because of the influence of the Qur'ān if nothing else, which in itself may create some effect. The freedom is clearly acknowledged among the points of rhetoric in a modern Arabic rhetoric book, for example. A perusal of the same work will show that this is also a feature of classical Arabic poetry.[33] Aside from this, the implications of such passages as (40) and the difficulties of Bell in (41) and (46) include a preference of Arabic in the Qur'ān at least for word economy, a laudable tendency that now seems to be reversed in both Arabic and English in this age of long-winded jargon. In this sense we must recall that it is not entirely just to judge the pithiness of the Qur'ānic style on the basis of both languages as they are at present. This also may account for some of the difference in effect, just as Shakespeare, now considered a bit archaic from the linguistic point of view although the first of the classics, has a different effect no doubt on his present readers than he did on his original hearers.

---

33 Bībānī, 78–79. The same point is demonstrated in Ibn al-Muʿtazz, 73–74; Ibn al-Athīr, *Mathal*, II, 178–180, 187.

CHAPTER 3

Indicative in Place of Imperative or Jussive

A second category of *iltifāt* is the use of the imperfect indicative in place of the imperative or the jussive in both positive and negative imperatives or the reverse.[1] Here, I will only be dealing with the shift from the indicative to the imperative, which is a repeated feature in the Qurʾān. Although also considered one of the points of the "production of speech in opposition requirement of the obvious" (*ikhrāj al-kalām ʿalā khilāf muqtaḍā l-ḥāl*;[2] cf. p. 70, below), it does not really cause that much difficulty because of its parallels in English. First we will take an example of a negative imperative effected by the indicative rather than the normal jussive, as it is more congenial to English, in verse 2:84:[3] Al-Hāshimī notes that the indicative replaces the jussive here for emphasis,[4] while al-Bībānī states that this is done in this verse emphatically to persuade the hearers to obedience.[5]

(54) wa-idh akhadhnā mīthāqakum lā tasfikūna dimāʾakum wa-lā tukhrijūna anfusakum min diyārikum ...

Bell translates this verse rather literally:

(55) "When We made a covenant with you: 'Ye shall not shed your own blood; ye shall not expel your own people from your dwellings.' ... "

Arberry reduces it slightly:

(56) And when We took compact with you: 'You shall not
shed your own blood, neither expel your own
from your habitations'; ...

---

1 Ibn al-Athīr, *Mathal*, II, 183–184; Zarkashī, III, 247–249. Interestingly, Abdel Haleem cites only the latter type: a shift from the indicative to the imperative. Abdel Haleem, *Understanding*, 200–201.

2 Bībānī, 75–76.

3 Az-Zamakhsharī's comment on the rhetorical feature here begins under the previous verse, 2:83. Zamakhsharī, I, 159–160. Cited in Sakkākī, 325; Zarkashī, III, 248.

4 Hāshimī, 92.

5 Bībānī, 76.

 | DOI:10.1163/9789004417441_005

The parallel with the commandments of the Old Testament is clear: "Thou shalt not …" Hence the use of the imperfect indicative in negative imperatives in place of the jussive presents no problem because of the similar case in English, other than giving the translation a slight impression of archaism, which, it could be argued, might be appropriate in view of the antiquity of the Qur'ān.

However, the case of positive commandments is not always so simple, as demonstrated by the well-known verse 3:110:

(57) kuntum khayra ummatin ukhrijat li-n-nāsi ta'murūna bi-l-ma'rūfi wa-tanhawna 'an al-munkari wa-tu'minūna bi-llāh …

This verse has generated a great deal of commentary, as classical commentators have often been anxious to explain it in a self-congratulatory way as a flat statement that the Muslims are the best people naturally. For example, al-Qurṭubī cites several possibly contradictory attempts to support this viewpoint, i. e., 1) that *kuntum* is inscribed on the "preserved tablet" which is with Allah, hence perfect, 2) that it was given as good news to the Prophet in order to inform him that his people would turn out the best, 3) that *kuntum* really means *khuliqtum*, "you were created," or *wujidtum*, "you came into existence," *khayra ummatin* being an adverbial *ḥāl* clause, and 4) even that, "You have become for mankind the best people," because you drag them in chains to Islam.[6] Indeed, this latter explanation is found in a *ṣaḥīḥ* hadith in al-Bukhārī, which probably explains the favor that Muslim commentators show to the opinion that the Muslims *are* the best community, or at least that their earliest coreligionists (*as-salaf*) were.[7] Certain other hadiths, such as one graded as *ḥasan* (fair) by at-Tirmidhī, in which the Prophet is reported to have stated that the Muslims are the last and best of seventy peoples which have appeared on earth, are also cited to support this position.[8] All seven translators I am using have also adopted this position, that the verse is a statement of fact. For example, Pickthall gives:

6 Abū 'Abd Allāh Muḥammad b. Aḥmad al-Anṣārī al-Qurtubī, *al-Jāmi' li-aḥkām al-Qur'ān*, Cairo: Dār al-Kitāb al-'Arabī li-ṭ-Ṭibā'ah wa-n-Nashr, 1387/1967, Vol. IV, pp. 170–171.

7 Indeed, Khan's translation of this very hadith states, "You are the best of people …" Muḥammad b. Ismā'īl al-Bukhārī, *The Translation of the Meanings of Sahīh al-Bukhārī: Arabic-English*, translated by Muhammad Muhsin Khan, Riyadh: Darussalam Publications, 1997, Vol. VI, pp. 73–74 (Kitāb at-tafsīr, bāb kuntum khayra ummah, hadith no. 4557).

8 Qurṭubī, IV, 170.

(58) 110. Ye are the best community that hath been raised up for mankind. Ye enjoin right conduct and forbid indecency; and ye believe in Allah.

Pickthall's translation, like that of Dawood, sunders the two parts of the verse into independent sentences, which clearly de-emphasizes the rather obvious connection between them.

Muhammad Ali, followed by Muhammad Asad, links Pickthall's two sentences with a colon:

(59) 109. You are the best nation raised up for men: you enjoin good and forbid evil and you believe in Allāh.

The colon here connects the two clauses, showing the second to be subordinate to and perhaps an effect of the first. By connecting them, unlike the separate sentences of Pickthall and Dawood, there is an implication that the Muslims should live up to these characteristics with which they have been described.

Arberry, like Yūsuf ʿAlī, connects the two sentences of Pickthall with a comma:

(60) You are the best nation ever brought forth
to men, bidding to honour, and forbidding
dishonor, and believing in God.

Despite his dubious use of the words "nation," "honour," and "dishonor," Arberry has at least shown that the status of "best" is at least described by and perhaps dependent on the existence of the three following characteristics.

Like Arberry and Yūsuf ʿAlī, Bell uses subordinate participial phrases to connect the second clause with the first, but even without a comma.

(61) 106. Ye have become the best community ever produced for the people urging what is reputable and restraining from what is disreputable, and believing in Allah.

Unlike all of the other six translations, Bell translates the perfect verb *kuntum* into the English present perfect rather than the present tense. This has the effect of making the Muslims the best community a result of their actions, which draws an even firmer connection between the three actions and the declaration of their excellence. Yet it also makes their status the result of their history, which not only materializes it, but also relates it seemingly to the generation which first heard the Qurʾān, namely the Companions of the Prophet.

Despite their general agreement and the particular nuances of their efforts, however, the seven translations do not nearly exhaust or cover the semantic possibilities of the verse. For instance, az-Zamakhsharī proposes a completely different interpretation, explaining the verse rather as constituting a command, with the perfect *kuntum* being used in place of the imperative *kūnū*.[9] If this explanation is accepted, we could revise Pickthall's translation here to read:

(62) Be the best community raised up for mankind; enjoin right conduct, forbid indecency, and believe in Allah.

Unfortunately, az-Zamakhsharī gives no further explanation about why this is the correct understanding of the verse. However, the fourth/tenth century rhetorician Abū al-Ḥusayn Isḥāq b. Ibrāhīm al-Kātib (fl. c. 335/c. 947) also includes this verse in a section of his book on imperatives, stating how the verse enjoins doing good and prohibiting evil.[10]

We can further analyze this verse by considering the grammatical status of the first verb in the verse, *kuntum*. Because of this verb, if we translated the verse literally, it ought to read, "You were the best community …" Yet this is not possible, in view of the following present indicatives, as in Pickthall's second sentence, as it would then make no sense. Because it cannot be taken in this obvious, unmarked way, another explanation must be sought. One way, that used by the bulk of the classical commentaries and by our seven translators, is to take the word *kuntum* as meaning "You were ever …," just as *kāna allāhu ʿalīman ḥakīmā* means "Allah was ever Knowing, Wise" (Qurʾān 4:11, etc.). While that might be comforting and complimentary to the Muslim hearers, it is only one possible interpretation and not likely to be the best one, as the Qurʾān is exhortative, constantly emphasizing that all are judged according to their actions and none are given a pass just because of their very being. This is why az-Zamakhsharī rather boldly took it instead to be an imperative. But I think that the existence of this perfect form here is hard to explain unless it is taken as implying a conditional sense for the whole verse. If we accept the idea that this is really a conditional expression, we could then link Pickthall's two sentences in something like the following way:

---

9 Zamakhsharī, I, 397; in I, 400, however, az-Zamakhsharī also includes the usual explanation.

10 Abū al-Ḥusayn Isḥāq b. Ibrāhīm b. Sulaymān b. Wahb al-Kātib, *al-Burhān fī wujūh al-bayān*, ed. by Aḥmad Maṭlūb and Khadījah al-Ḥadīthī, 1st ed., Baghdad: Maṭbaʿat al-ʿĀnī, 1387/1967, p. 275.

(63) You would be the best community brought forth for mankind, provided that you enjoin right conduct, forbid indecency; and believe in Allah.

This possibility is strongly supported first of all by another Qurʾānic verse which similarly describes the Muslims as the highest, but only conditionally (Qurʾān 3:139). Furthermore, a number of traditions found in aṭ-Ṭabarī, especially those from ʿUmar b. al-Khaṭṭāb and Mujāhid, even use the word for a condition (*sharṭ*) to describe the second clause of the verse and clearly state that the sense is conditional.[11] These traditions are also cited by al-Qurṭubī.[12] Also, al-Qurṭubī himself assumes that the verse is conditional, the first part depending on the latter.[13]

In light of the different possible interpretations of this verse I have cited, one can see that the translations here all fail to give two of the three potential interpretations of the verse. Indeed, in this case the translations fail to present the explanation that appears to be the more likely on linguistic grounds. And even if the interpretation given by the translations were to prove the correct one, the Arabic language would still admit the other two translations as well. Thus in any case, here we have another instance of the inability of translations to convey the meaning of the original Qurʾānic text fully.

---

11 Ṭabarī, IV, 29–30. Although aṭ-Ṭabarī does not himself favor explaining the verse as a conditional, he is forced to resort to a special argument to account for the otherwise odd usage of *kuntum*.

12 Qurṭubī, IV, 171–172.

13 Qurṭubī, IV, 173.

CHAPTER 4

Indefinite Nouns

A category related tangentially to *iltifāt* is the use of indefinite instead of definite nouns for a kind of broader generalization or emphasis. In Arabic, this is referred to as *tankīr* = making indefinite, and it is a feature of Arabic rhetoric.[1] Here, we are considering a subcategory of *tankīr* called *tankīr al-musnad ilayhi*, where the subject of a clause or sentence has been placed in the indefinite by choice rather than necessity.[2] This is fairly common in the Qurʾān, as in verse 2:2[3]

(64) dhālika l-kitābu lā rayba fīhi hudan li-l-muttaqīn.

Arberry has rendered this:

(65) That is the book, wherein there is no doubt,
a guidance to the godfearing …

Here, the use of the indefinite article with "guidance," while perhaps conveying a possible grammatical meaning of the verse, clearly goes astray from the intent mentioned above, as "a guidance" can hardly be taken as singling out the importance of this particular guidance as opposed to any other. But "guidance" in the indefinite suggests a general concept, which "a guidance" does not. Likewise in the Arabic, *hudā* in the indefinite as a general concept actually has a more sweeping meaning and greater power than the more particularized *al-hudā*. This is already briefly noted by az-Zamakhsharī, who suggests regarding this verse that the indefinite *hudā* is used to emphasize the limitlessness of Allāh's guidance.[4] Later, this idea is further developed by as-Sakkākī and al-Qazwînî, both of whom indeed cite this very construction in this particular verse as an example of the indefinite greatly amplifying the concept.[5] Furthermore, aside

1 Zarkashī, IV, 90–93; Mir, *Understanding*, 74, 86, 135.
2 Ṭabānah, *Muʿjam*, 692–694; Bībānī, 50–51; Abdul-Raof, *Arabic Rhetoric*, 145–146; Abdul-Raof, *New Horizons*, 184.
3 Ibn Mālik, 40; Bībānī, 82–83.
4 Zamakhsharī, I, 37.
5 Sakkākī, 268; Qazwīnī, 184–186. Al-Qazwīnī explains this principle at greater length using other examples in 76–78.

 | DOI:10.1163/9789004417441_006

from the greater power of the indefinite noun in this place, the word "guidance" is also an uncountable noun in English, so speaking of "a guidance" is somewhat ungrammatical and sounds odd, because the normal way of rendering an uncountable noun as a particular indefinite would be to say "a piece of guidance," which would obviously not be suitable in this place.

While Pickthall and Asad follow Arberry in translating "a guidance," Muhammad Ali and Dawood have preferred a less literal alternative that keeps the indefinite article but better preserves English usage by substituting the countable word "guide" for "guidance." Thus, Dawood (1990 and 2014) offers:

(66) This Book is not to be doubted. It is a guide for the righteous, …

Smoothness here is bought at the cost of distancing from the original, for the Arabic *hudā* is "guidance," not "guide." Thus, using "guide" can be considered a somewhat exegetical rendering.[6]

Bell, followed in this point by Asad, attempts to stay literally close to the text without using any article:

(67) That is the Book, in which there is no doubt, guidance for those who act piously.

Now, it appears here that the emphasis found in making the noun indefinite is to generalize it, making it more encompassing by being more vague, something like saying, "Faith is mighty," which surpasses the other two alternatives, "The faith is mighty," and "A faith is mighty." But "faith" may be countable. If the reader substitutes, for example, "honesty," he will quickly perceive that the first is the only possibility, thus vindicating Bell's treatment of "guidance," to some extent, as the best equivalent for uncountable concepts without article in the Arabic original.

Perhaps it is worth comparing as well where the Qur'ān itself uses *al-hudā* with the definite article, as in verse 53:23:

(68) wa-laqad jā'ahum min rabbihim al-hudā.

The interpretation of this verse seems quite straighforward: *al-hudā* here, as in 2:2, refers to the guidance provided by Allāh in the Qur'ān.[7] But the translation

6 Although this interpretation does receive some support from the *tafsīrs*. Ṭabarī, I, 76; Zamakhsharī, I, 37.

7 Ṭabarī, XXVII, 37.

is once again problematic, as the use of articles in Arabic and English does not match up. Pickthall, with Muhammad Ali and Dawood being similar, has:

(69) And now the guidance from their Lord hath come unto them.

Just as "a guidance" seems clumsy and ungrammatical, "the guidance" does not seem much better in English, despite the definite article in Arabic, for "guidance," unless specifically marked as a particular type or instance of guidance in previous discourse, is usually taken as an indefinite uncountable concept. Noticing this, Arberry has:

(70) ... and yet guidance has
come to them from their Lord.

This sounds better but seems insufficiently to distinguish the Arabic usage with the definite article (*al-hudā*) from the indefinite form (*hudā*). Three other translations use various devices in attempting to do this. Bell and Yūsuf ʿAlī respectively capitalize the term as "the Guidance" and "Guidance." This device obviously has its limitations. Arabic has no capital letters, so their use cannot be linked properly to any Arabic feature. The distinction between a capitalized "Guidance," perhaps divine, and a more general lower-case "guidance" is not one that is made by the Arabic Qurʾān.

However, Muhammad Asad has a more interesting proposal:

(71) ... although right guidance has now indeed come unto them from their Sustainer.

Thus, in both instances Asad has shunned the dubious use of articles for this general term, but has still managed to distinguish *hudā* = guidance from *al-hudā* = right guidance. That he should feel constrained to resort to such a device to express the carefulness of his translation is ample testimony to how these usages do not match up across the languages, just as the variety of the translations I have cited illustrates the same point.

A further example of the use of indefinite noun for emphasis is found in verse 81:14:

(72) ʿalimat nafsun mā aḥḍarat.

This refers to every soul finding out what it has earned on Judgment Day, and concludes the series of cataclysmic events that begin with verses 81:1–4 (see number (8) above). The feature at work is *al-iqlāl al-mutaʿammad* or deliberate understatement.[8] This is considered part of the points of the "production of speech in opposition to the requirement of the obvious" (*ikhrāj al-kalāmi ʿalā khilāfi muqtaḍā ẓ-ẓāhir*).[9] Az-Zamakhsharī describes this feature as a modest understatement freeing the speaker from blame for exaggeration but at the same time more effective than a flat statement in broadcasting the meaning of numerousness to the point of uncountability. If we quote the reply of the military commander in az-Zamakhsharī's example to the question, "How many horsemen do you have?" We find:

(73) rubba fārisin ʿindī.

This might be translated, for example:

(74) Oh, I happen to have a few horsemen with me.

As in the Arabic, the understatement gives off an imprecision of uncountable numbers that will not be exhausted.[10] It seems some of the effect comes from the singularity of the noun, which gives the impression to the reader of considering each horseman individually, which of course emphasizes his importance, as a single human being is important to himself, and how many are we considering! This feature works quite naturally in English, a language known for its preference for understatement, for example:

(75) Quite a few brave men fell that day on the field of battle!

The intent is obviously emphatic, yet the "few" implies a small number.

Turning then to our translations of (72), we find Arberry has:

(76) Then shall a soul know what it has produced.

Pickthall, on the other hand, gives a version that is more of a flat statement, hence farther from the original:

(77) 14. (Then) every soul will know what it hath made ready.

---

8 The expression *al-iqlāl al-mutaʿammad* is Dr. al-Nowaihi's, given to me verbally in 1975, and does not occur in the classical rhetoric books.

9 For this feature, see Qazwīnī, 48–49.

10 Zamakhsharī, IV, 709–710.

His inclusion of the explanatory word "every," while seemingly fitting with the meaning of the verse, nevertheless constitutes an exegetical addition to the text.

The only confusion that could arise from (76) is if the reader supposed somehow that a particular soul was intended. The figure of speech in it is not as close to normal English as (74), but it may be that (72) is a bit more unusual in Arabic than (73).

CHAPTER 5

Non-Consequential Exception

Related to *iltifāt* in that it also involves a sudden shift of attention for the reader is the emphatic rhetorical device known as *istithnāʾ munqaṭiʿ*, which might be translated as as "non-consequential exception."[1] This feature is often described by the grammarians from the earliest times, but is only rarely mentioned in books of rhetoric.[2] Nevertheless, it really appears to operate as a rhetorical device and certainly deserves a place here in our consideration of the translation of such devices into English. Common in the Qurʾān,[3] this feature may sometimes appear strange if rendered directly into English. It consists of making an exception to a generalization just stated, where the exception is not actually part of the generalization.[4] However, in some cases of *istithnāʾ munqaṭiʿ*, the exception may also be part of the generalization, and, moreover, the same statement may apply to both. In this latter case, it is closer to English usage than the first. The connection in any case seems to be a form of emphasis or changing direction of attention rather than constituting a true exception. A usual model example of *istithnāʾ munqaṭiʿ* is *jāʾa l-qawmu illā ḥimārahum* (the people came except for their donkey), which is very commonly cited.[5] Classical grammarians state that the word *illā* = except (or one of its synonyms), which is always used in this feature, has the meaning of *lākin* (but or however) here.[6]

---

1 This translation is Dr. al-Nowaihi's, from 1975.

2 Ibn Mālik, 125–128.

3 Abū al-Barakāt Kamāl ad-Dīn ʿAbd ar-Raḥmān b. Muḥammad Ibn al-Anbārī, *al-Inṣāf fī masāʾil al-khilāf bayn an-naḥwiyyīn al-Baṣriyyīn wa-l-Kūfiyyīn*, Beirut: al-Maktabah al-ʿAṣriyyah, 1424/2003, Vol. I, p. 218.

4 Abū ʿAlī al-Fārisī, *al-Īḍāḥ al-ʿAḍudī*, ed. by Ḥasan Shādhilī Farhūd, n. p.: n. p., 1389/1969, p. 211; Zamakhsharī, II, 276; Fāḍil Ṣāliḥ as-Samarrāʾī, *Maʿānī n-naḥw*, Amman: Dār al-Fikr li-ṭ-Ṭibāʿah wa-n-Nashr wa-t-Tawzīʿ, 1420/2000, Vol. II, p. 247. It is identified in Ṭabānah, *Muʿjam*, 122, as *al-istithnāʾ min ghayri mūjib*.

5 This example sentence was conveyed to me by Dr. al-Nowaihi in 1975. A similar example sentence can be found as *lā aḥada fīhā illā ḥimār* as early as Abū Bishr ʿAmr b. ʿUthmān b. Qanbar Sībawayh, *Kitāb Sībawayh*, ed. by ʿAbd as-Salām Muḥammad Hārūn, Cairo: Maktabat al-Khānjī, 1408/1988, Vol. II, pp. 319–320, and as *mā jāʾanī aḥadun illā ḥimārā* in Abū ʿAlī al-Fārisī, 211. The modern writer Samarrāʾī, II, 247, has *ḥaḍara l-qawmu illā ḥimārā*.

6 Abū Bakr Muḥammad b. as-Sarī Ibn as-Sarrāj, *al-Uṣūl fī n-naḥw*, ed. by ʿAbd al-Ḥusayn al-Fatlī, Beirut: Muʾassasat ar-Risālah, [1973?], Vol. I, pp. 290–291; Yūsuf b. Abī Saʿīd al-Ḥasan as-Sīrāfī, *Sharḥ abyāt Sībawayh*, ed. by Muḥammad ʿAlī ar-Rīḥ Hāshim, Cairo: Maktabat al-Kulliyāt al-Azhariyyah, 1394/1974, Vol. II, p. 63.

 | DOI:10.1163/9789004417441_007

However, that simple equating does not quite solve the problem of translation to English for this feature.

Among the easier examples of *istithnāʾ munqaṭiʿ* to translate into English, perhaps, is 74:38–39:

(78) kullu nafsin bi-mā kasabat rahīnah.
illā aṣḥāb al-yamīn.

This is translated without much variation in the translations we are using. Pickthall gives us:

(79) 38. Every soul is a pledge for its own deeds;
39. Save those who will stand on the right hand.

Whatever the grammatical fine points, it is plain that the translation (79) gives no particular difficulty in English, as "those who will stand on the right hand" will be assumed by the English-speaking reader to be an exception from among the encompassing group intended by "every soul." The commentators generally agree with this view, but al-Qurṭubī also cites a hadith from Ibn ʿAbbās stating that this group consists of the angels,[7] in which case the verses would seem strange in English, if the meaning really were:

(80) Every soul is a pledge for its own deeds, except the angels.

Then we might encounter a theological problem as to whether or not the angels have souls, but the possibility that an Arabic speaker could even state the hadith of Ibn ʿAbbās shows that the feature at work in (78) is of a different nature from the English of (79), even though the English of (79) happens to accord in form and by general agreement in the meaning with the Arabic of (78). We might also note that al-Qurṭubī brings forth a great variety of other hadiths which endeavor to explain who these are who are to be miraculously excepted from the Last Judgment, to which the Muslims as well as all others are to be subjected (though another hadith from Ibn ʿAbbās related by Abu Ẓabyān contradicts that as well).[8] So it is uncertain whether those on the right are to be considered a subcategory of the generalization or not, though it appears probable, but it is mandatory to consider them so in English.

7 Qurṭubī, XIX, 86.
8 Qurṭubī, XIX, 87.

A clearer example of where this feature causes difficulty for translators into English is found in verses 17:86–87:[9]

(81) wa-la-in shiʾnā la-nadhhabanna bi-lladhī awḥaynā ilayka thumma lā tajidu laka bihi ʿalaynā wakīlā.
illā raḥmatan min rabbika inna faḍlahu kāna ʿalayka kabīrā.

In these two verses, Allah states that, if He willed, he could take away the entire Qurʾān revealed to Muhammad, here addressed in the second person singular directly, and then Muhammad would not find anyone who could recover it, and that if Allah chose not to take it away, it would only be out of mercy.[10] The exception of *raḥmatan min rabbika* = "mercy of your Lord" is non-consequential because it is not a part of or related to *wakīlā* = a guard or agent; indeed, it is a quality rather than a person, and thus does not follow as a normal exception. The translations of these two verses vary somewhat from each other. Yūsuf ʿAlī gives a rather literal rendering, especially of the feature in question:

(82) 86. If it were Our Will,
We could take away
That which We have
Sent thee by inspiration:
Then wouldst thou find
None to plead thy affair
In that matter as against Us,—

87. Except for Mercy from thy Lord:
For His Bounty is
To thee (indeed) great.

In this work, the non-consequential exception is separated from the main text by a comma, a dash, a space, and a separate verse number, but the operative word "Except," the term normally used to render the Arabic *illā*, is used. All these features emphasize the discontinuity caused by the non-consequential exception; the one addition Yūsuf ʿAlī has included is the word "for," which is

9 Cited by Zamakhsharī, II, 691; Nāṣir ad-Dīn Abū Saʿīd ʿAbd Allāh b. ʿUmar ash-Shīrāzī al-Bayḍāwī, *Anwār at-tanzīl wa-asrār at-taʾwīl*, ed. by Muḥammad ʿAbd ar-Raḥmān al-Marʿashlī, Beirut: Dār Iḥyāʾ at-Turāth al-ʿArabī, 1418[/1997], Vol. III, p. 266, as a possible case of *istithnāʾ munqaṭiʿ*.

10 Zamakhsharī, II, 691.

not really in the Arabic text, though it might be read into it. This "for," however, detracts from the parallelism in the Arabic between *wakīlā* and its exception *raḥmatan*, both of them direct objects of *tajidu* = "find." Also, *wakīlā* is rendered as "one to plead thy affair," negated into "None" by the particle *lā* before the verb, which not only also detracts from the simplicity of the single word but furthermore confines its signification to only one of the word's possible meanings.

Meanwhile, Arberry has:

(83) If We willed, We could take away that
We have revealed to thee, then thou
wouldst find none thereover to guard
thee against Us,
excepting by some mercy of thy Lord;
surely His favor to thee is great.

While similar to Yūsuf 'Alī in some respects, Arberry's treatment of the exception phrase seems more continuous and less jolting, because he has introduced the word "by," transforming the noun *raḥmatan* into an adverbial phrase, a possibility in the Arabic. On the other hand, Arberry's antecedent clause, "then thou wouldst find none thereover to guard thee against Us," certainly seems obscure itself.

As often, Pickthall finds it necessary to add some words in parentheses:

(84) 86. And if We willed, We could withdraw that which We have revealed unto thee, then wouldst thou find no guardian for thee against Us in respect thereof.
87. (It is naught) save mercy from thy Lord. Lo! His kindness unto thee was ever great.

Pickthall's treatment of the obscure clause "then wouldst thou find ..." seems clearer than Arberry's, but he has chosen to separate the exception phrase into a completely separate sentence, and to provide it with a subject and verb in parentheses. However, by this he only pushes the problem back without solving it, for the antecedent of the "It" is not clear and cannot be the "guardian."

Dawood's two translations also illustrate the problematic of these verses. His 1990 edition reads:

(85) If We pleased We could take away that which We have revealed to you: then you should find none to plead with Us on your behalf. But your Lord has shown you mercy. His goodness to you has been great indeed.

This rendering, like that of Pickthall, separates the exception in its own sentence, interpolating "your Lord has shown you" in place of the latter's "mercy from thy Lord," which is observant of the wording in the original text, *raḥmatan min rabbika*. Of course, as usual with Dawood, it reads smoothly. Dawood's rendering of *thumma lā tajidu laka bihi ʿalaynā wakīlā* as "then you should find none to plead with Us on your behalf," parallel to and perhaps derived from Yūsuf ʿAlī, also specifies a particular possible interpretation that is other than the one given by az-Zamakhsharī and also completely drops the expression *bihi*, referring to the Qurʾān, which is the topic of the two verses.

Evidently unsatisfied with his 1990 version's lack of adherence to the original, Dawood (2014) has partially revised it to read:

(86) If We pleased We could take away that which We have revealed to you: then you should find none to plead with Us on your behalf, except through a favour from your Lord. His goodness to you has been great indeed.

Here, he has kept most of the translation the same, except that he has restored the connection of the exception phrase with its antecedent clause, even connecting it with the word "except," the most literal translation of the Arabic *illā*. But he has also replaced the word "mercy," the more literal rendering of *raḥmah*, with "favour." His translation now invites comparison with Arberry's, which it is fairly close to, but it still fails to represent the Arabic very closely, really undermining its connection with the revelation of the Qurʾān.

In the end, the various renderings of 17:86–87 are somewhat varied one from the other and also each show distancing from the original text in various ways, with those displaying the closest adherence to the Arabic rhetorical feature under discussion not being as smooth or acceptable in normal English as those who attempt a freer rehandling of the text.

An even more difficult problem for translation is presented by Qurʾān 18:50:[11]

(87) wa-idh qulnā li-l-malāʾikati sjudū li-ādama fa-sajadū illā iblīsa kāna min al-jinni fa-fasaqa ʿan amri rabbihi …

This verse is repeated a number of times elsewhere in the Qurʾān (2:34; 7:11; 15:30–31;[12] 17:61; 20:116) but without the words *kāna min al-jinni fa-fasaqa ʿan amri rabbihi*.

11 Specifically cited as an example of *istithnāʾ munqaṭiʿ* by Samarrāʾī, II, 247.

12 Mentioned by Ibn Mālik, 126, as an example of *istithnāʾ munqaṭiʿ*.

Translated into English, this sounds rather bizarre, assuming we know beforehand the difference between the jinn and the angels, who are two completely different registers of beings, the jinn having free will while the angels lack it, the jinn having both bad and good among them (Qur'ān 72:11), the angels being only good because always obedient to God (Qur'ān 16:49–50), the jinn being created from fire (Qur'ān 7:12; 15:27; 38:76; 55:15), the angels from light.[13] Also, Qur'ān 34:40–41 is cited as clearly distinguishing the angels from the jinn as two distinct, non-overlapping categories of beings.[14] The difference between the angels and the jinn is also confirmed by the main opinion of the Qur'ān commentators.[15] Pickthall, who is similar to most of the other translations, offers us:

(88) 51. And (remember) when We said unto the angels: Fall prostrate before Adam, and they fell prostrate, all save Iblîs. He was of the jinn, so he rebelled against his Lord's command.

So first we are told the angels fall prostrate except for Iblīs, but suddenly we find in Pickthall's next sentence, following a period, that he is really one of the jinn, who, as we have seen, are not the same as the angels. Knowing this difference, an English reader can hardly feel that this is a normal construction.

Dawood, with his preference for subordinate clauses, links the exception together in the same sentence:

(89) And when We said to the angels: "Prostrate yourselves before Adam," all prostrated themselves except Satan, who was a jinnee disobedient to his Lord.

By connecting the statement that Satan was one of the jinn directly with the main sentence, Dawood makes the apparent contradiction inherent in the English rendering of this Arabic rhetorical feature even more obvious.

---

13 Abū al-Ḥusayn Muslim b. al-Ḥajjāj al-Qushayrī an-Naysabūrī. *al-Musnad aṣ-ṣaḥīḥ al-mukhtaṣar bi-naql al-ʿadl ʿan al-ʿadl ilā rasūl Allāh* (SAAS). Ed by Muḥammad Fu'ād ʿAbd al-Bāqī. Beirut: Dār Iḥyā' at-Turāth al-ʿArabī, 1970, Vol. IV, p. 2994, (*k. az-zuhd wa-r-raqā'iq, b. fī aḥādīth mutafarriqah*, hadith no. 2996).

14 Samarrā'ī, II, 247.

15 ʿImād ad-Dīn Abū al-Fidā' Ismāʿīl al-Qurashī Ibn Kathīr, *Tafsir al-Qur'ān al-ʿaẓīm*, Beirut: Dār al-Fikr, 1389/1970, Vol. IV, p. 396. Ibn Kathīr draws the first piece of information from an early *ṣaḥīḥ* hadith, found in Muslim; the latter piece is of course from the Qur'ān (cf. 55:15). Zamakhsharī, II, 727, likewise denies that Iblīs could have been an angel, because angels cannot sin.

More daringly, Muhammad Asad has avoided the non-consequential exception here by translating:

(90) AND [remember that] when We told the angels, "Prostrate yourselves before Adam," they all prostrated themselves, save Iblīs: he [too] was one of those invisible beings, but then he turned away from his Sustainer's command.

Asad's effort here, by using the bracketed word "[too]" and the generalizing term "invisible beings," is able to cover both the angels and the jinn, thereby creating a category that is not in the Qur'ān. In this way, he avoids the incongruity of the non-consequential exception in English here, but only at the cost of a considerable distortion of the text.

Thus, while this device of non-consequential exception is clear enough in Arabic, in English it entails an incongruous internal contradiction, for Iblis or Satan cannot be of the jinn and the angels at the same time, but (88) and (89) necessitate just that. These translations can only be saved by ignorance of the difference between the angels and the jinn, as anyone who knows the difference is bound to be confused by it here.

However, it still might be possible to suggest an alternative that would convey the meaning. Modifying Pickthall, we might get:

(91) And (remember) when He said unto the angels: fall prostrate before Adam, and they all fell prostrate, though Iblîs, who was of the jinn, did not, and so rebelled against his Lord's command.

This translation would to a large extent represent the actual meaning of "but" in place of "except," as suggested by the classical Arabic commentaries cited above. Even thus, an English-language reader might ask "Why was Iblīs's refusal to obey an order to the angels rebellion?" Also, changing the Arabic to erase the decisive term "except" (*illā*) is really a domesticating move that erases an important difference of the Arabic text in the English translation. Thus, the sudden shift of attention appropriate for emphasis and drawing notice to Iblīs in Arabic is impossible to reproduce or fully imitate in English.

CHAPTER 6

Pleonasm and Redundancy

Pleonasm and redundancy are two overlapping terms which refer to using more words than necessary to convey an idea. According to a distinction proposed by Bernard Dupriez, pleonasm is the "repetition of an idea by the use of two or more different words within the same member of a sentence," while redundancy is the "repetition of an idea in two separate sentences or two separate members of the same sentence."[1] In Arabic rhetoric, these are part of the feature called *iṭnāb*, defined as saying things in more words than are normally necessary.[2] While pleonasm or loquacity can be used in English in specific cases where it may benefit, particularly in oratory, it is well-known about modern English that it prefers clarity, brevity, and concision,[3] so that eliminating excess wordage would obviously seem desirable, whereas other languages might in some of their phases prefer features such as parallelism that would result in a wordier text. On the other hand, English also employs various kinds of repetition in particular discourses.

Turning to specific examples, let us start with a feature that constitutes a kind of counterpart to the non-consequential exception or *istithnāʾ munqaṭiʿ* already discussed. But whereas non-consequential exception consists of making an exception not included in the original generalization, our first type of repetition consists of mentioning subordinate parts of a generalized item in a list as if they are separate, different items. Although such a list contains no actual repetition of the same lexical items, it does certainly contain a redundancy from the point of view of modern English. An example is found in verse 2:98:[4]

(92) man kāna ʿaduwwan li-llāhi wa-malāʾikatihi wa-rusulihi wa-jibrīla wa-mīkāla fa-inna llāha ʿaduwwun li-l-kāfirīn.

Arberry's rendition makes apparent the strangeness of this in English, assuming the reader realizes that Gabriel and Michael are angels:

1 Dupriez, 345; see also 382–383; Enos, 527–528.
2 Ibn al-Athīr, *Mathal*, II, 354–400; Ibn an-Naqīb, 218–225; Ṭūfī, 203–204; Bībānī, 93–94; Hāshimī, 201–206; Chowdhury, 199–200. Abdul-Raof, *Arabic Rhetoric*, 190–192, labels this feature "verbosity."
3 See my discussion of this point above on p. 8.
4 Bībānī, 97, describes this as an example of *iṭnāb*.

 | DOI:10.1163/9789004417441_008

(93) Whoever is an enemy to God and His angels
and His messengers, and Gabriel, and Michael—
surely God is an enemy to the unbelievers.

In English this doesn't make much sense, since the two angels were already included among "His angels" previously mentioned, and so their repetition seems useless. In Arabic, however, the repetition means a special honor to Gabriel and Michael,[5] and perhaps an emphatic reply to the Jewish opponents of Muhammad.[6] None of the English translations differs much from Arberry. Modifying the English by replacing the word "and" before "Gabriel" in (93) with "especially," for example, would bring the intent closer in the line with the intent of the Arabic and would make sense in English, but would not accord with the literal surface appearance of the Arabic. Another parallel example dealing with fruits is found in verse 55:68, although one of the words in question, *rummān*, happens to agree with the overriding rhyme pattern of the surah, a circumstance which does not obtain in (92).

Another form of *iṭnāb* is the repetition of an all-inclusive collective term for emphasis. This is a case of repeating the meaning but not the specific term, as two different words for "all" are used. Again, the repetition would probably be considered superfluous in English, as it has usually been omitted from the translations. Verse 15:30 provides an illustration:[7]

(94) fa-sajada l-malāʾikatu kulluhum ajmaʿūn.

This is typically rendered by Pickthall:

(95) 30. So the angels fell prostrate, all of them together

Here he avoids repeating the terms for "all," *kull* and *ajmaʿūn* by the use of "together." There is, however, a possible justification for considering his translation more exact. In verse 4:71, we see:

(96) fa-nfirū thubātin aw infirū jamīʿā.

5 Zamakhsharī, I, 169.
6 Qurṭubī, II, 36–37.
7 Bībānī, 52, citing this verse, calls this feature *tawkīd al-musnad ilayhi* (emphasizing the subject).

Arberry gives this as:

(97) ... then
move forward in companies or move forward
all together.

This is in agreement with the meaning of the Arabic as given by az-Zamakhsharī. *Jamīʿā* here means "all together in one group" rather than simply all, and stands in contrast to *thubātin*, which implies "in companies or successive raids."[8] Yet another similar example to (94) occurs in verse 10:99:

(98) wa-law shāʾa rabbuka la-āmana man fī l-arḍi kulluhum jamīʿā.

Here, however, the translations differ slightly. Striving to reproduce both words for "all (of them)" in the Arabic, Arberry gives us:

(99) And if thy Lord had willed, whoever
is in the earth would have believed,
all of them, all together.

Pickthall's expression is more economical and reflects the same understanding of the device shown in (95) as impled by verse 4:71 (96):

(100) 100. And if thy Lord willed, all who are in the earth would have believed together.

This is both less emphatic and less repetitious than Arberry in (99), producing a smoother texture that is more according to the usual textual expectations of English. But Arberry's translation here still might not be out of place in oratory as a kind of emphatic or exclamatory phrase, and, as we have see, the Qurʾān is an oral text. Whatever redundancy there may be for English in the possible semantic repetition for emphasis implied by the two words meaning "all" in (94) and (98), it does not seem to cause much of a problem.

There are still other cases where a different noun with the same semantic meaning as something which has preceded it in the sentence is mentioned for emphasis. This occurs, for example, in the famous night journey[9] verse 17:1:

8 Zamakhsharī, I, 532.

9 For the elaborated explanation of the night journey of the Prophet Muhammad given in the

(101) subḥāna lladhī asrā bi-ʿabdihi laylan …

This particular feature is among the points of rhetoric and is known as completion by bringing in something extra (*at-tatmīm bi-l-ityān bi-faḍlah*); in this case it is done to emphasize the shortness of the period.[10] The verb *asrā* means 'he sent by night' and *laylan* also means 'by night.' Arberry and Pickthall differ but little, the former putting forth:

(102) Glory be to Him, who carried His servant by night …

Bell offers a rather different version:

(103) 1. Glory be to Him who journeyed by night with His servant …

Bell's translation here differs from Arberry's in being anthropomorphizing, implying that God traveled with Muhammad on the night journey rather than that He just sent him,[11] an interpretation supported neither by the Arabic text nor the Muslim interpretive tradition. However, both Arberry and Bell fail to offer a translation that would differ from one of the same verse without the word *laylan*, and Muhammad Ali, Yūsuf ʿAlī, Pickthall, Asad, and Dawood (1990 & 2014) all likewise simply employ "by night." Yet Arabic rhetoric avers that this word slightly increases the emphasis.[12] Perhaps a phrase like "during a single night" would at least convey a greater degree of emphasis, although it is longer than the Arabic, heavier than the existing translations' short expression "by night," and would seem to change the meaning slightly by adding specification.

---

hadith, see Bukhārī, IV, 272–276 (K. bad' al-khalq, b. dhikr al-malāikah, hadith no. 3207), V, 132–136 (K. manāqib al-anṣār, b. al-miʿrāj, hadith no. 3887).

10 Zamakhsharī, II, 646–647; Bayḍāwī, III, 247; Bībānī, 102. Zarkashī, IV, 93, interesting contradicts az-Zamakhsharī by name on this point.

11 Bell, II, 539. It is apparent from Bell's comments here that he is trying to prove that Muhammad had a limited, anthropormorphic view of Allāh, at least early in his mission.

12 Bībānī, 102.

CHAPTER 7

Repetition for Emphasis

Another type of very common, emphatic Arabic rhetorical device, repetition for emphasis, also is defined as a kind of *iṭnāb*, but when it is repetition of the same words, it is more specifically called *tikrār*.[1] Repetition of words for emphasis is of course a common feature in many languages. It is first noted, perhaps, in both Greek and Latin books on rhetoric, starting with Aristotle in the 4th century BCE, who noted that repetition of the same word is not suitable for writing but is for speaking.[2] While Aristotle no doubt was referring to Greek, his observation appears to be often or mostly valid for other languages, including both Arabic and English, and is quite relevant to our discussion of this feature, as the Qurʾān is an oral text. Later ancient writers who elaborated further on repetition as a rhetorical device include Demetrius, the author of the *Rhetorica ad Herrenium*, and Quintilian.[3] In modern English, the repetition of the same word is called reduplication, which is one of the types of repetition.[4] Indeed, the kinds of repetition used in English, with names derived from ancient Greek rhetoric, are quite numerous.[5]

Arguments for and against repetition are very old, and there has probably always been an effort to eliminate redundancy and repetition in writing.[6] In the last century, despite the development of jargon or journalese with its technical terms and frequent verbosity, there has nevertheless perhaps been a trend away

1 For detailed descriptions of *tikrār* (also called *takrīr*) covering many Qurʾānic verses, see Ibn al-Athīr, *Mathal*, II, 358; III, 3–40; Ibn an-Naqīb, 226–237; Ṭūfī, 245–258; Zarkashī, III, 8–34; Hāshimī, 202–203; Chowdhury, 173–177. Abdul-Raof, *Arabic Rhetoric*, 250–251; Abdul-Raof, *New Horizons*, 202–204, calls this feature "epizeuxis."

2 Aristotle, *On Rhetoric: A Theory of Civic Discourse*. Tr. by George A. Kennedy. 2nd ed. New York: Oxford University Press, 2007, Bk. 3:12:2–4.

3 Demetrius, 66, 196–197, 211–214; *Rhetorica ad Herrenium*, 4:13:19–4:14:21; 4:25:34–35; 4:28:38–39; Quintilian, 9:3:28–36; 9:3:40–45; 9:3:54–57; 9:3:85–86. For a convenient listing of the different types of repetition in rhetoric with the ancient writers, see Peter Mack, *Rhetoric's Questions, Reading and Interpretation*. London: Palgrave Macmillan, 2017, p. 80.

4 Dupriez, 383–384; compare what Dupriez says about repetition, 390–392, and epanalepsis, 163–165. See also Enos, 600.

5 Harris, 125–130, 135–139, 147–151.

6 For example, Sakkākī, 591–592, while defending repetition by using Qurʾānic repetition (*tikrār*) as evidence, argues against an unnamed party who appear to have been critical of all textual repetition as useless already in the seventh/thirteenth century. Qazwīnī, 29–30, also criticizes excessive repetition.

 | DOI:10.1163/9789004417441_009

from such repetition for emphasis.[7] Indeed, it is asserted that the English language, as well as perhaps other languages, prefers to eliminate repeated words by transformational rules.[8] However, it is equally true that classical English literature contains plenty of repetition for emphasis. Besides this, it is interesting that addresses, speeches, and sermons, all oratory, are still most likely to contain this feature in the twentieth century, whereas it is the written genres that are less likely to have it.

If we go back to Shakespeare, we surely can scarcely find a piece of English oratory so famously outstanding as Anthony's funeral oration for Caesar in "Julius Caesar," Act III, Scene 2. Here it is just the device of repetition of the term "honorable man" or "honorable men" in referring to Brutus and his associates that is so effective; it is used about ten times in the scene in one form or another to bring a hostile crowd over to his side and into a frenzy against Caesar's murderers. Or, for example, take verses 91–92 in the same scene:

(104) But Brutus says he was ambitious;
And Brutus is an honorable man.

The basic effect of the repetition of Brutus's name here is to emphasize his connection with honor, perhaps to the point of implying the exclusion of others. This, of course achieves the high dramatic effect of making Brutus appear all the worse a scoundrel in the eyes of the Roman mob. However, repetition is much less necessary when the reader has time to ponder a text and return to the print for edification on any point he did not understand. But during a speech, the hearer has only one opportunity to catch what is said, so literal repetition for emphasis might be exactly the device called for, as in (104).

Repetition is also often characteristic of "biblical" style, which may be considered tedious by some, but is held to be sublime by others. Indeed, we can certainly find instances from the Old Testament that by current rhetorical standards might seem gratingly repetitious. For example, we find in Zechariah 1:3:

(105) Therefore say to them, thus says the Lord of hosts: Return to me, says the Lord of hosts, and I will return to you, says the Lord of hosts.

In this, the whole passage can be reduced by more than half and still retain its message; yet there are many readers who enjoy the Old Testament and find

7 Brooks & Warren, 46, 268, 387–388.

8 Mark Lester, *Introductory Transformational Grammar of English*. New York: Holt, Rinehart and Winston, Inc., 1971, p. 280.

it positively exciting, here perhaps from its emphasizing that it is God Who is speaking, and the whole passage represents an oral delivery. Presumably anyone who found no fault with (105) could not fault the Qur'ān nor its translations for tedious repetition either.

Thus, while a reader who is unaware of the oral nature of the Qur'ān might find some of the repetition monotonous, a more sympathetic reader who realizes the oral nature of the text would probably find the text more deeply resonant. However, as we shall see, there still may be some Qur'ānic passages that might seem monotonous to many readers. Also, it may be that the total effect of so much repetition in the Qur'ān when translated is to produce a feeling that it is overdone in English. But we need to examine specific cases in order to assess to what extent such a general preference for avoiding repetition in English might influence the reception of Qur'ān translations.

To start, one case similar to (104) in its power occurs in verse 11:81, where Lot is warned to hasten his departure from Sodom:

(106) inna mawʿidahum aṣ-ṣubḥu a-laysa ṣ-ṣubḥu bi-qarīb.

Like (104), the repetition involves a noun. Not differing much from the other six translators, Bell has rendered this:

(107) Their appointed time is the morning, is not the morning near?

It may be that the actual implication of the angels' warning, the intended semantic meaning, is something like:

(108) Their appointed time is the morning, so hadn't you better get moving?

It seems that the subtlety of (107) in not directly stating the threat actually increases the effect of it by leaving it for the reader's mind to fill in both the possible consequences of remaining behind and the actual necessity of beginning the flight immediately. This too can be considered a kind of emphasis by understatement, a feature also favored by English in certain cases, such as (38) above. After all, the morning is always near just before the dawn, every day. Only this particular morning meant in (107) has such ominous implications that the effect, though subtle, is really quite emphatic, exactly suitable for the situation. In Arabic there is a like effect. On the other hand, it might be mentioned here that aṭ-Ṭabarī and az-Zamakhsharī cite explanatory traditions which insert between the two sentences of (104) Lot saying, "I want it to happen sooner than that." In this case, we would understand the reply of the angels as meaning, "Isn't the morning soon enough?" Interestingly, the existence of these traditions suggests that even some early Muslim readers steeped in Arabic found the repetition of the word "morning" odd and chose to explain it by assuming that the second phrase was a reply to an interjection by Lot that is not in the Qurʾānic text. Although these traditions are traced back to very early authorities by aṭ-Ṭabarī, the rhetorical explanation of the repetition of "morning" appears to be better than a rather gratuitous addition to the text.[9]

An example that does not come across in English as well as (106) is shown in verses 36:20–21, where a verb phrase is repeated.[10]

(109) qāla yā qawmi ttabiʿū l-mursalīn.
ittabiʿū man lā yasʾalukum ajran wa-hum muhtadūn.

Arberry tries to adhere to the Arabic text quite closely:

(110) ... he said, 'My people,
follow the Envoys!
Follow such as ask no wage of you,
that are right-guided ...'

Arberry here repeats "follow" = Arabic *ittabiʿū*, and most of the other translations are similar.

However, Pickthall offers us:

(111) ... He cried: O my people! Follow those who have been sent!
21. Follow those who ask of you no fee, and who are rightly guided.

In the Arabic and in most of the other translations, only the verb has been repeated, but by translating *al-mursalīn* as those who have been sent, Pickthall increases the repetition from one to three words: "Follow those who ...;" in this he is followed by Dawood only. While this creates a repetition that is less faithful to the Arabic than Arberry's, Pickthall's amplified repetition conveys an urgency that is certainly part of the Qurʾānic text. This is an example of how a lack of adherence to the original sometimes may convey an aspect of the original that is lost in the more literal translation.

9 The traditions are traced back separately to Ismāʿīl b. ʿAbd ar-Raḥmān as-Suddī (d. 127/745) and Qatādah b. Diʿāmah as-Sadūsī (d. 117/735), and beyond him less probably to Ḥudhayfah b. al-Yamān (d. 36/656–657). Ṭabarī, XII, 54–55; Zamakhsharī, II, 416.

10 Qazwīnī, 186; Bībānī, 99.

Another example characteristic of the Qur'ān and having something in common with (105) is that it repeats the name of God in verse 33:3, which is similarly repeated elsewhere in the book in 4:81; 4:132, and 33:48:

(112) wa-tawakkal ʿalā llāhi wa-kafā bi-llāhi wakīlā.

Pickthall offers us:

(113) 3. And put thy trust in Allah, for Allah is sufficient as Trustee.

But Arberry has:

(114) And put thy trust in God; God suffices
as a guardian.

One translates the conjunction as "for," and the other renders it a semicolon. They are both "dealing with it" in some sense. Such repetition, to the English-speaking reader, is likely to remind the reader of the kind of writing represented in (105) above; probably he will react to it accordingly. Certain readers might regard repetitions of this kind as monotonous. If we employ subordination, the sentence can be reformed:

(115) And put your trust in Allah, Who suffices as a guardian.

This conforms to the supposed English preference in rhetoric for subordination.[11] In Arabic, this rewording sounds modern and prosy and causes a loss of emphasis, as all parallelism is lost:

(116) wa-tawakkal ʿalā llāhi lladhī yakfī wakīlā.

However, it must be conceded that by themselves (113) and (114) are not likely to be regarded as monotonous by anyone. Indeed, if this wording were not used elsewhere in the Qur'ān, it would likely be regarded as novel and emphatic to English readers of the Qur'ān. It is only through repeated use in many verses that it might become boring. And, as noted in the discussion of number (105), some readers brought up on the Old Testament and liking its style might even

11 Kaplan, 36.

be attracted by such a feature. We must recall, however, that the Qur'ān consists of revelations made over a period of more than two decades, and was not originally intended to be read in one or even several sittings.

Nevertheless, there are some repetitions of nouns in the Qur'ān that might be considered monotonous by most of the general audience of contemporary English-speaking readers, such as 55:7–9:

(117) wa-s-samā'a rafa'ahā wa-waḍa'a l-mīzān.
allā taṭghaw fī l-mīzān.
wa-aqīmū l-wazna bi-l-qisṭi wa-lā tukhsirū l-mīzān.

It should be noted that in the Arabic, in addition to the threefold repetition of *al-mīzān* at the end of each verse, there is also the use in the third verse of *al-wazna*, another, different noun having the same root as *al-mīzān*, *w-z-n*. While it might be objected that it is difficult to see the threefold repetition of *al-mīzān* as elegant, even in Arabic, and perhaps especially in modern Arabic, yet it must be conceded that different tastes exist and that we, as modern, literate people, are not really able to know what the reception of this feature by its first, non-literate hearers might have been. Az-Zamakhsharī states that the threefold repetition of *al-mīzān* is to strengthen and emphasize the commandment to be just in weighing.[12] Each of the translators has dealt with these verses a bit differently. Bell, less concerned with rhetorical beauty as promised in his introduction, does the least to try to suppress the repetition of *al-mīzān* of the Arabic:

(118) 6. The heaven He hath lifted up, and He hath set the Balance.
7. That ye may not transgress in regard to the Balance.
8. Establish the weighing in justice, and make not short the balance.[13]

Even though Bell has already lost one of the repetitions, by using "weighing" for *wazna* and the unrelated "balance" for *mīzān*, his repetition of "balance" may seem somewhat heavy-handed in English, as evidenced by the effort of both Arberry and Pickthall to modfiy it in their translations of these verses. Arberry does so by downgrading verses 8 and 9 with parentheses, while leaving the repeated word. Hence the effect differs only slightly from (118):

12 Zamakhsharī, IV, 444.
13 The failure to capitalize "balance" at the end of the passage could be a typo.

(119) ... and heaven—He raised it up, and set
the Balance.
(Transgress not in the Balance,
and weigh with justice, and skimp not in the Balance).

Now, the English-speaking reader will doubtless notice the intent of the original: to emphasize the Balance, especially as Arberry has thoughtfully supplied capital letters to ensure that this does not escape his or her attention. But the reader may wonder at the same time whether it was really necessary to have such repetition. Perhaps she or he might prefer Pickthall's slightly less literal rendering:

(120) 7. And the sky He hath uplifted; and He hath set the measure,
8. That ye exceed not the measure,
9. But observe the measure strictly, nor fall short thereof.

Still, Pickthall has not really reduced the repetition, only replacing the final *al-mīzān* with "thereof," while translating *aqīmū l-wazna* as "observe the measure," thus still ending up with three "measures." All these thus seem to be somewhat monotonous repetitions in English, though, again, they remind us of the other threefold repetition in Zechariah (105) above. Also, one must note that, in comparison with the original's repetition of *al-mīzān*, Pickthall's refrain in verse 9 of "thereof" certainly appears to fall flat.

In contrast to Bell, Arberry, and Pickthall, each of whom has preserved some of the original repetition of the Arabic, Dawood (1990) reads:

(121) He raised heaven on high and set the balance of all things, that you might not transgress that balance. Give just weight and full measure.

Dawood's version here offers bald readability and fluency and certainly represents the domesticating method of translation as described at length by Venuti. Here, although the word "balance" is still used twice, it loses its emphatic position at the end of each verse. While it still concludes the first sentence, Dawood has reduced the repetitive impact of its mate in the same sentence by inserting the non-Qur'ānic, exegetical phrase "of all things." In the final sentence of verse 9, Dawood has flattened out the original completely, reducing *wa-lā tukhsirū l-mīzān*, literally "and do not cause the balance to be lost" to just "and full measure." Probably many English-language readers would prefer Dawood as being in more fluent, easier, more contemporary language closer to their own speech than the other translations, which thus appear here more foreignizing in their various degrees.

In his revisions, Dawood seems to have changed his text to be more in line with the usual, less domesticating tradition of Qur'ān translation. In the case of these verses, Dawood (2014) presents us with:

(122) The heaven he raised on high and set the Balance of all things, that you might not transgress that Balance. Give just weight and measure, and do not cheat the Balance.

This version of Dawood shows us several of Dawood's choices, all of which have moved his text in a more traditional direction. In the first sentence, he has placed the direct object first, exactly as in the Qur'ānic Arabic, despite this leading to less clarity because the first clause is not longer parallel to the second, where the direct object "Balance" still follows the verb, also exactly as in the Arabic. This can only be seen as a foreignizing move. Similarly, the capitalization of Balance exits from normal English. Lastly, the final sentence is now included as in the other translations, more or less. One might suspect that this phrase was previously merely omitted by mistake, except that the 1990 version is the fifth edition, which certainly should have included it were its omission a mistake rather than a choice. While Dawood's translation still contains more domesticating features than the other translations, it is quite interesting that he felt constrained after all the success of his Penguin Classics work to move at last at least a little in a foreignizing direction.

It should be noted that there are other examples of repetition of words similarly likely to be monotonous in English in verses 69:1–3; 101:1–3; and 114:1–3 and 5–6, illustrating that this is a frequent feature in the Qur'ān. Unlike 55:7–9, however, all these latter cases could be examples of oracular utterances.

Finally, among repetition of words as a kind of *iṭnāb* of emphasis, we ought to note that words, phrases, and sentences can all be repeated for emphasis. A vivid example occurs in 102:3–7:

(123) kallā sawfa taʿlamūn.
thumma kallā sawfa taʿlamūn.
kallā law taʿlamūna ʿilm al-yaqīn.
la-tarawunna l-jaḥīm.
thumma la-tarawunnahā ʿayna l-yaqīn.

Here we note the repetition of *kallā* three times, *sawfa* twice, *taʿlamūna* three times, *thumma* twice, *al-yaqīn* twice, and *la-tarawunna* twice. Furthermore, verse 4 is a repetition of verse 3,[14] while verse 7 repeats the meaning of verse 6 and *al-yaqīn* of verse 5. Of course, in considering this repetition, we must remember, as we noted in the introduction, that the Qur'ān is an oral text, orally revealed and delivered. Thus features like this repetition will be more familiar to spoken English, particularly formal spoken English, than to written style. As for the translations Bell gives us:

(124) 3. Nay, but ye shall know,
4. And again, nay, but ye shall know!
5. Nay, but if ye knew with the knowledge of the Certainty,
6. Ye would see the Hot Place.
7. Then ye will assuredly see it with the eye of the Certainty.

This seems a reasonably smooth translation, our earlier comments about the usage of "Hot Place" notwithstanding. However, Bell has misunderstood the two verses after the third "nay" as a true improbable conditional with *law*, whereas actually the first of them is a conditional protasis with the real apodosis omitted (a feature that will be further dealt with below). The final two sentences are a substitute for that apodosis, but should be taken in the positive and emphatic sense rather than as the fulfillment of the conditional. Arberry has understood this better though he should perhaps have supplied some punctuation to separate the two verses to avoid confusion:

(125) No indeed; but soon you shall know.
Again, no indeed; but soon you shall know.
No indeed; did you know with the knowledge of certainty
you shall surely see Hell.
Again, you shall surely see it with the eye of certainty

The heavy emphatic sense of the Arabic, comes through quite clearly into English in both (124) and (125), though the degree of emphasis implied by *la-tarawunna* is only accounted for by the latter. On the other hand, while the oral Arabic of the Qur'ān contains no exclamation marks such as that used by Bell in (124), he may be quite justified in thus imparting a sense of urgency heard by the original listeners but lost in an unmarked written text, especially in English where some of the other devices still at hand for the Arabic reader,

14 Ibn Qutaybah, 235–236. Ibn Qutaybah here confirms that the repetition here is for emphasis.

such as the rhymed prose endings, are lost. In (125), one point that might cause annoyance is the "no indeed" followed by its semicolon three times, producing a heavy grating effect in the mind of the reader not found with the original's *kallā* and also avoided by Bell's "nay." One might well ask what Arberry is saying "no indeed" to, whereas the same question does not arise with "nay."

We might finally consider one more example of repetition of whole phrases for emphasis that occurs in the Qur'ān in verses 109:2–5:

(126) lā aʿbudu mā taʿbudūn.
wa-lā antum ʿābidūna mā aʿbud.
wa-lā ana ʿābidun mā ʿabadtum.
wa-lā antum ʿābidūna mā aʿbud.

We should mention that these are among the most outwardly repetitive verses the Qur'ān has to offer. Pickthall's choice of the two syllable word "worship," while paralleling the multisyllabic Arabic terms, also may seem to heavily overload the English, which prefers brevity:

(127) 2. I worship not that which ye worship;
3. Nor worship ye that which I worship.
4. And I shall not worship that which ye worship.
5. Nor will ye worship that which I worship.

His attempt to distinguish the last two sentences by placing them in the future in contrast to the first two for rhetorical variety is not borne out by the commentators. Az-Zamakhsharī assigns futurity only to the first of these, pointing out that the negative particle *lā* used with the imperfect implies futurity, *mā* the present time, *lan* being an emphatic particle.[15] Verses 3 and 5 in the Arabic are identical.

On the other hand, Arberry translates:

(128) I serve not what you serve
And you are not serving what I serve,
Nor am I serving what you have served,
Neither are you serving what I serve.

15 Zamakhsharī, IV, 808–809.

Unlike (124) and (125), where the reader feels some of the Qur'ānic urgency pressing in on him, some of the surety of the threat of the Judgment, which he may or may not like according to taste and religious prejudice, here one feels nothing of that excitement. And indeed, the usual interpretation of the Arabic here seems to be rather to prove the firmness of the Prophet in his faith. While that meaning comes across clearly in (128), one well may suppose that the repetition in these particular verses will be still seem monotonous to many English-language readers, consisting as it does of whole sentences and without visible rhetorical benefit in English. Perhaps Arberry's use of the present continuous in verses 3–5 does not help as well, stretching the text out longer than the simple present would.

In addition to all these cases of repetitions of words, there are the repetitions of whole sentences verbatim to serve as refrains in certain surahs, certainly the most obtrusive examples of repetition in the Qur'ān. These include especially the refrains of surahs 55 (31 repetitions), 77 (10 repetitions), 26 (3 verses with 8 repetitions each and 2 more with 5 each), 54 (2 verses of 4 repetitions each), and 27 (5 repetitions). Whatever one may think of this poetic or hymnic device, which would appear most to resemble the repeated chorus stanza of popular songs, it is not part of the repertoire of normal modern written English and may appear to be tedious to many readers, especially the cases with the most numerous and frequent repetitions.

In sum, in the Qur'ān there is considerable repetition, more than contemporary standards of English prose generally allow, but usually not more than befits an oral style. Hence, though much repetition is natural, expected, and effective in the Qur'ān, it may serve to alienate an English-language reader unless she or he understands the nature of the text beforehand and adjusts her or his expectations accordingly. However, there is also much great literature which, though it may have been oral in its original intent, like the plays of Shakespeare, is popular with a wide audience despite or perhaps partly because of its skillful use of repetition. An example of how this can come from the translations we are examining is (107) above. Other passages may have been made more repetitive and hence tedious by translator error, like (111), where it seems a different choice of words could have saved Pickthall's repetition. Of course, it is also in the nature of many translations to be awkward and stiff, although we note on the other side that this has not prevented the Bible from rising to the status of supreme literature and possibly even having a considerable effect on other compositions. So sorting out the true effect of Qur'ānic repetition in English will require further study. At most, we might allow the probable monotony of (118), (119), (120), (127), and (128) to most readers.

CHAPTER 8

Parallelism

Next, we must turn our attention to a type of repetition that constitutes another major area of rhetorical difficulty for translators of Arabic in English: parallelism. This term, denoting that "Correspondences between two parts of an utterance are emphasized by means of syntactic and rhythmic repetition," covers a very large number of diverse rhetorical devices whose explanation is quite complex.[1] Elaborate parallelism of various types often typifies Semitic writing and is particularly common in the Qur'ān. It may be, in fact, that the various kinds of Qur'ānic parallelism constitute the single most obvious difficulty for Qur'ān translation.

Of course, the use of parallelism in both speech and writing is widespread in human languages in general. Thus, parallelism is already taken into account by several ancient Greek and Roman authors, who mainly emphasize contrastive parallels.[2] Because of the varieties of parallel figures and devices, Arabic rhetoricians do not seem to have settled on one convenient term to cover all kinds of parallelism, though they developed many terms for its various types. Ḍiyā' ad-Dīn Ibn al-Athīr, considers parallelism to be a kind of *tanāsub al-maʿānī* = harmony of meanings, but he seems to prefer to term at least some forms of parallelism *muqābalah*. Ibn al-Athīr also divides *muqābalah* then into three kinds: paralleling a thing with its opposite, or with something different, or with something similar or the same.[3] While following Ibn al-Athīr considerably, Ibn an-Naqīb prefers to use the terms *tanāsub*, *tashābuh*, and *munāsabah*. Later, al-Qazwīnī places the whole question of parallelism under the third category of rhetoric, *ʿilm al-badīʿ*, and considerably elaborates the various kinds of parallelism into many separate types, starting with *muṭābaqah* and *muqābalah*.[4] Az-Zarkashī treats much of the parallelism in the Qur'ān as *muqābalah*.[5] Generally, Arabic rhetoric books defined *muṭābaqah* (also called *ṭibāq*) as any antithesis, that is, parallelism between two or more antithetical terms,

1 Dupriez, 318–319; Mustansir Mir, "Some Figures of Speech in the Qur'an," *Religion & Literature*, 40 (2008), 34–38.

2 Aristotle, 3:9:7–9; Demetrius, 22–29, 247–250; *Rhetorica*, 4:15:21.

3 Ibn al-Athīr, *Jāmiʿ*, 211–218; cf. Ibn al-Athīr, *Mathal*, III, 143–177. Ṭūfī, 259–266, mostly follows Ibn al-Athīr in all of this, even citing the same proof texts.

4 Qazwīnī, 383–390.

5 Zarkashī, III, 458–477.

 | DOI:10.1163/9789004417441_010

and *muqābalah* as parallels between two or more terms on each side of the parallel, that is, at least four terms.[6] To cover all synonymous parallelisms, the term *murāʿāt an-naẓīr* was developed, but seems to have been less used than *muṭābaqah* and *muqābalah*.[7] As noted by al-Qazwīnī, *murāʿāt an-naẓīr* is also called *tanāsub*, *iʾtilāf*, or *tawfīq*,[8] all of which seem to be suitable terms for parallelism. The editor of Ibn an-Naqīb, Zakariyyā Saʿīd ʿAlī, in a footnote specifically states that *tanāsub*, *tashābuh*, *munāsabah*, *murāʿāt an-naẓīr*, *tawfīq*, *iʾtilāf*, and *muʾākhāh* all describe exactly the same feature.[9] From all this, it appears that *muṭābaqah* and *muqābalah* may be considered as subcategories of *tanāsub*. More recently, Hussein Abdul-Raof also presents several different terms for parallelism, all different from the above: *jinās ṣarfī*, *muwāzanah*, *mumāthalah*, *tarṣīʿ*, and *sajʿ mutawāz*.[10]

The concept of parallelism in English is constructed somewhat differently. As was recognized by Professor Robert B. Kaplan, the parallelism present to this day in Arabic, to the extent that it even permeates Arab students' English compositions, is fundamentally a style preferred by the Old Testament and the Qurʾān, but not modern English. Citing several types of parallelism, he goes on to point out that it was the popular literary fashion in Elizabethan times but since the 17th century has ceased to be in vogue.[11] While even quite complex parallelism is certainly still employed to good effect in English,[12] elaborate and frequent parallelism is now discouraged and students are urged to use it sparingly.[13] Kaplan counts four classifications of different kinds of parallelism: synonymous, synthetic, antithetic, and climactic.[14] Similar to Ibn al-Athīr's third type, synonymous parallelism is a kind of coordination of two sentences or expressions having the same meaning, though different in form, as in Isaiah 43:25:

(129) I, I am He
Who blots out your transgressions for

6 Bībānī, 183–187; Hāshimī, 303–304.

7 Sakkākī, 424; Shihāb ad-Dīn Aḥmad b. ʿAbd al-Wahhāb an-Nuwayrī, *Nihāyat al-arab fī funūn al-adab*, Cairo: Dār al-Kutub wa-l-Wathāʾiq al-Qawmiyyah, 1423[/2002], Vol. VII, p. 106; Hāshimī, 304–305; Ṭabānah, *Muʿjam*, 261.

8 Qazwīnī, 390–392.

9 Ibn an-Naqīb, 177, fn. *, citing several other medieval authors as well.

10 Abdul-Raof, *New Horizons*, 208.

11 Kaplan, 35–39.

12 Williams & Colomb, 141–146, who prefer to call it "balance and symmetry;" Harris, 5–11.

13 Brooks & Warren, 381–385.

14 Kaplan, 39–40.

my own sake,
and I will not remember your sins.

Here two nearly synonymous ideas are linked by "and." Synthetic parallelism involves the completion of the idea of the first clause in the second, after implying a causal relationship. An example of this is Psalms 37:8–9:

(130) Refrain from anger, and forsake wrath!
Fret not yourself; it tends only to evil.
For the wicked shall be cut off;
but those who wait for the Lord shall possess the land.

This contains three kinds of parallelism, but the main message, "Fret not; for the wicked shall be cut off," is an example of synthetic parallelism. The third kind of parallelism, antithetic, is represented in Ecclesiastes 1:4:

(131) A generation goes and a generation comes, but the earth abides forever.

This is to emphasize a contrast. The form of the two clauses may also be the same for greater emphasis. Example (131) also has this feature in the two sentences joined by "but." The last type is climactic parallelism, where the effect is delayed until the end, as in the modern periodic sentence. This is a common feature especially in the writings of certain of the prophets, where the real prophecy is saved for last while the prophet is warming up his listeners with a series of ominous warnings. For example, in Amos 1:5, we read:

(132) I will break the bar of Damascus and cut off
the inhabitants from the Valley of Aven,
and him that holds the scepter from Beth-eden;
and the people of Syria shall go into exile to Kir.

Examples could be cited of each of these types of parallelism from the Qurʾān as well, but here we are concerned with the impact of Qurʾānic parallelism on English rhetoric, not to prove the identity of its style with the Bible. Hence, we will prefer to divide our examples according to scope, making three divisions of parallel words, clauses, and larger blocks of writing, while trying to concentrate on the first two. We may make occasional reference in our analysis to the above divisions of Kaplan, noting that parallelism is certainly a prominent feature in the Old Testament as in the Qurʾān.

The first feature we will examine, then, parallel words, commonly occurs at the end of a verse, where two nouns or adjectives of similar but differing meaning and in the same grammatical case as well as often of the same derivational pattern are paired without a connective conjunction. Instances of this are exceedingly frequent in the Qur'ān, as in the well-known *amānah* verse 33:72:

(133) … innahu kāna ẓalūman jahūlā.

This verse clearly shows the feature as just described and also exactly matches an example of *murāʿāt an-naẓīr* cited by modern rhetoricians.[15] While the parallel adjectives *ẓalūm* and *jahūl* have different meanings, the first connected with aggression and wrongdoing, the second with thoughtless anger and folly, they are similar in that both are undesirable qualities often connected with each other in the same person, in this case *al-insān*, generic man or human being. Hence, they would have to be taken as an instance of (nearly) synonymous parallelism. Both are in the indefinite accusative case, fulfilling the requirement for parallel grammatical case, and here both have the same derivational pattern, *faʿūl*, making for an intensification of the meaning. No conjunction connects the pair, as is common in Arabic in general and Qur'ānic usage in particular. While the two words here could be taken either as two substantive nouns, or as two adjectives describing the human, or as a noun modified by an adjective, the last is the least likely explanation, as all of the paired words at the end of verses are usually understood to be on an equal footing and not subordinate to each other, as implied in the Arabic name for the feature, *murāʿāt an-naẓīr* = consideration of the peer, or consideration of equal status.[16]

Another problem in this verse not directly related to parallelism is how to render the verb *kāna*, which is normally the past or perfect tense of the verb "to be." Thus, it might be translated "he was," yet it is unlikely that the text means only that the human being was aggressively wrongdoing and thoughtlessly angry in the past. So it is possible to take the verb as meaning either "was ever or always" or "has ever been," just as is the case in similar constructions when predicated of God, and in this way the perfective sense of *kāna* is kept. However, it appears that the structure can also be taken as emphatic in the present, meaning "indeed, he is …" as is supported by modern analysis of simi-

15 Hāshimī, 304; Ṭabānah, *Muʿjam*, 261.

16 Zamakhsharī, III, 565, sees the two as a pair of descriptives on an equal footing.

lar structures.[17] If then rendered "he is ever ...," both the emphatic element and the continuity will be covered.

The translators for their part differ considerably in their interpretations in this case, both in the point of the paired nouns and of the verb *kāna*, following one or another of the usages we have mentioned. Pickthall adheres to the majority emphasizing perfectivity by using the present perfect tense:

(134) Lo! he hath proved a tyrant and a fool.

He has also inserted the conjunction normally necessary in English to coordinate two nouns with each other, a feature not in the Arabic.

Dawood (1990 and 2014) has:

(135) ... but he has proved a sinner and a fool.

Thus Dawood is quite similar to Pickthall in adding the conjunction "and" and using the present perfect, while modernizing the language, as he does elsewhere, for greater fluency and ease of reading.

Bell keeps some of the same characteristics but with quite a different result:

(136) Verily he has become affected with wrongdoing and ignorance.

Like Pickthall, he has translated *kāna* with the English present perfect, but the word "affected" combined with "become" does not appear to fit here, as it implies affectedness, a translation that has no support in the Qurʾānic text. More infelicitous is the connection of "wrongdoing" and "ignorance" to the verb by the preposition "with." It almost appears from such a translation that he has tried to take the paired nouns as an adverbial phrase, entailing in Arabic the changing of the two adjectival nouns into *maṣdar*s (verbal nouns or gerunds) *ẓulm* and *jahl*. Thus, his translation here does not seem to give either the correct meaning nor much of the rhetorical art of the four-word original.

Arberry has chosen to be simpler:

(137) Surely he is sinful, very foolish.

---

17 Wolfgang Reuschel, "Wa-kāna llāhu ʿalīman raḥīman," *Studia Orientalia in Memoriam Caroli Brockelmann* (Sonderausgabe der Wissenschaftlichen Zeitschrift der Martin-Luther-Universität Halle-Wittenberg, Gesellschafts- und sprachwissenschaftliche Reihe), Heft 2/3, Jahrgang XVII, 1968, pp. 147–153.

While this seems obviously more attractive than the other two efforts for trying to reproduce the Arabic as closely as possible, especially in its word economy, it clearly demonstrates that in translating, everything cannot be conveyed, although some renditions may come closer to achieving this than others. Here we have six words, compared to the nine each of Pickthall and Bell. "Surely" provides us with a more contemporary emphasis word for *innahu* than either "Lo!" or "Verily," which are both archaic. But the formal pairing of the nouns, while more closely rendering the Arabic by avoiding the use of a conjunction, is done with the inclusion of the additional word "very." This is in order to convey that the word *jahūlā* is an emphatic adjective (*ṣifat mubālaghah*), but the same applies to *ẓalūman*. As for the verb, while Arberry's usage of the present tense is plain and simple, he has tried to convey the emphatic element by using "Surely," an extra word not in the Arabic. Arberry's text seems to convey the semantic meaning of the verse, but whether with quite the same rhetorical effect as the Arabic is open to question.

Yūsuf ʿAlī gives us:

(138) He was indeed unjust
And foolish;—

Like Arberry's version, this somewhat parallels the word economy of the Arabic's four words, but the simple past gives the impression that the human's error only happened at the time the trust was offered, whereas the Arabic *kāna* here would better taken to mean "was ever" rather than simply "was."

Interestingly, it is the oldest of our translations, that of Muhammad Ali, along with Muhammad Asad, who convey the idea of *kāna* as a permanent condition of the human being. Capturing some of the succinctness of the original in six words like Arberry and Yūsuf ʿAlī, Muhammad Ali gives us:

(139) Surely he is ever unjust, ignorant—

While Muhammad Asad has:

(140) ... for, verily, he has always been prone to be most wicked, most foolish.

With thirteen words, Asad's translation here is by far the wordiest. Both Muhammad Ali and Asad have to insert extra words, "ever" or "always prone," to convey the meaning of a permanent condition that they alone have. This further illustrates the difficulty of the translator in not being able to convey all the possible meanings of the original.

A similar example involves pairing two of the qualities that are among the divine attributes of Allah. As in (114), the translations differ considerably in dealing with only this small part of a single verse, which is repeated five times in the Qur'ān in 4:56, 158, 165; 48:7, 19, appearing as a refrain, the like of which are ubiquitous throughout the Qur'ān using different words:

(141) … wa-kāna llāhu ʿazīzan ḥakīmā.

Here again, the verb *kāna* cannot be translated simply as "was" in the past, because it concerns God. Rather, it means "was and remains," that is, continues to the present without a break.[18]

Thus, Muhammad Ali translates:

(142) Surely Allah is ever Mighty, Wise.

Pickthall has rendered this:

(143) And Allah is ever Mighty, Wise.

Pickthall, like the other translators, removes Muhammad Ali's "Surely," which translates the Arabic emphatic particle *inna*. Perhaps Pickthall felt that the normally unnecessary "And" in English produces a kind of emphasis.

Arberry even dispenses with Pickthall's "And," just leaving the bare statement:

(144) God is All-mighty, All-wise.

It is quite interesting that Arberry, normally rather literalist, inserts the possibly superfluous word "All-" to mark God's characteristics. Only Muhammad Asad among our translators has done likewise.

Meanwhile, Bell has:

(145) And Allah hath become sublime, wise.

---

18 Abū Saʿīd al-Ḥasan b. ʿAbd Allāh b. al-Marzubān as-Sīrāfī, *Sharḥ kitab Sībawayh*, ed. by Aḥmad Ḥasan Mahdalī and ʿAlī Sayyid ʿAlī, Beirut: Dār al-Kutub al-ʿIlmiyyah, 2008, Vol. 1, p. 296; Abū Ḥayyān Muḥammad b. Yūsuf al-Gharnāṭī al-Andalusī, *at-Tadhyīl wa-t-takmīl fī sharḥ kitab at-tashīl*, ed. by Ḥasan Hindāwī, Damascus: Dār al-Qalam, 1997–, Vol. 4, pp. 211–212; Samarrāʾī, I, 213.

Probably the most immediately noticeable problem here to the native English speaker would be Bell's notion of Allah "becoming" sublime and wise, which would be reprehensible to a Muslim reader, because it would imply God's changeability, a characteristic by no means supported in the Qur'ān (see 10:64; 17:77; 30:30; 33:38,62; 35:43; 40:85; 48:23). It is interesting that the present perfect, appropriate elsewhere as in (135) for example, here fails to carry the meaning of the Arabic across into English. Likewise Arberry's treatment of the verb, though better than Bell's, has the same quality of his translation of 33:72 (137), leaving one feeling something is missing. Pickthall, by rendering the identical surface structures of Arabic of (133) and (141) into English differently has tried most closely to adhere to the semantic intent of the original rather than the Arabic structure and at the same time has produced something of suitable rhetorical effect in English, as (143) represents some of the idea of permanence inherent in the verb *kāna*, but still at the cost of inserting an extra word. As for the paired nouns here, we find all translators deal with them similarly, finding no necessity of putting in an extra connective particle as Pickthall did in (134). Their consensus indeed seems to point to the effect of this: though unusual in English without a coordinating or contrasting particle, it seems to produce a suitable effect in the English reader. We might note, however, that if (143) were read out loud without a pause after "Mighty," the hearer might hear "Allah is ever mighty wise," where "mighty" would seem to be the colloquial intensifier meaning "very," as in, "That was a mighty nice dinner." Thus we can understand how English, especially oral, would prefer a connective here. We could imagine the use of either "and" or "but" in this place, depending on the translator's attitude towards the relationship of the two words "mighty," and "wise." In order for this pair of nouns to be separated by a "but," they must in some sense be contrastive, as the two in question undoubtedly are. It is probably in the interests of readability that Dawood (2014), alone among our translators, inserts a conjunction:

(146) Surely God is mighty and wise.

There are, however, many cases in which the two nouns are not so apparently contrasting, but are nearly synonymous. We read in 16:7 for example:

(147) … inna rabbakum la-ra'ūfun raḥīm.

The two attributes here, generally included among ninety-nine beautiful names of Allah, are similar in meaning; almost synonymous, both contain the concept of mercy, although derived from different roots. So the translators must use their skill to come up with synonyms to reproduce both words, not always an easy task. Pickthall gives for this verse:

(148) Lo! your Lord is Full of Pity, Merciful.

Arberry has, repeating his tendency to amplify God's characteristics with "All-":

(149) Surely your Lord is All-clement, All-compassionate.

And Bell:

(150) Verily your Lord is kind and compassionate.

While keeping the adjectives of Bell, Dawood splits the double Arabic refrain words in both of his versions. His 1990 version reads:

(151) Compassionate is your Lord, and merciful.

By 2014, he had revised this to read:

(152) Surely kindly is your Lord, and compassionate.

By splitting the Arabic expressions thus, Dawood has certainly altered the structure if not the meaning of the original, and he has also produced a version that is not the unmarked form of English, by placing one of the predicate adjectives first. In doing so, he attracts the attention of the reader to his words and thus achieves something of the emphatic aspect of the original, but at the cost of wiping away the structure of the original.

One might say that Bell's (150) is the closest to normal twentieth-century English prose, despite the archaic "Verily" because he has used a coordinate particle as well as the very common words "kind and compassionate." But this is really the least accurate in meaning and perhaps least effective rhetorically as well. Why? Example (150), though ordinary, is just for that reason a pedestrian type of statement. On the other hand, it is just possible that the Arabic rhetorical feature of parallel adjectives with no conjunction present in (148) and (149) may be effective, for some readers, though exotic in English. At least we can say it offers no problem to the clear conveyance of the semantic meaning. As for choosing between Arberry and Pickthall, the latter is closer to the semantic meaning, but has somewhat broken the appearance of the Arabic by translating *ra'ūfun* in three words. On the other hand, there is reason to object to Arberry's rendition of *raḥīm* as 'compassionate,' as we shall presently see.

So far, while we have seen how translation cannot convey the whole meaning of the original even in examples containing very few words, we have nonetheless encountered no problem very difficult in English in this chapter. But other cases may cause more strain for the translators, such as even that most common phrase which opens all the surahs except the ninth, and occurs as well in 27:30:

(153) bismi llāhi r-raḥmāni r-raḥīm.

It may come as a surprise to some that a phrase a common as this, one of the most often repeated word groupings in the Arabic language, could be a source of any difficulty, yet it is. The matter turns on the fact that the paired words *ar-raḥmān* and *ar-raḥīm* are both derived from the same root, *r-ḥ-m*, having to do with mercy. Their difference in meaning can partly be ascertained from the fact that *ar-raḥmān* refers only to Allah in the Qur'ān, being one of his most preferred names in the Book, as it appears 57 times.[19] On the other hand, *raḥīm* may be used to refer to others as well, as it does in the singular, describing the Prophet (9:128), and in the plural form "*ruḥamā'*" in verse 48:29. According to classical exegesis, *ar-raḥmān* denotes the permanent quality of mercy, while *ar-raḥīm* refers to mercy in specific instances. Thus, internal evidence as well as the commentators both agree that *ar-raḥmān*, is stronger or wider than *ar-raḥīm* in meaning.[20] But how can this be dealt with in English, while attending to the semantic, rhetorical, and oral aspects of the phrase at the same time? Starting with Bell, Arberry, and Dawood (2014), we find:

(154) In the Name of God, the Merciful, the Compassionate

Muhammad Ali and Pickthall give, however:

(155) In the name of Allah, the Beneficent, the Merciful.

As often, Muhammad Asad suggests a wordier version:

(156) In the name of God, the Most Gracious, the Dispenser of Grace.

---

19 Muḥammad Fu'ād 'Abd al-Bāqī, *al-Mu'jam al-mufahras li-alfāẓ al-Qur'ān al-karīm*, Cairo: Dār al-Ḥadīth, 1422/2001, pp. 376–377.

20 Zamakhsharī, I, 6. See also Ibn Kathīr, I, 37–38.

Asad has tried to preserve some of the Arabic parallelism of *ar-raḥmān ar-raḥīm* by rendering each using words from the same root (Gracious, Grace), but at the cost of increasing the number of words and not observing the parallelism of form otherwise.

Meanwhile, Yūsuf ʿAlī has:

(157) In the name of God, Most Gracious, Most Merciful.

This last translator acknowledged, in a footnote, the inadequacy of his use of the superlative, which implies comparison with other beings, yet finds himself unable to come up with a different term to translate *ar-raḥmān*, which, as we have seen, is applied to Allah only.[21] We note here that none of the terms suggested translate either of the paired Arabic nouns, except "merciful." "Compassionate" refers more to *ḥanān* and *shafaqah* in Arabic than to *raḥmah*. "Beneficent" implies, *al-muḥsin* or *al-munʿim* more than *ar-raḥmān*, and other of Allah's attributes closer to *al-munʿim* in meaning. "Gracious" might do, though normally given as *laṭīf*. But suppose we were to write "the Gracious, the Merciful" or "the Merciful, the Gracious" as the nearest approximation. We still would have 1.) failed to account for the difference in emphasis between the two words and 2.) given two words of different roots, though synonyms, distorting some of the formal parallelism of the Arabic *ar-raḥmān ar-raḥīm*. Nor can we say "the Most Merciful, the Merciful," as we would lose both the formal parallelism and the rhetorical elegance of the original. Nor will "the Merciful, the Merciful" do, for obvious reasons. This is not a trivial problem, either, considering the frequency and importance of this phrase in Arabic, but no satisfactory solution exists, so this will have to be recognized as one case of paired-word parallelism, where, because of the two words being from the same derivational root but having differing emphasis, it is impossible to render them into English adequately.

Next, we will examine the various kinds of parallelism we may find in a single surah, al-Muṭaffifīn, number 83. Many of the early Makkah surahs which appear near the end of the Qurʾān exhibit extensive parallelism, including numbers 77, 78, 80, 82, 84, 85, 87, 88, 91, 92, and others, besides 83. These surahs, thought to be the earliest in chronological order, are those containing the most fervent style and the most varied rhyming, resulting in a richness and variety of parallelism among other features. It may be that 83 does not contain the most obvious parallelism in the Qurʾān, but nevertheless it does contain some ele-

21 Yūsuf ʿAlī, 14, fn. 19.

ments of this feature characteristic of many of the book's latter pages. While only in verse 12 is there an occurrence of the parallelism of two nouns we have been considering, verses 9, 20, and 25 each contain a noun with adjective. As we have mentioned above, the distinction between the noun and adjective is often unclear, as in verse 12; where it is more clear, the pairing of two still produces a notable effect. The first word of a pair will probably be taken as the noun. Next, we might note pairs of verses joined by a conjunction for parallel or contrastive meaning and often similar in form. In surah 83, these include vv. 2/3, 5/6, 14/15 16/17, and 25/27–28. Finally, we note that these words and verses are some of the building blocks of longer passages which are parallel to each other, like 7–17 which parallel 18–28 and 29–33 which stand in contrast to 34–35. In both these cases of parallel alignment of passages, the purpose is contrastive, comparing the state of the ingrates with that of the believers. We will endeavor to look briefly at an example of each level of parallelism found in the surah.

First, then, if we turn to verse 83:12, we will see a case that does not differ greatly from 33:72 (133):

(158) wa-mā yukadhdhibu bihi illā kullu muʿtadin athīm.

Pickthall finds the parallel words here easier to translate concisely, his version according more closely in form with the original than in his translation of 33:72 (134):

(159) 12. Which none denieth save each criminal transgressor.

Here the paired adjectives used as nouns *muʿtadin athīm* are not of the same derivational pattern either, though both are indefinite genitives in case. Each may be taken ordinarily in Arabic as either a noun or an adjective, the distinction being mainly one of usage; likewise "criminal" in English may serve as a noun or an adjective. But the native English speaker still may feel that the use of the two words "criminal transgressor" together in (159) constitutes verbal overkill. Repeated in form frequently throughout the Qurʾān, the refrains consisting of two words, as here, may not appeal to the reader, though accurately translated.

On the other hand, Bell translates:

(160) 12. No one counts it false but each ill-disposed and guilty (one).

The distracting use of parentheses, the translation of the two end nouns as two words each instead of one, the insertion of a superfluous "and," and the clumsiness of the expression "guilty one," usually only used in cases of identification as when the victim emphatically points out the criminal saying, "He's the guilty one," all combine to make this translation less effective than Pickthall's, although it does nevertheless convey the overall meaning.

A typical example of sentence parallelism is provided by verses 83:1–3 in the same surah denouncing fraudulent practices of merchants:

(161) waylun li-l-muṭaffifīn.
alladhīna idhā ktālū ʿalā n-nāsi yastawfūn.
wa-idhā kālūhum aw wazanūhum yukhsirūn.

Here, as in 7:131 (169) below, we have a pair of parallel conditional sentences, except that these are both conditionals of the same kind with *idhā*, parallel in form except for the presence of two verbs instead of one, also parallel in form, with each other in the second conditional. In (169), an effort was being made to distinguish between the different probabilities of the two conditionals; here the probabilities are the same, as indicated by the use of the same *idhā* and the same verb forms in both sentences. Also the verbs *iktālū* and *kālū* are from the same trilateral root *k-y-l*, dealing with the semantic area of measurement. This is one of the features that are indeed difficult to translate from Arabic, as noted in the discussion of *ar-raḥmān* and *ar-raḥīm* above: the juxtaposition of words which are of the same root yet different derivational patterns. English also has a derivational system for many verbs based on latinate stems, e.g., impose, oppose, depose and the rest. But it is less regular, does not cover all verb stems by any means, and does not have the same semantic correlates as the complex Arabic system. Some of the effect of the correlation between the two verbs in the Arabic derivational system is lost when it cannot be carried into English according to a like patterning. The translators vary somewhat on these two verses, Arberry giving:

(162) Woe to the stinters
who, when they measure against the people, take full measure
but, when they measure for them or weigh for them, do skimp.

A possible cause of dullness here is the threefold repetition of the word "measure," a two-syllable word of relatively low frequency in English, whose overuse produces a boring effect, as in all the translations of 55:7–9 (117) above. Also, it does not reproduce the Arabic, which has no such repetitions in the two verses. The correctness and effectiveness of "do skimp" might also be questioned, even though "do" helps the rhythm in English. Although Arberry's translation conveys the semantic meaning, and although his use of the conjunction "but" instead of "and" is appropriate, his overall effect makes the Arabic parallelism seem deadly. Bell gives us another example:

(163) 1. Woe to the scrimpers,
2. Who, when they measure for themselves against the people, fill full,
3. But, when they measure or weigh to them, scant!

The exclamation mark is evidently put in because the three verses, constituting one long sentence, starts with "Woe," but the mark is so far from the word "Woe" that its emphatic intent seems strained or shrill. One is also doubtful about the word "scant," whose position as a verb in this example is not even clearly established. Does it mean "do scant" or possibly "fill scant"? In either case, it is inferior to (162). Also, as in Arberry's version, the repetition of "when they measure" is likely to seem simplistic and unsophisticated to the English-speaking reader, who would prefer variety. But what about these verbs "measure or weigh to them"? Such usage is awkward, making the reader hesitant about their sense. Indeed, neither Bell nor Arberry seems fortunate in his choice of prepositions to represent the two kinds of transactions the verses are discussing, and the failure to distinguish the meaning of *iktālū* from *kālū* is striking.

Pickthall, however, may have come nearest to the original in this case:

(164) 1. Woe unto the defrauders:
2. Those who when they take the measure from mankind demand it in full,
3. But if they measure unto them or weigh for them, they cause them loss.

Again, one is not wholly satisfied. Pickthall has repeated the word "measure" just like Arberry and Bell. Furthermore, his inclusion of the third "they" is grammatically dubious in view of "Those who" at the beginning of the first line, since if we omit the intervening conditional, we get, "Those who they cause them loss." Also, the use of two "theys" and three "thems" in the second conditional sentence is a bit much. Arabic avoids such repetition of pronouns by often, as here, having the subject pronoun contained in the verb and therefore not formally expressed, but English usually cannot do this, so that is another way in which English translation from Arabic, especially in the verb-filled Qurʾān, is difficult.

Dawood (2014) in this case presents greater word economy but has to grammatically alter the verses:

(165) WOE BETIDE the unjust who, when people measure for them, exact in full, but when they measure or weigh for them, defraud them!

Unlike the other translators, who try to preserve the structure of the Arabic more completely, Dawood, makes "people" the subject of the first "when" clause, which it is not in the Arabic because of the character of the Arabic verb *iktālū*. This has led the other translators to use more or less cumbersome locutions to follow the Arabic sentence structure, whereas Dawood gives a simple solution, but at the cost of not representing the Arabic verb more exactly. Many verbs having to do with buying and selling in Arabic present similar problems, as does the verb *raḍiya yarḍā* and its derivative *irtaḍā yartaḍī*, all requiring circumlocutions or extra words to convey their meaning in most cases. Apart from Dawood's reversal of the first "when" clause, he also still has one more "them" than the Arabic and also repeats "measure" twice, thus also failing to observe the distinction between the two verbs.

Space will not permit us to quote from the longer parallel passages of 83:7–17 and 18–28. We will merely note that verse 7 is similar to 18, though contrastive in meaning, 8 is like 19 in form, 9 is identical to 20, and 14–17 similar to 22–28. The effect of this is to reinforce the conviction in the English-speaking reader that the Book is full of dualism; it is inescapable that he will notice many passages balanced by others. Probably he will also notice that moral dichotomy is the frequent arbiter of this dualism. Examples of this are common throughout the Qur'ān, especially in the thirtieth *juz'* or part of the Qur'ān, as we have noted above.

One final example should complete our demonstration of Qur'ānic parallelism and its effect in English. Verse 12:6 is notable for bringing so many elements together in a single verse and putting them in parallel:

(166) wa-kadhālika yajtabīka rabbuka wa-yuʿallimuka min ta'wīli l-aḥādīthi wa-yutimmu niʿmatahu ʿalayka wa ʿalā āli yaʿqūba kamā atammahā ʿalā abawayka min qablu ibrāhīma wa-isḥāqa inna rabbaka ʿalīmun ḥakīm.

In this single verse addressed to Joseph there are at least four instances of parallelism, especially of form. We have first of all the verbs with objects *yajtabīka* and *yuʿallimuka*, then *yutimmu niʿmatahu ʿalayka wa ʿalā āli yaʿqūba* and later *ʿalā abawayka min qablu ibrāhīma wa-isḥāqa*. The first two verbs, meaning "choose" and "teach," are parallel in meaning in being indications of God's bounty to Joseph, and in form, both being in the imperfect indicative followed by the second person masculine singular pronominal suffix. Then, four prophets are mentioned (except that it is the family of Jacob, i.e., Joseph's broth-

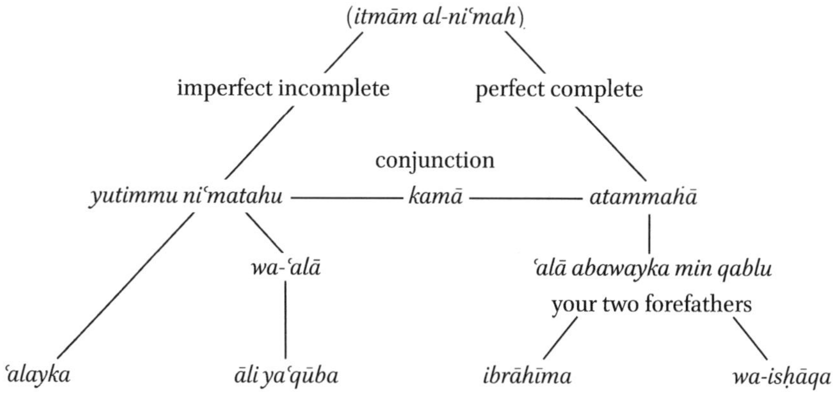

FIGURE 2 The balancing elements of Qur'ān 12:6

ers as well, who receive distinction with their father), being divided into two pairs, those whose blessing has been completed, Abraham and Isaac, and those whose blessing is still being completed, Joseph and the family of Jacob. The difference is indicated by the verb *atamma*, repeated twice, in the imperfect in the case of the first two, the perfect in the case of the others. This is represented schematically for clarity in Figure 2, above.

The verse is completed with parallel adjectives or names of Allah as we have seen above, here *ʿalīmun ḥakīm*.

Here the translations of Pickthall, Bell, and Arberry are quite similar in accurately following the organization of the verse as shown above. But let us not suppose that the results must be normal English. Pickthall is typical:

(167) 6. Thus thy Lord will prefer thee and will teach thee the interpretation of events, and will perfect his grace upon thee and upon the family of Jacob as he perfected it upon thy forefathers, Abraham and Isaac. Lo! thy Lord is Knower, Wise.

This consists of seven kernel sentences connected by five conjunctions, the last refrain sentence being disconnected. On the other hand, there is no subordination at all unless "as," a dummy subordinator like "although" that really coordinates here, is taken as the beginning of a subordinate clause. Of course, we find subordination elsewhere in the Qur'ān, and this may be considered an extreme example, but nevertheless the resulting structure does not conform to the rhetorical conventions of modern written English, nor can it really be rendered into the English idiom without deviating much more from the text of the original. The effect of this verse in English is likely to be heavy and monotonous.

Textbooks on rhetoric strongly discourage this type of coordination in English, labelling it "weak coordination."[22]

By contrast, Dawood (1990)[23] deals with this verse somewhat differently:

(168) You shall be chosen by your Lord. He will teach you to interpret visions, and will perfect his favor to you and to the house of Jacob, as he perfected it to your forefathers Abraham and Isaac before you. Your Lord is all-knowing and wise.

In what must be considered a domesticating move, here Dawood removes the first "weak coordination" by separating the first two verbs into two separate sentences, reducing the coordinating complexity of the whole verse by a little. The rest of his translation here is remarkably similar to Pickthall's, however, showing how otherwise Dawood has modified the Qur'ān translation tradition in English in this case rather little, even using the verb "perfect" just like Pickthall, leaving the main sentence still somewhat overloaded from the viewpoint of English rhetoric, particularly the phrase, "as he perfected it to you …," where the "to" seems at least odd.

Another series of problems is caused by the Arabic conjunctions and how they are translated into English. There are complex distinctions made in Arabic rhetoric regarding coordination (*al-waṣl*)[24] which need not concern us here yet, except for the general requirement also present in English that the two coordinated words or phrases be connected somehow semantically in the mind of the reader while not being exactly the same.[25] But it may be in some cases that the use of coordination by the particle *wa-* in Arabic would not be appropriate with the parallel "and" in English, the latter preferring either another conjunction or subordination. Indeed, as indicated above in the preceding chapter on parallelism, the frequency of coordinate compound sentences in the translations of Qur'ānic verses can be monotonous to the English-speaking reader. This is partly because of the excessive literalness of the translators, who do not realize or do not wish to realize that classical Arabic often has *wa-* where modern Arabic should say *wa-lākin*, the equivalent of "but," and so on.

22 Hulon Willis, *A Brief Handbook of English*, New York: Harcourt, Brace, Jovanovich, Inc., 1975, p. 232.

23 Dawood, 2014, 154–155, contains the same text, except that he now begins the first sentence with "Even thus shall you be chosen …," replacing his bald sentence with one introduced by a transition that is actually there in the Arabic, thus conforming more closely to the Arabic text. This is another case of Dawood moving away from some of the domesticating tendencies in his previous versions.

24 Bībānī, 85–93.

25 Jurjānī, 224–226.

CHAPTER 9

Juxtaposition of Contrasting Conditional Sentences

A particular kind of paralleleism in Arabic rhetoric that is very common in the Qurʾān is the juxtaposition of two conditional sentences in which both their respective conditional clauses and result clauses are contrasting. This would appear to be another part of the feature mentioned in the last chapter called *muqābalah*.[1] While it falls in a general way under the classical[2] and modern rhetorical category of antithesis,[3] its Qurʾānic form develops more elaborate parallels. This feature is not so common in contemporary English, but it is quite characteristic of the parallelism of Hebrew poetry in the Bible. Its existence there could help to give English Qurʾān translations a biblical air.

An example of such *muqābalah* is provided by verse 7:131:

(169) fa-idhā jāʾathum al-ḥasanatu qālū lanā hādhihi wa-in tuṣibhum sayyiʾ-atun yaṭṭayyarū bi-Mūsā wa-man maʿahu …

Here we note that neat coordinate arrangement of the two parallel conditionals, the first headed by the particle *idhā* followed by the verb in the perfect, the definite article attached to the subject noun of the condition clause, and the placing of the particle *li* and its object before the noun of the *jawāb* or result clause of the conditional. The second conditional uses the particle *in* followed by the verb in the jussive mood of the imperfect, no article attached to the subject noun of the condition clause, and no object parallel in form to *lanā*. Indeed, the verse contains an elaborate *muqābalah* similar to what is described as *muqābalat al-arbaʿah bi-l-arbaʿah*, the coordination of four with four, as each conditional contains four elements.[4] Those of the first conditional are represented by *jāʾathum*, *al-ḥasanatu*, *qālū*, and *lanā hādhihi* and those of the second conditional by *tuṣibhum*, *sayyiʾatun*, *yaṭṭayyarū*, and *bi-Mūsā wa-man maʿahu*. Each element in the first conditional parallels the corresponding element in the second, but every one of these parallel elements is in a different form from the other, *jāʾathum* a verb in the perfect tense, while *tuṣibhum*

1 Ṭūfī, 259–260.

2 Aristotle, 3:9:9–10, 3:10:5, 7; Demetrius, 24, 27–28; *Rhetorica*, 4:15:21, 4:18:25–26; Quintilian, 9:2:100–101, 9:3:81–86, 92.

3 Dupriez, 50–52; Enos, 13.

4 Ṭabānah, *Muʿjam*, 537–538.

 DOI:10.1163/9789004417441_011

is in the jussive, *al-ḥasanatu* being a definite noun, while *sayyiʾatun* is in the indefinite, *qālū* being again a perfect verb while *yaṭṭayyarū* is jussive, and *lanā hādhihi* being an emphatic direct quote introduced by the preposition *li-* while *bi-Mūsā wa-man maʿahu* is indirect object introduced by the prepostion *bi-*. All these differences emphasize that the two separate conditionals are not equivalent to each other, but rather that each has a different intent, the first emphasizing the inconstancy and ingratitude of the people of Pharaoh by magnifying their illegitimate claim to the good, the second minimizing the pretended evil which causes them to blame Moses and his people.[5] Az-Zamakhsharī states a similar explanation: that the purpose of the rhetorical arrangement of this verse is to emphasize the greater prevalence and likelihood of the blessings of Allāh's provision compared to the lesser occurrence and probability of disasters.[6] This effect is achieved by making the first conditional more definite, the second more unlikely, by the use of the above-mentioned formally differentiated devices.

The translations handle this slightly differently. Muhammad Ali, Pickthall, Yūsuf ʿAlī, Bell, Dawood, and Asad are similar in form of expression, Bell suggesting:

(170) 128. So when good came to them they said: "This is ours," and when evil hit them they drew bad omens from Moses and his followers; …

Here, we find the conditional particles, in this case "when," the same in both conditionals. The verbs are all in the simple past and no distinction by use of any articles is made between "good," and "evil," although the accompanying verbs are at least different. The *jawāb* phrases, "they said, 'this is ours'" and, "they drew evil omens," are not differentiated into a nominal and a verbal clause as in the Arabic. There are four grammatical differences in the Arabic, but not a single one is noted in Bell and the translations similar to his. While it is true that English has no particles *idhā* and *in* differentiated according to meaning, as well as no jussive mood, and the uses of the article are different in the two languages, there are nevertheless other ways of conveying the original intent of the Arabic. In this, Arberry has shown himself more meticulous:

5 Sakkākī, 241, 246; Ibn Mālik, 53–54; Qazwīnī, 121; Zarkashī, II, 262–263; Bībānī, 23–24.

6 Zamakhsharī, II, 144–145; see also Niẓām ad-Dīn al-Ḥasan b. Muḥammad an-Naysaburī, *Tafsīr gharāʾib al-Qurʾān wa-raghāʾib al-furqān*, on the margin of Abū Jaʿfar Muḥammad b. Jarīr aṭ-Ṭabarī, *Jāmiʿ al-bayān fī tafsīr al-Qurʾān*, Būlāq: al-Maṭbaʿah al-Kubrā al-Amīriyyah, 1323–1329, Vol. IX, p. 29.

(171) So, when good came to them, they said,
'this belongs to us'
but if any evil smote them, they would augur
ill by Moses and those with him.

Now it is clear that in this case Arberry, unlike Muhammad Ali, Pickthall, Yūsuf 'Alī, Bell, Dawood, and Asad, has distinguished between the probability of *idhā* and the lesser probability of *in* and between the perfect and jussive of the Arabic verbs by using different conditional particles (when vs. if) and different verb tenses (said vs. would augur). He has also differentiated the lack of any article attached to *sayyi'atun* by writing "any" before "evil." Thus, he has captured more of the meaning and feeling of the Arabic,[7] even if he still does not represent all the nuances of the Arabic text. That Arberry picked up on these nuances of Arabic must be accounted an example of his attention to fine details in his translation effort. But one still wonders if his "came" is a good translation of *jā'at* here. In Arabic, the perfect may state a condition removed from time, and thus sometimes be closer to the present than the past in English. If we also modified Arberry's second conditional to increase its power, we would get:

(172) So whenever good comes to them, they say, 'this belongs to us,' but if any evil were to smite them, they would augur ill by Moses and those with him.

Perhaps this would be nearer to the content of the original Arabic. Still, it lacks the extra emphasis of *lanā hādhihi* which might be better rendered, "This is ours alone," for the precedence of the predicate before the subject indicates the limitation of that predicate to its subject, just as it does in English. This feature, *ḥaṣr* in Arabic, is common in the Qur'ān, as we have seen in the earlier example (11).[8] In English, there is a parallel means of expression, i.e., "His is the glory, mine is the loss, and yours is the gain," although the parallel is not precise, as this placement of the possessive first has a more restricted use. Thus, to say, "Ours is this," while not grammatically incorrect, still sounds awkward, which is probably why Arberry disdained to use it in this case, despite his carefulness with regard to the other literary devices in the verse and generally.

7 Bībānī, 24.
8 Bībānī, 35.

CHAPTER 10

Coordination

Coordination through the use of conjunctions of course is an important part of language generally, and one might imagine that its usage is straightforward. However, this is not the case, and it has been an important rhetorical consideration since ancient times.[1] Among classical Muslim scholars, coordination (*waṣl*) was generally considered together with lack of conjunctive (asyndeton, Ar. *faṣl*) and constituted a very substantial part of rhetoric.[2] According to the Arabic rhetoricians, the understanding of *waṣl* and *faṣl* is complicated (*ṣaʿb al-maslak*) and can only be attained by those who have a large measure of eloquence.[3] Connection through a conjunction (*waṣl*) is usually effected by the letter *wāw*, pronounced *wa* and meaning "and," which is described as simply adding together related terms,[4] though these do require a connecting factor (*jāmiʿ*) between them, whereas all the other conjunctions add something more.[5]

English does not greatly differ from Arabic in these formal rules for the use and interpretation of conjunctions, which are also more complicated than they may appear on the surface. However, the difference between the two languages is greater in the actual use to which conjunctions are put, as they have a role in parallelism, which we have just described in Chapters Eight and Nine above. One result of this is that the use of the conjunctive *wa-*[6] is rather more frequent in Arabic than "and" is in English, and English-language students are discouraged from overuse of "and," being rather constantly and consistently instructed to vary their sentences for greater complexity with more use of subordinate clauses.[7] One can see the penetration of this stylistic prescription into modern Arabic writing as well; nevertheless, a difference remains.

1 Aristotle, 3:5:2–3, 7; Longinus, 21; Quintilian, 9:3:51–53.

2 Jurjānī, 222–248; Sakkākī, 271–276; Ibn al-Athīr, *Mathal*, II, 235–240; Ṭūfī, 241–242; Zarkashī, IV, 101–117; Hāshimī, 179–182; Jenssen, 116–123; Abdul-Raof, *New Horizons*, 210.

3 Jurjānī, 222; Qazwīnī, 181; Hāshimī, 179.

4 Jurjānī, 224.

5 Hāshimī, 179–180; Abdul-Raof, *Qur'an Translation*, 125–127; Abdul-Raof, *Arabic Rhetoric*, 177–184; Jenssen, 121–122.

6 For the multiple uses of the *wāw* by itself, see Jamāl ad-Dīn Ibn Hishām al-Anṣārī, *Mughnī al-labīb ʿan kutub al-aʿārīb*, ed. Māzin al-Mubārak, Muḥammad ʿAlī Ḥamd Allāh, and Saʿīd al-Afghānī, Damascus: Dār al-Fikr, 1384/1964, Vol. I, pp. 391–408.

7 Brooks & Warren, 385–387; Strunk & White, 25.

 | DOI:10.1163/9789004417441_012

There is more than one function for which coordination can be used; one of the most important is comparison and contrast. In the Qur'ān, this is very frequent, as for example in verses 82:13–14:[8]

(173) inna l-abrāra la-fī naʿīm.
wa-inna l-fujjāra la-fī jaḥīm.

The two sentences contrast the conditions of two groups in the afterlife. Such contrasts constitute one of the conditions demanding the use of coordination.[9] The translations more or less follow what they consider to be the literal equivalent of the Arabic coordination. For example, Arberry has:

(174) Surely the pious shall be in bliss,
and the libertines shall be in a fiery furnace.

Unfortunately, much of the emphatic contractive sense is lost for English readers by the blandness of the conjunction "and." "Whereas" or "while," contrastive conjunctions of English, would normally be preferable in this place.

Pickthall tries in incorporate the emphatic sense in his translation by using the emphatic additional words "lo" and "verily" as well as exclamation marks:

(175) 13. Lo! the righteous verily will be in delights.
14. And lo! the wicked verily will be in hell.

Thus, at least the emphasis is repeated by other devices. Perhaps the separation of the second sentence, with its coordinating conjunction, from the first gives it more independence and contrastive sense. But one may still feel that coordination by "and" is basically weak for contrastive purposes in English.

Nevertheless, we note that this feature of coordination with "and" has been occasionally used in literature to good effect. We read in Henry VI, Pt. 2, Act V, Sc. 1, verse 143:

(176) I am thy king, and thou a false-heart traitor.

On the surface, this doesn't appear to differ form the example we have just been discussing. But actually there are several reasons why (176) is effective but (174)

8 Sakkākī, 271; Ibn Mālik, 68; Qazwīnī, 192; Hāshimī, 181; all citing this verse.

9 Jurjānī, 225.

and (175) are not so much. First, in the Shakespearean line, the king himself is directly addressing the person he refers to. All the drama of the theater is present to heighten the effect of this confrontation, even to readers of the play. The simple contrast is made only once to denounce the treason, not to repeat the truth many times as in the Qur'ān, and is effected by the readers' personal knowledge of the characters in the play. As an emphatic device, it can only be occasionally used or it would lose its effect, but the Qur'ānic verses of (173) use *inna* as an emphasizer, not *wa-*, which is merely a conjunction. To sum up, "but" or "whereas" are normally better contrastive coordinators in general and often better in translations of Qur'ānic verses in particular to render the contrastive *wa-*, although it may be that "and" can occasionally be used successfully as a contrastive conjunction in literature if noticeable rhetorical benefit is derived from it.

Among the other uses of coordination is emphasis, which may be rendered into English sometimes more easily than our preceding example, as in verse 11:54:[10]

(177) qāla innī ushhidu llāha wa-shhadū annī barī'un mimmā tushrikūn.

As az-Zamakhsharī explains, the emphasis here is in the two verbs connected by *wa-*, because the first is indicative and the second imperative, which shows that Allah's witness is not to be compared to that of the unbelievers, whose swearing, if they did it, would be inferior.[11] Here the translators, despite some other weaknesses in their renditions, have produced a sense which is moving in its emphasis and not confusing. Arberry has:

(178) He said, 'I call God to witness,
and witness you, that I am quit of
that you associate ...'

This is the most literal and perhaps less immediately resonant with English-language readers because of the strangeness of "witness you," the usage of "quit," and the possible ambiguity and bareness of "that you associate," although the meaning is completed in the next verse, 11:55.

Bell gives however:

10 Hāshimī, 181.

11 Zamakhsharī, II, 403–404; Ibn al-Athīr, II, *Mathal*, 183–184, *Jāmiʿ*, 101.

(179) He said: "I call Allah to witness and do ye witness that I am clear of what you associate (as gods) …"

The choice of "clear" is ambiguous, as is "associate," despite the insertion of the parenthetical phrase.

Mostly following Muhammad Ali, Pickthall produces a version perhaps closely in accord with the semantic intent of the original, but at the cost of too many distracting parenthetical insertions:

(180) He said: I call Allah to witness, and do ye (too) bear witness, that I am innocent of (all) that ye ascribe as partners (to Allah) …

As with Arberry, Pickthall's grammatical use of commas to set off the coordinated command "do ye (too) bear witness" seems to give that phrase a greater degree of importance. "Innocent," though longer, is probably a more familiar term than either "quit" or "clear," but Arberry's "quit," containing the implication of active rejection rather than passive non-involvement, seems closer to the sense. But the power of the speaker, the Prophet Hūd, calling Allah to witness and then asking his interlocutors to witness against themselves as well that he is will have nothing to do with their religion, a true, dramatic challenge to illustrate their disbelief, is quite striking even in these English renditions.

Another example of emphatic coordination in Arabic is when a second sentence is added with the particle *wa-* to a first sentence, to emphasize its intent. This may or may not translate easily into English. For example, in 7:169:

(181) a-lam yu'khadh mīthāqu l-kitābi an lā yaqūlū ʿalā llāhi illā l-ḥaqqa wa-darasū mā fīhi …

The words *wa-darasū mā fīhi* are to assure us that the Jews not only accepted the revealed covenant but have also studied it,[12] which emphasizes its incumbency upon them.

Our translators mostly have very similar renditions of this, all translating the conjunction *wa-* of *wa-darasū* as "and," or "And" if beginning a new sentence, except for Dawood (1990), who reads:

(182) Are they not committed in the Scriptures, which they have studied well, to tell nothing of God but what is true?

12 Qurṭubī, VII, 312; cf. Zamakhsharī, II, 174; Bayḍāwī, III, 41.

Here, Dawood has summed up the Arabic in succinct, direct English, keeping it noticeably brief, exceeding the Arabic word count only slightly, if we count the Arabic particles as words as in English. Yet he has significantly altered the text by subordinating the independent, coordinate clause *wa-darasū mā fīhi* as "which they have studied well" and also abridging *mīthāqu l-kitābi* = "the covenant of the book" as just "the Scriptures." It is quite interesting that by 2014 Dawood felt impelled to revise his translation here to read:

(183) Are they not committed in the Book to tell nothing of God but what is true? And they have studied it well; …

Thus, Dawood has realigned his text with both the word order and the rhetorical point of the Arabic that our other six translators have all followed while still trying to maintain the brevity and simplicity of his English.

For comparison, Pickthall translates this text as:

(184) … Hath not the covenant of the Scripture been taken on their behalf that they should not speak ought concerning Allah save the truth? And they have studied that which is therein …

This passage is fairly normal, without special difficulties, requiring none of the parenthetical insertions Pickthall resorts to so often. However, it is also considerably wordier than Dawood. Of interest to us here is that the coordinate "And," when heading a separate sentence as here and in Dawood's 2014 version, has a slightly emphatic meaning that reflects the feeling of the Qur'ānic passage, as, for example, "He never lent me the money. And he had sworn he would." Such an "And" could be underlined in writing to indicate voiced emphasis. Thus, the translations in this case somewhat reproduce the impact and even the syntactic form of the original.

However, this same type of coordination elsewhere can produce different results for translators, as in verses 53:11–13:

(185) mā kadhaba l-fu'ādu mā ra'ā.
a-fa-tumārūnahu ʿalā mā yarā.
wa-laqad ra'āhu nazlatan ukhrā.

Al-Jurjānī states that the existence of *wa-* between two sentences must denote a connection between them,[13] between the second and third of these three

13 Jurjānī, 224–225.

verses. But here, unlike in the preceding example, the second sentence is a reply to the first, a refutation of the ingrates' disputation, whereas above it was simply a further detail added to emphasize the point already made.

The translations are somewhat at variance in rendering these verses.

Bell offers:

(186) 11. The heart did not falsify what it saw.
12. Do ye debate with it (heart) as to what it sees?

13. He saw him, too, at a second descent.

Arberry follows Bell to a considerable extent, translating:

(187) His heart lies not of what he saw,
what, will you dispute with him what he sees?

Indeed, he saw him another time …

Pickthall, with Muhammad Ali and Muhammad Asad somewhat similar, gives:

(188) 11. The heart lied not (in seeing) what it saw.
12. Will ye then dispute with him concerning what he seeth?
13. And verily he saw him yet another time …

Here we are offered three different possible ways of relating the third verse of (185) to the preceding ones. Bell, followed by Arberry, proposes no connection at all, as he has not only omitted the connecting conjunction, but left a space between the verses as well, assigning 53:12 to the preceding grouping (vv. 1–12) and 53:13 to the following grouping (vv. 13–18), describing the Prophet's second vision. By doing this, Bell and Arberry negate the possibility of any direct rhetorical connection between the second and third verses we are concerned with here, for the vague link implied by the transitional word "Indeed" used by Arberry, which may actually only be to connect the two groupings of verses. Thus, presumably Arberry would explain the initial *wa-* of verse 53:13 as a connector for the two groupings of verses in his arrangement only. On the other hand, Pickthall preserves the *wa-* we are concerned with in the original by deploying an initial "and," adding to that a "yet" to strengthen the tie with the previous verse and indicate that his last verse is a reply to the rhetorical question embodied in the middle one, v. 12. Bell also applies the pronoun "it" for *al-fu'ādu* from verse 53:11 in verse 12 while returning to "he" for verse 13, further sundering any connection between verses 12 and 13 but emphasizing his contention about the disconnectedness of the Qur'ān. Considering the repetition of the same verb (*ra'ā* in Arabic and "to see" in English) in each of the two verses, the use of the coordinate conjunction between them, the emphatic sense of *laqad*, and the suitability of the meaning, it seems far more likely that there is a direct connection between the two verses of the kind implied by Pickthall, and Arberry's revisions of Bell, also implying a greater connection than Bell has, should be seen in this light. However, this is clearly not so simple a matter as (181), because it is also possible that the junction is actually with the first verse, 11, and that v. 12, the middle verse, is a mere parenthetical question.

Another kind of coordination is where the coordinate conjunction is used to connect a number of parallel noun phrases; this does not differ from English, except that in English the conjunction itself is normally replaced by commas to separate all but the last two items in a series of three or more. The exceptional repetition of the conjunction in linking a series of items in English constitutes a rhetorical feature called polysyndeton, which is especially known in the Bible.[14] In the Qur'ān, an example of a list of several items on more than one level is provided by verse 2:83:[15]

(189) wa-idh akhadhnā mīthāqa banī isrā'īla lā taʿbudūna illā llāha wa-bi-l-wālidayni iḥsānan wa-dhī l-qurbā wa-l-yatāmā wa-l-masākīni wa-qūlū li-n-nāsi ḥusnan wa-aqīmū ṣ-ṣalāta wa-ātaw az-zakāta …

A complication in this verse is immediately apparent owing to the omission of a word, either *tuḥsinūna* or *aḥsinū* before *bi-l-wālidayni*. Otherwise, we must take the phrases following *mīthāqa banī isrā'īla* as appositive to it.[16] This difficulty is transmitted by Arberry:

(190) And when we took compact with the Children of Israel:
'You shall not serve any save God;
and to be good to parents, and the near kinsmen,
and to orphans, and to the needy;
and speak good to men, and perform the prayer,
and pay the alms.'

14 Quintilian, 9:3:50–54; Dupriez, 348–349; Enos, 542; Harris, 18–19.
15 Bībānī, 87.
16 Zamakhsharī, I, 159; Bayḍāwī, I, 91.

The terms of this compact as translated by Arberry can be presented in outline form:

I. You shall not serve any save God
II. To be good to
  A. Parents
  B. The near kinsmen
  C. Orphans
  D. The needy
III. And[17]
  A. Speak good to man
  B. Perform the prayer
  C. Pay the alms

All of these terms are linked to one another by the coordinate conjunction "and" as they are by *wa-* in the Arabic; in addition Arberry has separated the major term divisions, the Roman numerals of our outline, by semicolons, in his original translation of 1955.[18] However, these major terms, though all ultimately commandments, are given in different forms. "You shall not …" is an emphatic prohibition, as explained in the similar case of (56) above, a case of using the indicative in place of the imperative. The second, "to be good to …" would not even be construed as grammatical English unless it is taken as an appositive to "compact," in which case it would have to come outside the quotation marks. Only the last three, "speak good to men, and perform the prayer, and pay the alms," are direct commands in the imperative. One has to acknowledge here that Arberry has carefully reproduced as many of the original Arabic distinctions of form as possible. But it is notable that this lack of correct parallelism in coordinate sentences is most disliked in contemporary English rhetoric and is even labelled "faulty parallelism."[19]

Because of this, Pickthall presents a translation with similar meaning but parallel forms, that submits in greater degree to rhetorical conventions in English than Arberry's does.

(191) And (remember) when We made a covenant with the Children of Israel, (saying): Worship none save Allah (only), and be good to parents and to

17 Zarkashī, III, 13, cf. 347–348, adding another possibility. Here I follow az-Zarkashī's first choice.

18 Cf. Arberry, 1955 ed., I, 38, with Arberry, 1964 ed., 10. For some reason the latter edition has replaced Arberry's fine distinctions in punctuation with all commas.

19 Willis, 207.

kindred and to orphans and the needy, and speak kindly to mankind; and establish worship and pay the poor-due.

Here, all of Pickthall's verbs are in the imperative, and he has provided an imperative verb "be" where a verb is lacking in the Arabic without indicating that this is an addition. Pickthall, like Arberry, has also bothered to distinguished the Roman numeral terms in our outline but using commas instead of semicolons for the major items, while omitting the commas from the subordinate items under "be good to …," connecting them with the conjunction "and" alone. Pickthall has, however, linked the final two imperatives about worship and the poor-due to the rest with a semicolon. While Pickthall's translation of this verse reads fairly smoothly in English, the passage could still be criticized for the excessive number of "ands" that Pickthall has faithfully preserved from the occurrences of *wa-* in the Arabic; these "ands" would normally be reduced to commas in English.[20]

Indeed, this is exactly what Dawood (1990) does in his translation of 2:83, getting rid of all but two of Pickthall's seven "ands":

(192) When We made a covenant with the Israelites We said: 'Serve none but God. Show kindness to your parents, to your kinfolk, to the orphans, and to the destitute. Exhort men to righteousness. Attend to your prayers and render the alms levy.'[21]

But is this colloquializing English a fair representation of the original? The respect he shows for the English preference for brevity, while certainly effective enough in English, is bought at the cost of making the transitions between the various list items too abrupt, in effect disconnecting them by placing them in separate sentences marked off by periods rather than linking them. Only the items under "Show kindness …" are linked by commas. Also, all of Dawood's verbs are imperatives: "Serve," "Show," "Exhort," "Attend," and "render," all except the last capitalized, as they stand at the beginning of separate sentences, which gives even a further emphasis to their imperative demandingness that is not found in the original. Thus, despite his smoothness, Dawood fails to represent the nuances of the Arabic, including the use of the indicative instead of the imperative in the first verb and the omission of the verb for the second item.

20 Willis, 89.

21 Dawood, 2014, 8, includes very few changes, mainly replacing "kinfolk" with "kin" and "the alms levy" with "alms." "Men" (Ar. *an-nās*) is changed to a more gender-neutral "people." The article "the" is omitted from before "orphans," more in line with normal English.

Furthermore, the harmonization of all the verbs to direct imperatives and the inclusion of the fifth verb "Show" are characteristic of Dawood's tendency to reduce and render uniform differences in the original Arabic text in the interests of producing English readability, certainly a domesticating move.

Thus, we see that coordination, though a frequently used feature of English and Arabic and while it may be closely parallel in usage and form at times, may cause great difficulty to translators. The excessive use of "and," though normally objectionable in modern English, may be resorted to by writers, ancient and modern, to achieve a certain rhetorical effect, as we have seen in examples (176) and (184). This may be done to achieve epic or biblical force, but it risks becoming bathetic or boring if not skillfully handled. Also *wa-* in Arabic may have manifold purposes as we have noted above and need not always be rendered as "and." Indeed, in Arabic, as in the Bible, "and" is often just a way of beginning a sentence, a new thought, as in the phrase, "And it came to pass …" Perhaps this developed as an unconscious verbal punctuation device in an age when there were no others, as a substitute for periods and paragraphing. For example, we see in II Chronicles 3:8–9, describing Solomon's construction of his temple in Jerusalem, a paragraph separated from what stands around it:

(193) And he made the most holy place; its length, corresponding to the breadth of the house, was twenty cubits, and its breadth was twenty cubits; he overlaid it with six hundred talents of fine gold. The weight of the nails was one shekel to fifty shekels of gold. And he overlaid the upper changers with gold.

Remarkable in this passage to the English reader is the lack of coordinating conjunctions considering the overall amount of coordination. More surprising is the fact that of the three "ands" that are used, one is at the beginning of the passage where it is not needed, and another, heading the last sentence, stands at the head of the least connected sentence in the text and likewise could be dispensed with. This is in agreement with the rhetorical rule in Arabic whereby *kamāl al-ittiṣāl* or total semantic identity requires that no particle be used.[22] Hence *wa-* can only be inserted where there is some difference of meaning.

22 Sakkākī, 252; Bībānī, 82; Ṭabānah, *Muʿjam*, 516.

CHAPTER 11

Lack of Conjunctive (Asyndeton)

Apart from complex varieties of coordination that we have just described, another important and complex rhetorical feature is the lack or absence of such coordination, which is called asyndeton and is more specifically defined as the separation of two words, utterances, or sentences without transition or a normally expected coordinating particle.[1] Most of the ancient rhetoricians already discussed this rhetorical device, which was especially used for forceful oral presentation and argument.[2] This same feature also continues to be used as a rhetorical device in English, where it is limited, however to "omitting conjunctions between words, phrases, or clauses in a list."[3] In Arabic rhetoric, asyndeton is called *faṣl* = separation. Two other features which often contain *faṣl* are *iltifāt* (Chapter Two) and *iʿtirāḍ* (Chapter Twelve), which both involve a discontinuity that sometimes includes a lack of transition, but in this chapter I will deal only with other types of *faṣl*.

It is natural to expect that the lack of conjunction between two sentences or expressions would owe to a lack of semantic connection between the sentences preceding and following the break, just as coordination by conjunction requires some relationship or shared factor in the coordinated elements. But as al-Jurjānī insists, there may be many reasons for the omission of a conjunction, the case is not so simple, and in fact this is the most difficult aspect of rhetoric (*al-balāghah*).[4] The amount of space devoted by other Arabic rhetoricians to this feature also bears witness to its variety and complexity.[5] For example, it may be that the second sentence is adjectival or an emphatic confirmation to the first sentence, hence connected in meaning but not in form, since lack of conjunctive is required in such cases.[6] A few examples will suffice to demonstrate the result of rendering this into English.

For example we have in verses 2:14–15:[7]

---

1 Dupriez, 73–74; Enos, 41.

2 Aristotle, 3:12:2–4; Demetrius, 64, 269; Longinus, 19; *Rhetorica*, 4:30:31; Quintilian, 9:3:50, 62.

3 Harris, 16–18.

4 Jurjānī, 231.

5 Sakkākī, 249; Qazwīnī, 182–189; Hāshimī, 179, 183–193; Ṭabānah, *Muʿjam*, 295–297, 512–516, 600–604; Abdul-Raof, *Arabic Rhetoric*, 184–188; Abdul-Raof, *New Horizons*, 201–202; Mir, "Some Figures," 33.

6 Jurjānī, 227, 243.

7 Jurjānī, 228, 233–235; Sakkākī, 262; Ibn Mālik, 59; Qazwīnī, 182, 185; Ṭabānah, *Muʿjam*, 515.

DOI:10.1163/9789004417441_013

(194) ... wa-idhā khalaw ilā shayāṭīnihim qālū innā maʿakum innamā naḥnu mustahziʾūn.
Allāhu yastahziʾu bihim wa-yamudduhum fī ṭughyānihim yaʿmahūn.

The structure here is a conditional clause beginning with *wa-idhā* followed by its apodosis beginning with *qālū*, followed by a break of *faṣl* with another independent clause of the quotation, followed by an independent clause being with *Allāhu* and separated from what precedes a break of *faṣl*. After these, the independent clause beginning with *wa-yamudduhum* is joined to the preceding independent clause by *wa-* of coordination. Thus, there are two breaks illustrating lack of conjunction. Al-Jurjānī regards the separation between *maʿakum* and *innamā* as owing to the fact that the meaning of the following clause is really equivalent to the preceding, which requires lack of conjunctive.[8] Continuing, he attributes the second separation between *mustahziʾūn* and *Allāhu* to the confusion that would arise if they were joined by *wa-*, as the two clauses would then be taken as the speech of the hypocrites though they contradict each other in meaning.[9] The sentence beginning with *Allāhu* may be interpreted as a curse retort, a sharp reply by God in this case to the unbelievers, as proposed by Devin Stewart.[10] In this case, the asyndeton is not only clarifying but also heavily emphatic. The translations handle this feature variously in the case of these two verses, Pickthall giving the following interpretation:

(195) ... but when they go apart to their devils they declare: Lo! we are with you; verily we did but mock.
15. Allah (Himself) doth mock them, leaving them to wander on blindly in their contumacy.

Here, Pickthall solves the first case of *faṣl* with a semicolon and the second with a period making the next sentence separate, as well as marking the separation with the intrusive verse numbering he employs throughout his text, which mirrors the actual verse numbering in most Arabic Qurʾāns.

Arberry, by contrast, eschews using obtrusive verse numbers in the text itself, confining them rather to once every five verses in the page margins, because he would evidently prefer the text to be continuous, and of course

8 Jurjānī, 228.
9 Jurjānī, 233–235.
10 Devin J. Stewart, "The Cognate Curse in the Qurʾan." *Journal of the International Qurʾanic Studies Association* 2 (2017), 74–75.

verse numbers were not in the original revelations of Muhammad. Nonetheless, he likewise treats the two asyndetons with a semicolon and a period respectively:

(196) ... but when they go privily to their Satans, they say,
'We are with you; we were only mocking.'
God shall mock them and shall lead them on
blindly wandering in their insolence.

A number of points can be made here. First, it seems the semicolon in English may be able at least occasionally to play a role similar to the *faṣl* in Arabic, separating two clauses with basically the same meaning yet placing them in juxtaposition, which makes the second emphasize and explain the first, as in the Qur'ānic verse. Indeed, putting a conjunction "and" in place of the semicolon would render the effect of the English far weaker for basically the same reason al-Jurjānī gives for its prohibition in the Arabic of the verse. This is likewise the case in some English literature. For example, in Shakespeare's *Romeo and Juliet*, Act I, Scene 1, verses 14–16, we have two independent clauses of similar meaning, separated by a colon:

(197) A dog of that house shall move me to stand: I will take the wall of any man or maid of Montague's.

Again, the purpose is forceful emphasis, in this case the speaker being in an excited mood. The second separation in the Qur'ānic verses cited here, however, could be replaced by a "but" before "Allah" in the English. However, this is not necessary and also might reduce the effectiveness. The suddenness of the bringing of Allah's mocking into contrast with that of the hypocrites achieves a powerful, startling effect not too unlike the Arabic. We may also note that in a case of contrast such as this, the repetition of "mock" is emphatic and effective, as if throwing the hypocrites' mockery back on them. Pickthall's insertion of "Himself" in parentheses, omitted by Arberry, is perhaps unnecessary but demonstrates that the former was aware of the emphatic nature of the verse. Bell differs slightly:

(198) ... but when they go apart to their satans they say: 'We are on your side; we are only making fun.'
14. Allah will make fun of them, and will let them go on for a while in their proud transgression blindly wandering.

We note the same basic features as Pickthall's rendition has, including the semicolon, the period, and the prominent verse number. Even here, the effect is not lost by the too unserious "making fun,"[11] nor by the coordination rather than the subordination as in Pickthall, of the last clause.

There are, however, other cases of *faṣl* in Arabic that may not always meet the expectations of English-language readers so readily. One such case occurs in verses 23:81–82.[12]

(199) bal qālū mithla mā qāla l-awwalūn.
qālū a-idhā mitnā wa-kunnā turāban wa-ʿiẓāman a-innā la-mabʿūthūn.

What follows *al-awwalūn* is called a *badal kull* in Arabic,[13] meaning an appositive that replaces or includes all of what is intended by the proceeding noun phrase. In both languages, the appositive is a device for emphasis or explanation, but in English, where it is considered a normal and desirable rhetorical feature, it is usually preceded by only a single noun or short phrase, not a long phrase as in this verse. Willis gives as an example of this:[14]

(200) A black hole, an astronomical body of such mass that not even light can escape from its gravitational pull, is composed of matter so dense that a thimbleful of it would weigh tens of millions of tons on earth.

Longer noun phrases may precede appositives of course, but the type of (200) is most common.

Arberry renders the verse we are considering:

(201) Nay, but they said the like of what
the ancients said.
They said, 'What, when we are dead
and become dust and bones, shall we be
indeed raised up? ...'

11 However, his might not be so far astray in view of Qur'ān 83:29, 34, and is indeed a possible literal translation of the participle *mustahzi'ūn* and the verb *yastahzi'u*.

12 Cited in Ibn Mālik, 61; Bībānī, 82.

13 Sakkākī, 259 (found only in the al-Maktabah al-Shāmilah version of this text and not in the print version on this page; possibly, the editors of al-Maktabah al-Shāmilah have put back in a text that was dropped from the printed version); Yaḥyā b. Ḥamzah al-Ḥusaynī al-ʿAlawī aṭ-Ṭālibī al-Mu'ayyad bi-llāh, *aṭ-Ṭirāz li-asrār al-balāghah wa-ʿulūm ḥaqā'iq al-iʿjāz*, Beirut: al-Maktabah al-ʿAṣriyyah, 1425[/2004], Vol. III, p. 169.

14 Willis, 226–227.

The threefold repetition of "said," which reproduces the three instances of the Arabic verb, twice preceded in the translation by "they," is not likely to appeal much to the English-speaking reader, even allowing for the verbal tale-like quality of the verses. Despite Arberry's attempt to follow the Arabic closely that we have seen, he is unable to preserve the parallel between the Arabic verbs *mitnā* = are dead and *kunnā* = become (actually literally "are"), because the English verb structure is quite different from Arabic verb structure, and the other translators fare no better on this point.

Bell, by converting the second "said" into "did say," manages a version closer to English normalcy:

(202) Nay, they said just what those of old did say. They said: 'what! when we have died and become dust and bones shall we be raised up?'

Perhaps this is not so ineffective, considering the smooth assurance of "just" coupled with the delay in telling us what "they," whether the ancients or the present ones in the verse, really did say. This is a point of rhetoric in English for increasing suspense and holding up the interest to the end.[15]

Dawood (2014) here presents a version in more modern English:

(203) Indeed, they say what the ancients said before them. 'After our death, when we are dust and bones,' they say, 'shall we be raised to life? …'

As elsewhere, Dawood's version is easier on the reader and contains only common vocabulary items. But note how he has subtly altered the text, splitting the quotation that is unified in the Arabic by moving the "they say" to the middle of it from its beginning, in order to reduce the repetitious element, exchanging the archaic "Nay" of Arberry and Bell for "Indeed," which might however be farther from the sense of the Arabic *bal*, and subordinating the "when we are dead" clause as well as completely eliminating its verb by changing it to "After our death." While the semantic meaning is clearly present, the effect is significantly altered.

Probably the effect of this is similar in other verses containing a similar appositive, such as 26:131–134:

(204) fa-ttaqū llāha wa-aṭīʿūn.
wa-ttaqū lladhī amaddakum bimā taʿlamūn.

15 Brooks & Warren, 389.

amaddakum bi-anʿāmin wa-banīn.
wa-jannātin wa-ʿuyūn.

This passage differs from (199) in that the words following *taʿlamūna* constitute a *badal baʿḍ* rather than a *badal kull* because they are an appositive covering part but not all of the meaning of *bimā taʿlamūn*.[16] The second *ittaqū* would begin yet another *badal kull* appositive, as the one above in (199), if not for the interposition of *wa-aṭīʿūn* which breaks the sequence and necessitates the coordinate *wa-* that joins it with what follows. The translations do not differ on this point, Arberry rendering:

(205) So fear you God, and obey you me,
and fear Him who has succoured you
with what you know,
succoured you with flocks and sons,
gardens and fountains.

Again, the normal tendency in modern English is to omit the repeated words "succoured you" and possibly "with" according to the duplicate deletion rule.[17] Any deviation from the normal pattern is emphatic, as in this case. But devices of emphasis must be used sparingly to retain their effect, or the result is likely to impress the reader as shrill.[18] We can only consider it highly probable that the tendency to repeat words previously mentioned in these Qur'ānic appositives tends to give the translations some of their characteristic flavor in English.

A different impression of these verses is produced by Muhammad Asad:

(206) "Be, then, conscious of God and pay heed unto me: (131) and [thus] be conscious of Him who has [so] amply provided you with all [the good] that you might think of (132)—amply provided you with flocks, and children, (133) and gardens, and springs: (134) ..."

16 Sakkākī, 259 (found only in the al-Maktabah al-Shāmilah version of this text and not in the print version on this page; apparently, the editors of al-Maktabah al-Shāmilah have restored a text that was dropped from the printed version); Ibn Mālik, 62; Qazwīnī, 186; Bībānī, 82. The reader's attention is also drawn to the parallelism of grouping the four nouns of the appositive into two groups of two items each, first two of the animal kingdom (*anʿāmin* and *banīn*), then two associated with physical nature (*jannātin* and *ʿuyūn*), reminiscent of (166) above.

17 Lester, 280.

18 Brooks & Warren, 383.

Although the rhetorical features are similar to Arberry here, the effect is rather different because of the different vocabulary used. Asad more strongly emphasizes the appositive by repeating not one word like Arberry ("succoured") but two ("amply provided"). His words also certainly give a milder impression, translating the problematic polysemic word *ittaqū* as "be conscious of" rather than "fear," which most of the other translators have preferred.

There are other cases in which the *faṣl* and *waṣl* of the Arabic may be reversed exactly in English. This is the case in verse 2:5–6:[19]

(207) ulāʾika ʿalā hudan min rabbihim wa-ulāʾika hum al-mufliḥūn.
inna lladhīna kafarū sawāʾun ʿalayhim a-andhartahum am lam tundhirhum lā yuʾminūn.

These two verses present a certain amount of complexity. The first verse here, from *ulāʾika* to *al-mufliḥūn* continues the description of those for whom the Book was sent down as guidance (see 64 above), either as a *khabar* (predicate) or an *istiʾnāf* (nominal resumption) of what precedes. The two halves of the verse are joined by *wa-* of coordination because the two predicates *ʿalā hudan* and *al-mufliḥūn* are not synonymous in meaning, referring to the condition of the believers in this life and the afterlife respectively. Because this verse constitutes a continuation of the description of the Book by describing the kind of people it was sent down for, it is different from the following verse beginning with *inna* both in intent and style; the latter describes the disbelievers and is not directly related to the description of the Book and believers. Hence, the relationship of the two verses of (207) to each other is not like that of (204) above.[20] As for the final words *lā yuʾminūn*, they may be taken either as a predicate, if the phrase from *sawāʾun* to *tundhirhum* is taken as an *iʿtirāḍ*, or as an emphatic expression having or summing up the same meaning as that of the immediately preceding phrase, in which case that phrase would be the predicate. In either case, there is no coordinator. ʿAbd al-Qāhir prefers the latter explanation,[21] which is the one followed by all three translators. Arberry offers us:

(208) ... those are upon guidance from their Lord,
those are the ones who prosper.

19 Cited on this point by Jurjānī, 228; Ibn Mālik, 65; Qazwīnī, 185–186.
20 Zamakhsharī, I, 46. See also Ibn Kathīr, I, 78–80.
21 Jurjānī, 228. See also Zamakhsharī, I, 47.

As for the unbelievers, alike it is to them
whether thou hast warned them or hast not warned them,
they do not believe.

Here we find to our surprise that the conjunction between "Lord" and "those" found in the Arabic has been omitted and replaced by a comma, which, though a common usage, actually should be a semicolon in grammatical English as a comma here constitutes a comma-splice error. Placing the two sentences back to back like this with a semicolon would achieve a slightly greater emphasis than inserting "and," which might dilute the effect of the words to some extent.

On the other hand, in place of the lack of conjunctive between the two Arabic verses, we find in (208) that Arberry has marked the split with the insertion of an additional line space. By doing this, he is trying to domesticate his text to modern expectations by creating a greater hiatus as well as the transition "As for the unbelievers," both of which constitute expansions not directly paralleled in the Arabic text. However, despite the lack of a conjunctive, the use of the emphatic *inna* alerts the Arabic reader to the intended strong contrast which is coming. Hence, a translator may be justified in translating "As for" or "However" for fluency and to avoid excessive literalness, although this transition directly connects the description of the unbelievers with what precedes, a connection played down by az-Zamakhsharī as we have seen above.

Finally, we note the last separated phrase "they do not believe" is also not coordinated and should be separated by a semicolon, colon, or dash, not a comma. However, it may be that the effect of the latter verse is telling in English, particularly the simple summing up of "they do not believe" following the longer phrase describing them. Pickthall gives:

(209) 5. These depend on guidance from their Lord. These are the successful.
6. As for the disbelievers, whether thou warn them or thou warn them not it is all one for them; they believe not.

Here two points may be mentioned. First, the separation of the first verse into two sentences by a period seems to reduce its effectiveness considerably. It is notable in English that ideas closely connected like these are often best left in the same sentence separated only by a semicolon,[22] as this reduces the choppiness that might otherwise result. Second, the phrasing "they believe not," by

22 Willis, 107–108.

placing the "not" at the end, achieves a greater impact than that of Arberry at the expense of being slightly archaic and pompous. Again, Bell differs slightly:

(210) Such (stand) upon guidance from their Lord, and they are the ones who prosper. As for those who have disbelieved, it is all one whether thou hast warned them or not; they will not believe.

Despite his attempt to vary the text of the original with different words to translate *ulāʾika*, Bell's interpretation does not seem to surpass those of Arberry and Pickthall. Rather one feels that the repetition of the word "those" in a sentence coordinated with a semicolon produces a more emphatic effect.

Thus, we see in this case that English probably prefers a translation somewhat like that of (208), but where the first coordination in Arabic involves a separation by semicolon in English, and the first place lacking a conjunctive in the original entails a transition like "As for" in the translations. From this it is clear that the points of coordination and of lack of conjunctive are not necessarily the same in the two languages, and that there may be a resultant difference in rhetorical effect, as for example the difference between (208) and (210) above. Likewise, we have seen that the *wa-* coordinator of Arabic need not necessarily be translated as "and," that that would constitute a literalness not to be sought which might well fail to convey the rhetorical beauty contained in the original, and that often *wa-* fulfills the role in English of punctuation, which was not developed in classical Arabic. Thus, translators' inattention to rhetorical differences may be sometimes be responsible for inelegance rather than the differences themselves.

CHAPTER 12

Parenthesis (*iʿtirāḍ*)

Another feature freely occurring in the Qurʾān that may cause difficulty to translators by sounding unnatural in English is that known as *iʿtirāḍ* in Arabic,[1] parallel to parenthesis in English,[2] of which asides in literature are one kind. While cases of *iltifāt*, dealt with above in Chapter Two, can also sometimes be considered a type of parenthesis, *iʿtirāḍ* as we are discussing it here does not have the changes in person that characterize *iltifāt*. The *iʿtirāḍ* we are considering here occurs as a definite break in the sentence, verse, or train of thought for various reasons, such as a prayer, drawing attention to something, drawing emotion, showing the reason for something strange, etc.[3] It may consist of a single word, a phrase, a sentence, or more than one sentence. Ibn al-Athīr states that legitimate *iʿtirāḍ* must only be used for emphasis (*tawkīd*).[4] Parenthesis was already recognized by Quintilian in ancient times; he refers to it as interiectio = interjection, a feature often used by orators and historians, and comments that such insertions must not be too long lest they impede comprehension.[5] This feature is not often used in contemporary written English, being inappropriate to the demand for unity and immediate relevance of all parts to the whole, although it has a well-known place in plays and other oral genres. This is probably because these reflect to some degree the freedom of conversation, where speakers change subjects suddenly at will, as opposed to writing, where the reader expects to be presented with a more united whole. In *A Brief Handbook of English*, Hulon Willis, speaking about coherence, which is, of course, a desirable a characteristic in writing, says, "Coherence means that all parts of each sentence and all sentences in a passage stick together, making the writing clear, intelligible, and smooth,"[6] a principle that exists in some tension with parenthesis.

1 For *iʿtirāḍ* in the Qurʾān general, see Ibn al-Muʿtazz, 108; Sakkākī, 428, who places *iʿtirāḍ* in *ʿilm al-badīʿ*; Ibn al-Athīr, *Mathal*, III, 40–49; Ibn an-Naqīb, 194–201; Ṭūfī, 170–177; Qazwīnī, 239–242, who seems to be be the first to classify *iʿtirāḍ* in *ʿilm al-maʿānī*, Zarkashī, III, 56–64; Ṭabānah, *Muʿjam*, 413–417, Abdel Haleem, *Exploring*, 227; Abdul-Raof, *New Horizons*, 187–188.

2 Dupriez, 325–327; Enos, 492; Harris, 79.

3 Bībānī, 99–100.

4 Ibn al-Athīr, *Mathal*, III, 41; Ṭūfī, 171.

5 Quintilian, 8:2:15.

6 Willis, 236.

 | DOI:10.1163/9789004417441_014

An example of *iʿtirāḍ* of a single word into a verse is given in 16:57:[7]

(211) wa-yajʿalūna li-llāhi l-banāti subḥānahu wa-lahum mā yashtahūn.

The word *subḥānahu* might seem like a superfluous exclamation at first to the uninformed Western reader, though its emphatic sense is readily evident. It is placed here to show not only that Allah is above such conceptions as his having daughters, but that he is indeed far above all anthropomorphism.[8] In English, however, it seems to interfere with the flow of the sentence, though the translations of the verse are similar; Arberry for examples gives:

(212) And they assign to God
daughters; glory be to Him!—
and they have their desire.

While this has some similarity to the English interjection "God forbid!" which might be more suitable in place of "glory be to Him" here, the latter is indeed the meaning of the Arabic and is foreign-sounding to English ears. Arberry's unbalanced punctuation does not make things easier, though this tool can obviously be of service, if handled properly, in isolating *iʿtirāḍ* insertions from the context.[9] But, mostly, here the English-speaking reader would be likely to dislike the shock of sudden shifts and prefers transitions, as we have seen in the chapter on *iltifāt*, unless the shift or insertion is one of those idiomatically allowable in English, like "God forbid!" Arabic, with *ḥāshā lillāh* to translate this term and a large variety of others like *subḥānahu* of (211) presents a greater richness of such insertions, but the success or failure of the translation may well depend on whether the translator can find a corresponding idiomatic expression in English.

Dawood (1990, 2014) isolates the phrase using parentheses:

(213) They foist daughters upon God (glory be to Him!), but for themselves they choose what they desire.

The parentheses do help to remove the insertion from the flow of the sentence, but at the cost of introducing a feature not found in the Arabic text which in effect demotes the words of the insertion to a lower status.

---

7 Cited in Ibn al-Athīr, *Mathal*, III, 42; Qazwīnī, 239; Ṭabānah, *Muʿjam*, 414.
8 Ibn al-Athīr, *Mathal*, III, 42; Bībānī, 100.
9 Strunk & White, 2–5, on marking off *iʿtirāḍ* in English with punctuation.

Muhammad Asad tries a different strategy:

(214) And [thus, too,] they ascribe daughters unto God, who is limitless in His glory—whereas for themselves [they would choose, if they could, only] what they desire.

First, this is not strictly comparable to the other translations because of its big exegetical insertions and expansions. On the point in question here, however, Asad chooses to make the interjection *subḥānahu* into a subordinate clause, which also appears more congenial to the flow of the text, although he then follows it with a hyphen separating the following contrasting clause. At least these three translations illustrate that there are numerous choices in rendering the Arabic interjection here, though each of them seems to come with a cost.

A longer *iʿtirāḍ* insertion, really consisting of two insertions, are placed after the other, is given in verse 3:36:[10]

(215) fa-lammā waḍaʿathā qālat rabbi innī waḍaʿtuhā unthā wa-llāhu aʿlamu bi-mā waḍaʿat wa-laysa dh-dhakaru ka-l-unthā wa-innī sammaytuhā maryama wa-innī uʿīdhuhā bika wa-dhurriyyatahā min ash-shayṭān ar-rajīm.

Here at least the two successive asides of *wa-llāhu aʿlamu bi-mā waḍaʿat* and *wa-laysa dh-dhakaru ka-l-unthā* are obviously related to the thread of the text and are not exclamatory. All the translations employ punctuation to mark and to ameliorate the suddenness of the three breaks; Arberry uses parentheses and quotation marks, Pickthall dashes and a semicolon, Muhammad Ali dashes and a comma, Bell dashes, quotation marks, and a semicolon, Dawood dashes, quotation marks, and colon, Yūsuf ʿAlī dashes, quotation marks, and a period, and Muhammad Asad dashes, quotation marks, and a comma. Even with Arberry's parentheses to isolate the inserted sentences and demote them in importance, a move away from the Arabic text, the English-speaking reader is likely to consider them a digression far from the subject:

(216) And when she gave birth to her she said, 'Lord, I have given birth to her, a female.' (And God knew very well what she had given birth to; the male is not as the female.) 'And I have named her Mary, and commend her to Thee with her seed, to protect them from the accursed Satan.'

---

10 Qazwīnī, 240; Bībānī, 100–101.

Pickthall offers the following, which Muhammad Ali resembles in setting off the first parenthesis with dashes:

(217) And when she was delivered she said: My Lord! Lo! I am delivered of a female—Allah knew best of what she was delivered—the male is not as the female; and lo! I have named her Mary, and lo! I crave Thy protection for her and for her offspring from Satan the outcast.

Pickthall's rendering differs from Arberry's in that he evidently considers "the male is not as the female" to be a resumption of Mary's mother's speech, as do Muhammad Ali and Yūsuf ʿAlī, whereas Arberry, Bell, Dawood, and Muhammad Asad regard it as a continuation of the parenthesis, or rather a second parenthesis. Even if it is part of Mary's mother's speech, it is still another parenthesis.

Indeed, it seems there is no way of escaping a certain strangeness for English language readers in these insertions, particularly with the second of the two parentheses, "the male is not as the female," which seems irrelevant and does not appear to follow the preceding statement about God's knowledge, because of course God would know that. Indeed, that is why it is emphatic in the Arabic, but the English reader is not so likely to get that. Also, the various punctuation devices resorted to by all of the translations have no counterparts in the Arabic text, particularly not those which subordinate some text. This also reminds us that punctuation must be considered along with the other features when analyzing translations.

Another case of *iʿtirāḍ* insertion of sentence length that causes some confusion in the translation occurs in verse 12:53:[11]

(218) wa-mā ubarriʾu nafsī inna n-nafsa la-ammāratun bi-s-sūʾi illā mā raḥima rabbī inna rabbī ghafūrun raḥīm.

Here the *iʿtirāḍ* is usually interpreted as a continuation of the speech of the same speaker, unlike the preceding example, where the speech of Mary's mother was cut by the two asides. The confusion turns on whether the phrase *illā mā raḥima rabbī* should be taken as part of the aside or the beginning of the resumption of the thread of speech,[12] as is apparent from the translations. Arberry includes this phrase in the resumed speech:

11 There is a difference of opinion as to whether this is the speech of Joseph or of Zulaykha, the former interpretation being favored, but that does not concern our present study. See Zamakhsharī, II, 480–481.

12 See Zamakhsharī, II, 480, for a discussion about this. He admits seven possibilities.

(219) Yet I claim not that my soul was innocent—surely the soul of man incited to evil—except inasmuch as my Lord had mercy; truly my Lord is All-forgiving, All-compassionate.

The *iʿtirāḍ* as rendered by Arberry here requires the reader to make three sudden jumps in the same verse, from "innocent" to "surely," "evil" to "except," and "mercy" to "truly." This might slow down the reader's progress, distract him from his concentration, and reduce his interest, all features of foreignization brought about by Arberry's attempt to translate quite literally.

Pickthall, however, includes the phrase in the aside:

(220) 53. I do not exculpate myself. Lo! the (human) soul enjoineth unto evil, save that whereon my Lord hath mercy. Lo! my Lord is Forgiving, Merciful.

Again, as in (215), the aside is clearly connected in meaning to the thread of the text, but it appears nevertheless to be a moralistic digression. Perhaps it is more acceptable in English than some cases of *iʿtirāḍ* because it occurs in the speech of a person admitting he has committed some wrong, and then musing on the condition of man generally.

Indeed, Dawood (2014) has modified the Arabic in this direction:

(221) '... Not that I claim to be free from sin: man's soul is prone to evil, except his to whom my Lord has shown mercy. My Lord is forgiving and compassionate.'

While Dawood seems smoother here than the others, the parenthesis still clearly stands as a digression, albeit one closely related to the subject at hand.

A case where the semantic connection of the *iʿtirāḍ* sentence is not so clear occurs in verse 7:42:

(222) wa-lladhīna āmanū wa-ʿamilū ṣ-ṣāliḥāti lā nukallifu nafsan illā wusʿahā ulāʾika aṣḥābu l-jannati hum fīhā khālidūn.

Az-Zamakhsharī says that this *iʿtirāḍ* is to increase the attraction of paradise to the believers as well as being an indication of man's very great capacity for believing and doing good works,[13] thus showing by this view his Muʿtazilite

13 Zamakhsharī, II, 104.

bias, emphasizing the necessity of doing good works. But Ibn Kathīr points out rather that the verse urges to belief and good works by pointing out how God has made doing them easy in the aside, not by magnifying man's capacity for faith and righteous deeds.[14] It is also possible to take *wa-lladhīna āmanū wa-ʿamilū ṣ-ṣāliḥāti* as a subject with predicate omitted, thus making the sentence beginning with *ulāʾika* independent. In that case all three parts of the verse would be independent of each other without *iʿtirāḍ*, but this view appears very unlikely, as it requires introducing too many ad hoc elements. Whatever the case, any connection is not so obvious in English, as demonstrated by the translations. In this verse, all of the translations except Bell set off the parenthesis with dashes.[15] Pickthall, for example, has:

(223) But (as for) those who believe and do good works—We tax not any soul beyond its scope—Such are the rightful owners of the Garden.

Quite plainly, we have here in English two ideas with slight visible connection between them and no transition or other device to give a hint of their belonging to each other.

Because of the foreignness of the insertion to the rest of the sentence, Bell here, rejecting the uses and implications of *iʿtirāḍ* in the Arabic language, literally tears the verse apart, rearranging it to look something like this:

(224)

	40a. But those who have be- lieved and wrought the works
....	of righteousness—40c. these are
40b. We lay not upon anyone	the inmates of the garden,
more than he is capable of	therein abiding;
....	

The lines of dots are Bell's method of showing that the text within is not related to what precedes or follows it and that it is an irrelevant accidental insertion which occurred due to a mixing up of the leaves or scraps that the verses were written on from which the Qurʾān was compiled, according to Bell.[16] Bell's reception of this verse certainly could indicate the reaction of a typical English-speaking reader to the verse, as it takes a moment of reflection to see how the

14 Ibn Kathīr, III, 169.

15 Except that Arberry uses one dash and one semicolon.

16 Bell, I, vi–vii, 141.

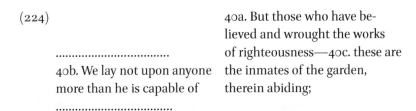

iʿtirāḍ fits with the rest of the verse. That Bell could even suggest rearranging the verse the way he does shows that the Arabic of (222) violates normal English rhetorical expectations, even though it is quite a normal example of the frequent feature of *iʿtirāḍ* in the Qur'ān.

In many cases, even the refrains at the end of verses can be considered as cases of *iʿtirāḍ* when they do not appear connected to the part of the verse preceding them nor to the following verse, especially when the latter continues the same topic found in the former verse. A case of this is found, for example, in parts of verses 2:222–223:[17]

(225) … fa idhā taṭahharna fa-'tūhunna min ḥaythu amarakum Allāhu inna
    llāha yuḥibbu t-tawwābīna wa-yuḥibbu l-mutaṭahhirīn.
  nisā'ukum ḥarthun lakum …

Az-Zamakhsharī passes quickly over this, pointing out that the refrain of 2:222, which begins with *inna* and ends with *al-mutaṭahhirīn*, refers to the preceding commandment enjoining only normal sexual relations with women. Thus, the aside *inna llāha yuḥibbu t-tawwābīna wa-yuḥibbu l-mutaṭahhirīn* urges the believers to repent of wrong they many have committed and to be pure in their sexual relations, or to purify themselves with proper repentance.[18] This case is remarkable in that it elicits such a small comment in the Arabic, but violates the expectations of English rhetoric when translated, as in Arberry:

(226) '… When they have cleansed
  themselves then come unto them as God
  has commanded you.' Truly, God loves
  those who repent, and He loves those
    who cleanse themselves.
  Your women are a tillage for you …

"Those who cleanse themselves" is not really an adequate translation of *al-mutaṭahhirīn*, which has more to do with purification, and this could mislead us as to the relevance of the digression in English. The command against abnormal sexual intercourse is followed by this digression about purity, but unless the reader gets this first connection, he or she may miss the point of the *iʿtirāḍ*

17 Cited as a case of *iʿtirāḍ* by Qazwīnī, 240; Zarkashī, III, 58; Bībānī, 100; Ṭabānah, *Muʿjam*, 414.

18 Zamakhsharī, I, 266.

insertion. Should he or she then find describing women as a "tillage" objectionable, that reader will probably find the reference to cleanness and purity rather strange.

Bell, similar to Arberry, uses distracting quotation marks to complete the declaration from the preceding verse:

(227) "… but when they have purified themselves, come to them as Allah hath commanded you."
Verily Allah loveth those who turn continually in penitence, and loveth those who keep themselves pure.
Your women are to you (as) cultivated land; …

In sum, the parenthesis here in both (226) and (227) seems to be at best a moralistic aside with an unclear connection to the thread of the text. This is partly because the readers cannot encompass the full occasion of the original revelation and are likely to miss the connection. Of course, anyone who reads the Qur'ān will become familiar with the frequency of such asides and other semantic jumps, but it is still a feature difficult to accept in English for a reader not thoroughly versed in the environment in which the Qur'ān was revealed, and likely to lead to as much confusion as *iltifāt*.

However, there is also another type of *iʿtirāḍ* called *tadhyīl*, which consists of appending a short independent clause containing the same meaning after a verse to emphasize the meaning presented in the first sentence,[19] as in the addition of *nisāʾukum ḥarthun lakum* in (225) above. Sometimes the added sentence takes the form of a rhetorical question,[20] as in verses 21:34–35:[21]

(228) wa-mā jaʿalnā li-basharin min qablika l-khulda a-fa-in mitta fa-hum al-khālidūn.
kullu nafsin dhāʾiqatu l-mawt …

19 Abū Hilāl al-Ḥasan b. ʿAbd Allāh al-ʿAskarī, *Kitāb aṣ-ṣināʿatayn: al-kitābah wa-sh-shiʿr*, ed. by ʿAlī Muḥammad al-Bajāwī and Muḥammad Abū al-Faḍl Ibrāhīm, Cairo: Dār Iḥyāʾ al-Kutub al-Arabiyyah, ʿĪsā al-Bābī al-Ḥalabī, 1371/1952, pp. 373–374; Zakī ad-Dīn Abū Muḥammad ʿAbd al-ʿAẓīm b. ʿAbd al-Wāḥid Ibn Abī al-Iṣbaʿ, *Taḥrīr at-taḥbīr fī ṣināʿat ash-shiʿr wa-n-nathr wa-bayān iʿjāz al-Qurʾān*, ed. by Ḥanafī Muḥammad Sharaf, Cairo: al-Majlis al-Aʿlā li-sh-Shuʾūn al-Islāmiyyah, Lajnat Iḥyāʾ at-Turāth al-Islāmī, [1383/1963], pp. 387–392; Qazwīnī, 233–234.

20 Indeed, two of the three Qurʾānic examples cited by al-Qazwīnī, 233–234, are rhetorical questions.

21 Cited by ʿAskarī, 373; Ibn Mālik, 217–218; Qazwīnī, 234; Bībānī, 101.

Again, there is no transition to the appended phrase, yet its relevance to the preceding verse is clear. Indeed, part of its stature as a classical example of *tadhyīl* is its play on the final word of the first sentence, *al-khulda* = immortality, by ending the interrupting sentence with *al-khālidūn* = the immortal ones, a different word based on the same root.

Arberry has somewhat tried to preserve this figure in his translation by ending both the first clause and the second, interrupting question clause with "forever." However, because this is an exact word-for-word repetition, it does not have the same effect as the Arabic:

(229) We have not assigned to any mortal before thee to live forever; therefore, if thou diest, will they live forever? Every soul shall taste of death.

Also, Arberry's insertion of "therefore," which is not exactly expressed in the Arabic, is too weak to translate *a-fa-in*, as it loses the emphasis.

Pickthall certainly has more emphasis with his "What!":

(230) 34. We appointed immortality for no mortal before thee. What! if thou diest, can they be immortal?
35. Every soul must taste of death.

And he has also tried to save something of the Arabic figure by using the words "immortality" and "immortal," compounding them into three by also using the English cognate word "mortal," which is from a different root in the Arabic. But the effect is still not the same, for he has not placed "immortality" at the end of the first sentence.

Meanwhile, Dawood (1990 & 2014) has:

(231) No man before you have We made immortal. If you yourself are doomed to die, will they live on for ever?
Every soul shall taste death.

Here, in his typical way, Dawood places no connectives at all between the three sentences. The third sentence, "Every soul shall taste death," shares no connective with Arberry's and Pickthall's versions, as all three translators reproduce the Arabic asyndeton. But for the second sentence, he reduces its complex transition *a-fa-in* to just "if," which illustrates his flattening out of Arabic figures and phrases in the interests of simplicity and directness. But the result, in this case, seems choppy. Also, Dawood has rearranged the word order of the first sentence significantly and has made no effort to reproduce the *tadhyīl* using words of the same root, preferring the diversity of "immortal" and "live on for ever" to using words of the same root.

Whatever is best on these points, however, each of these three translators clearly conveys some of the rhetorical excellence of the original. "Every soul must taste of death" sums up the human condition so succinctly that the reader can scarcely help being attracted by its simplicity; also, it admirably binds up the more specific words of the preceding sentences. So it may be that an Arabic rhetorical device translated directly into English can retain some of its original impact while conveying the originally intended meaning. But on the other hand, as we have seen, none of the translations here exactly conveys the impression of the Arabic either.

CHAPTER 13

Succinctness, or *ījāz al-qiṣar*

One point of rhetoric which is important in the Qur'ān is *ījāz*, meaning succinctness, concision, or brevity. Here, a succinct or abbreviated form still carries the basic intent and thus enhances the effectiveness of the message. Like *iṭnāb*, *ījāz* requires references to context; it may not be taken totally out of context, for then confusion might result. *Ījāz* became established as a significant category of rhetoric as early as ar-Rummānī,[1] who also detailed its division into the two subcategories we are dealing with here: succinctness and ellipsis. In Arabic, these two subcategories are traditionally defined as *ījāz al-qiṣar*, in which the words are epigrammatically fewer but still carry a full meaning and are complete in themselves,[2] and *ījāz al-ḥadhf*,[3] which involves omission of certain words without loss of the meaning, which is still implicit. The latter is particularly noticeable to the English-speaking reader of translations of the Qur'ān, so understanding of it is essential, but the former is also very frequent, particularly in the earlier surahs revealed at Makkah, where short verses may be heavily charged with meaning.

Succinctness[4] is a rhetorical virtue in many languages, of course. Among the ancient Greeks, it is mentioned by Aristotle, Demetrius, and Longinus.[5] It is also of course considered a major virtue in modern English rhetoric.[6]

Like poetry, which involves expression prized as rhetorically beautiful first because it sums up a certain idea or line of thought succinctly and precisely, occurrences of *ījāz al-qiṣar* may present a formidable problem to the translator, who may or may not find equivalent expressions in English. We have already seen the succinct quality of the feature of *tadhyīl* above in the final sentences of examples (225) and (228). Other examples are frequent; we shall only be able to examine a few.

---

1 Rummānī, 76.

2 For *ījāz al-qiṣar*, see Rummānī, 77–78; ʿAskarī, 175–179; Bāqillānī, 262–263; Sakkākī, 277–278; Ibn al-Athīr, *Mathal*, II, 265–279; 332–354; Ibn an-Naqīb, 139–145; Ṭūfī, 178–179, 199–202; Qazwīnī, 215–218; Zarkashī, III, 220–232; Ṭabānah, *Muʿjam*, 711–713, 556–557; Abdul-Raof, *Arabic Rhetoric*, 188–189; Jenssen, 128–129, Abdel Haleem, *Exploring*, 231.

3 For *ījāz al-ḥadhf*, see Chapter Fourteen, below.

4 Mir, *Understanding*, 7, 67, refers to this feature as "terseness." My translation of "succinctness" comes originally from Dr. al-Nowaihi.

5 Aristotle, 3:9:3; Demetrius, 137–138, 241–243; Longinus, 42.

6 Williams & Colomb, 100–105, 107–111, 113–117, referring to concision.

 | DOI:10.1163/9789004417441_015

One such instance occurs in verse 15:94:

(232) fa-ṣdaʿ bi-mā tu'maru wa-aʿriḍ ʿan al-mushrikīn.

This is considered *ījāz al-qiṣar*, as there is no omission. In the three words *fa-ṣdaʿ bi-mā tu'maru*, it includes a command that encompasses all the conditions of the Prophetic mission.[7] The point of brevity and hence eloquence here turns on the word *iṣdaʿ*, which is packed with meaning. The verb *ṣadaʿa-yaṣdaʿu* may mean break, crack, split, divide, split off, manifest a thing, or declare the truth, which latter meaning is obviously a figurative connotation developed from the original, physical denotation.[8] The basic concept includes the idea of splitting, breaking, or bursting. Part of the meaning contained in the verse is abstract, though conveyed by a tangible metaphor implicit in *fa-ṣdaʿ*. But the power of the verse truly comes from the very graphic image carried by this word. The second half of the verse tells the Prophet to oppose those who partner anything with Allah and hence to let loose with all the inspiration that is in him without restraint.

The translators have conveyed this with varying degrees of success; Yūsuf ʿAlī gives us:

(233) Therefore expound openly
What thou art commanded,
And turn away from those
Who join false gods with God.

This has a kind of nice rhythm to it, but does it really represent the Arabic original? First, as often with Yūsuf ʿAlī, it is rather wordy, containing seventeen words in comparison with the original's six. Therefore, succinctness here is compromised or lost.

Arberry has managed to use fewer words:

(234) So shout that thou art commanded and turn away from the idolaters.

By using "that," Arberry may have intended the rendition to be ambiguous, containing the two possible meanings, "shout the thing which thou art com-

7 ʿAskarī, 176; Ibn al-Athīr, *Jāmiʿ*, 144; al-Mu'ayyad bi-llāh, II, 49; Zarkashī, III, 226, 437; Bībānī, 95.

8 J.G. Hava, *al-Farā'id ad-durriyyah ʿarabī-inklīzī: Al-Faraid Arabic-English Dictionary*, Beirut: Catholic Press, 1964, p. 392.

manded" and "shout the fact that thou art commanded." In modern English the second is the far more likely understanding of Arberry's sentence, but in the Arabic original, the first is really the proper meaning. It may be that Arberry was trying to save a word here, using "that" instead of "that which."

Pickthall avoids this ambiguity by using exactly that phrase:

(235) So proclaim that which thou art commanded, and withdraw from the idolaters.

The word "proclaim" is more tepid than Arberry's "shout," which is also imprecise in conveying the Arabic. Also, one supposes the meaning "don't pay attention to," as Ibn Kathīr interprets the second half of the verse,[9] would be more closely give the meaning of *aʿriḍ* than "withdraw from."

Dawood (1990 & 2014) paraphrases Pickthall, using shorter words:

(236) Proclaim, then, what your are bidden, and let the idolaters be.

None of these translations really conveys the meaning or the impact of *fa-ṣdaʿ*.

Bell, on the other hand, gives:

(237) Burst forth with what thou art commanded, and turn from the polytheists.

Bell's interpretation conveys some of the shock or suddenness of movement implicitly in "break" or *fa-ṣdaʿ*. Only Bell has attempted thus to carry the Arabic metaphor into English, giving some of the excitement of the early bursts of revelation experienced by the Prophet. It is perhaps a matter of personal taste whether or not the attempt is successful.

Another case which constitutes *ījāz al-qiṣar* occurs in verse 2:179:[10]

(238) wa-lakum fī l-qiṣāṣi ḥayātun …

This is considered a clear example of brevity because, although the words are few, the meaning is much. For example, if a man knows there will be retribution if he kills or maims, he will restrain himself and hence live.[11] At another

9 Ibn Kathīr, IV, 176.

10 Cited by Rummānī, 77; Bāqillānī, 263; ʿAskarī, 175; Ibn al-Athīr, *Mathal*, II, 352; Ibn Abī al-Iṣbaʿ, 468; Ibn Mālik, 76; Qazwīnī, 215; Jenssen, 128–129.

11 Bībānī, 95.

level, it implies that because the justice of legalized retribution on specific terms has been revealed, the blood feuds of pre-Islamic times have stopped, thus saving many lives.[12] It may be also that the verse was an eye-opener for the original hearers of the Qur'ān, startling because it brings together the apparently opposed concepts of "retribution" and "life." Indeed, aside from being considered an example of succinctness, this verse is also often cited as an example of *muṭābaqah* (antithetical juxtaposition) by classical rhetoricians.[13] Some of the translations mimic the laconic expression of the original, but without the contextual implications, inevitably. Context, of course, is one of the points of rhetoric that is hard, if not impossible, to convey in another language, unless the translator resorts to extensive glosses or footnotes by way of explanation.

In this case, the verse (238) comes after a more detailed verse on *qiṣāṣ* or legal retribution, so the reader of the English translations may extract the meaning and its various connotations, according to the context and his knowledge of the matter. The native reader of the original steeped in his own culture is more likely to discover the nuances than the foreigner reading a translation.

Keeping to the feature of succinctness, Bell renders the verse in the briefest English:

(239) In retaliation is life for you.

Pickthall and Arberry differ little from this, the latter giving:

(240) In retaliation there is life for you.

Here we note only the inclusion of the superfluous "there." Perhaps this makes Bell's brevity closer to the spirit of the original, in which every word counts.

Yūsuf ʿAlī presents a slightly longer translation:

(241) In the Law of Equality
There is (saving of) Life
To you …

While his translation raises questions and avoids rendering *al-qiṣāṣ* as "retribution" or "retaliation" by substituting the undefined "Law of Equality," it still

12 Qurṭubī, II, 256.

13 Ibn al-Muʿtazz, 48; Bāqillānī, 80.

constitutes an ideological choice representing Yūsuf ʿAlī's liberal and pacific view of the Qurʾān's message. Furthermore, the neat antithesis in the original between "retaliation" and "life," presenting the reader or hearer with a kind of paradox about how there can be life in killing, is lost.

Dawood (1990 & 2014) also presents a somewhat exegetical translation:

(242) In retaliation you have a safeguard for your lives ...

By converting the element "life" into "a safeguard for your lives," Dawood has also abandoned the form of antithesis of the original. While his interpretation could possibly help the reader's understanding, the beauty of the brevity and succinctness of the original is of course lost.

Other instances of *ījāz al-qiṣar* are perhaps more difficult to translate into English. In 55:1–4, we read:

(243) ar-raḥmān.
ʿallama l-qurʾān.
khalaqa l-insān.
ʿallamahu l-bayān.

The variety of interpretations by the translators shows how rich these lines are with various possible meanings. Yet they are certainly not obscure; they simply admit a variety of interpretations. Indeed, we are reminded continually in the Qurʾān in such verses as 12:1 that this is the book which explains clearly. These particular lines seem to cause little difficulty to az-Zamakhsharī, for example, and are among the oft-quoted verses for modern Egyptians. They contain information put in the fewest possible words about the revelation of the external Qurʾān, the creation of man, and the instilling in him of logical thought or reason, which distinguishes him from the animals.[14] Arberry renders them:

(244) The All-merciful has taught the Koran
He created man
and He has taught him the Explanation.

We note here particularly the rendering of *al-bayān* as "the Explanation," which does not quite convey the intent of the verse as described by az-Zamakhsharī yet is perhaps an acceptable literal translation of the Arabic word. Also, while

14 Zamakhsharī, IV, 443.

Arberry has striven to be concise, not adding extra explanatory words, his English still has more words than the Arabic, and of course the original's rhyme and rhythm disappear.

Pickthall gives us:

(245) 1. The Beneficent
2. Hath made known the Qur'ân.
3. He hath created man.
4. He hath taught him utterance.

Verse 4 in this version is an example of what may happen when the translator attempts to maintain the laconic Qur'ānic expression in English. "Utterance" here presumably means the power of speech, but we suspect from az-Zamakhsharī's explanation that the meaning of *al-bayān* is intended to be wider than that, and az-Zamakhsharī's interpretation, while it is not the only one possible, certainly is a plausible one. Thus, the translation, by specifying, tends to exclude some of the possible meanings, always a problem in translation. Furthermore, "utterance" could be taken in ways other than Pickthall may have intended, such as "to utter a grunt" or "to utter any sound," rather than simply "speech" or "the ability to speak." "Taught" does not quite cover the meaning of *ʿallama*, "to cause to know," either, yet the alternative is to use more words and thus dispense with the Qur'ānic brevity.

Bell, despite his disclaimer of any striving to achieve rhetorical beauty and perhaps because of it, gives the briefest version:[15]

(246) 1. The Merciful
Taught the Qur'ān,
2. Created Man,
3. Taught him the Explanation.

We have noted the problem of rendering *ar-raḥmān* above in the discussion of parallelism. While Bell's version appears short, he felt constrained to append a footnote to make "the Explanation" intelligible. It reads, "Usually taken to mean the power of intelligible speech; but cf. III, 132, XXV, 19, which suggest it has reference to the Qur'ān." The latter idea would appear less likely, as the Qur'ān was just mentioned in verse 2, but the point is that Bell's brief translation by itself conveys neither of the meanings given in the footnote to the reader, as they

15 Muhammad Ali's version of these verses is equally brief, however.

are not obvious. However, Bell, by omitting connective words and pronouns, has managed to render something of the Arabic figure of succinctness at least, although the long word "Explanation" does not fit in very well. Still, Bell's striving to stick to the form of the original is a foreignizing move, and, after all, Bell is trying to present the Qur'ān as a foreign text.

Yūsuf ʿAlī overcomes the problem of the other translations choosing either "speech" or "reason/logic" for *al-bayān* by giving both meanings:

(247) 1. (God) Most Gracious!
2. It is He Who has
Taught the Qur'ān.
3. He has created man.
4. He has taught him speech
(And Intelligence).

This is accompanied by two long footnotes for further elucidation. Now we have what az-Zamakhsharī described as the meaning, approximately, but the succinct quality of the original is gone. The contrast between (246) and (247) represents to some extent the problem of the conflict between form and clarity of rendering in translation. In this case, the clarification is brought about by exegetical expansions that do not translate words found in the original.

Meanwhile, Dawood (1990 & 2014) completely flattens out the succinctness of the separate verses of the original:

(248) It is the Merciful who has taught the Koran.
He created Man and taught him articulate speech.

Though not as wordy as Yūsuf ʿAlī's version, Dawood's still represents an expansion in the size of the text. He conflates the four verses into just two sentences, the first by subordination of a clause and the second by coordination, all of it made to sound more like normal English. This is plainly a domesticating move, and the figure of Qur'ānic succinctness, as well as the poetic rhythm and rhyming, are completely absent.

Another difficult problem is caused by the *ījāz* of verses 95:4–5:

(249) laqad khalaqnā l-insāna fī aḥsani taqwīm.
thumma radadnāhu asfala sāfilīn.

These few words are also rich with meaning. They may refer to the creation of man in the best of form, stature, beauty, or symmetry, then his being sent to

Hell when he shows ingratitude. On another level, rather than Hell, the second verse may refer to a man's decline when he reaches old age.[16] Yet still another interpretation would refer to his moral turpitude despite his being endowed with a rational mind and having superiority in that sense over the beasts.

For these two verses, Arberry gives us:

(250) We indeed created Man in the fairest stature
then We restored him the lowest of the low—

"Stature" does not really convey the full meaning of *taqwīm*, especially not the connotation of straightness or uprightness that would go with any of the meanings given above. "Restored" is inadequate because it implies "returned to its proper place." While it is true "the lowest of the low" is an acceptable, commonly-used English expression somewhat pejorative in sense, one wonders if it has conveyed the full pejorative sense of *sāfil*.

Bell gives more of the physical meaning for the term *taqwīm*:

(251) 4. Surely We have created man most beautifully erect,
5. Then have rendered him the lowest of the low,—

This is expanded on by him in two footnotes containing five explanations.

Yūsuf ʿAlī typically has a more spiritual explanation, again in more words:

(252) 4. We have indeed[17] created man
In the best of moulds,
5. Then do We abase him
(To be) the lowest
Of the low,—

Like Bell's version, this is expanded by two footnotes, one of which gives five meanings for *taqwīm*: mould, symmetry, form, nature, and constitution. The Arabic admits all of these meanings, as an educated native speaker must be aware. But to give them all in English is impossible without footnotes, and then the brevity is transformed into a long exposition.

The version of Dawood (1990) here illustrates a domesticating interest in fluency and readability in English, paying no attention to the verse form, lump-

16 Zamakhsharī, IV, 774.

17 The original reads "inneed," which is a typo that I have corrected here.

ing all of the passage into a single prose sentence, and it is also rather loose in translation:

(253) We created man in a most noble image and in the end We shall reduce him to the lowest of the low:[18]

Dawood limits the meaning of the original by suggesting *taqwīm* is "image," a physical term and one that may be informed by English Bible translations, and then makes man's being "the lowest of the low"—an expression shared by all five translations we are considering here—into a future event, thus apparently following the explanation that man's reduction is in the afterlife in Hell, something suggested by one possible interpretation by classical commentators, even though the Arabic verb for "reduce him" here, *radadnāhu*, is in the perfect tense, and so it has been rendered by most of the other translators.

In short, in instances of *ījāz al-qiṣar*, the meaning may be given in English if enough words are used, provided the translator is skilled enough, but rhetorical beauty of the original inherent in the very brevity of expression will be mostly or completely lost. It is not merely that Arabic has the quality of brevity while English is verbose, because English too has its epigrams, some of which might turn out longer in Arabic than in English if translated. Rather, there are certain expressions in a language that are appropriate and striking just because they do sum up a certain point so briefly, and putting the same point across with equal brevity and suitability of expression in another language is a source of difficulty.

18 Dawood, 2014, 417, has: "We created Man in a most noble image, and then We shall reduce him to the lowest of the low:" which capitalizes "man" and replaces "in the end," a kind of exegetical translation, with "then," the commoner rendering of the Arabic *thumma*.

CHAPTER 14

Ellipsis, or *ījāz al-ḥadhf*

Ellipsis or deliberate omission is possibly the most noticeable and dramatic of all the devices we have been examining, because it consists of actual omissions of words, phrases, or clauses, in some cases quite lengthy ones. Indeed, it would seem logical to conclude that the shock of the disruption increases in proportion to the size of the omission. This feature was already described in ancient times by Demetrius, the *Rhetorica ad Herrenium*, and Quintilian.[1] Ellipsis is also a heavily mentioned, described, and used feature in modern English rhetoric, although the form and extent of its usage differs from Arabic, especially Qurʾānic Arabic. Ellipsis is defined as omitting text whose meaning is easily understood by the context of the other words.[2] Such a concept may work well enough in one language where the innate language competence of the speakers provides some agreement about what may be immediately understood when some text is omitted, but in another language, that concept inevitably differs somewhat.

In Arabic, ellipsis forms a second type of *ījāz* or brevity called *ījāz al-ḥadhf*, or "the brevity of omission,"[3] contrasted with *ījāz al-qiṣar* or "the brevity of succinctness (or concision)" that we have just seen. Ibn al-Athīr divides it into two subcategories according to whether the omission consists of sentences[4] or single words.[5] *Ījāz al-ḥadhf* provides a number of examples that present the translator with obstacles similar in difficulty to some of those listed above in the chapter on *iltifāt*. This characteristic *ḥadhf* or omission is a feature that recurs with considerable frequency throughout the Qurʾān, also exhibiting a certain amount of variety in what may be omitted. In general, the occurrence of ellipsis in the Qurʾān is vastly more than English readers are accustomed to.

1 Demetrius, 253; *Rhetorica*, 4:30:41; Quintilian, 9:3:18, 58–64.

2 Dupriez, 149–152; Enos, 211.

3 Rummānī, 76–77; Jurjānī, 146–172; Ibn al-Athīr, *Mathal*, II, 279–332; Ibn an-Naqīb, 145–165; Ṭūfī, 179–198; Qazwīnī, 218–227; Zarkashī, III, 102–220; Ṭabānah, *Muʿjam*, 155–159, 713; Abdul-Raof, *Qurʾan Translation*, 77, 127–128, 173; Abdul-Raof, *Arabic Rhetoric*, 189–190; Jenssen, 76–83, 129–130, Abdel Haleem, *Exploring*, 226.

4 Ibn al-Athīr, *Mathal*, II, 280–295.

5 Ibn al-Athīr, *Mathal*, II, 295–332.

 | DOI:10.1163/9789004417441_016

Certain cases of omission cause little difficulty in English owing to the smallness of what is left out, such as verse 18:79, which nevertheless constitutes an example of how concise the Qur'ān can be, no words being wasted.[6]

(254) ammā s-safīnatu fa-kānat li-masākīna ya'malūna fī l-baḥri fa-aradtu an a'ībahā fa-kāna warā'ahum malikun ya'khudhu kulla safīnatin ghaṣbā.

What is missing is immediately visible in the English translation of Bell, from whom the other translators differ but little:

(255) 78. As for the ship, it belonged to poor men who toil in the sea, and I wished to damage it, for there was behind them a king, taking every ship by force.

This captures the brevity of the original as adequately as a translation can, no word being wasted. One might ask why the speaker (al-Khiḍr) should wish to damage the ship if the king was taking every ship by force. Here then is the omission: we must supply an understood adjective such as "good" or "complete" for the ship.[7] However, this seems to cause no great difficulty either to translator or reader, as the inference is readily taken. Arberry's rendition scarcely differs:

(256) As for the ship, it belonged
to certain poor men, who toiled
upon the sea, and I desired
to damage it, for behind them
was a king who was seizing
every ship by brutal force.

The only comment to be made here is that the addition of the words "certain," "who was," and "brutal" appears to add nothing to the meaning presented by Bell, upon whom Arberry seems to be dependent in this instance, and none of these words is directly present in the Arabic original. The last of these added words in particular seems to throw off an appealing rhythm found in (255) somewhat reminiscent of that in the original Arabic verse.

Another of the well-known points of Qur'ānic ellipsis which may be sometimes paralleled in English is the omission of the apodosis or *jawāb ash-sharṭ*

6 Cited by Ibn al-Athīr, *Mathal*, II, 315–316; Qazwīnī, 219; Bībānī, 95.
7 Ibn al-Athīr, *Mathal*, II, 315–316; Bībānī, 95; cf. Zamakhsharī, II, 741.

of a conditional sentence, a very frequent feature in the Qur'ān. In English this may be realized in an incomplete conditional of warning such as, "If you do that ..." or, "If you do that, I'll ..." leaving the hearer to fill in the consequences in his own mind. In Qur'ānic Arabic, the potential scope of such uncompleted conditionals is greater, but may also somewhat fit the rhetorical expectations of English, as in verse 32:12:[8]

(257) wa-law tarā idh al-mujrimūna nākisū ru'ūsihim ʿinda rabbihim rabbanā abṣarnā wa-samiʿnā fa-rjiʿnā naʿmal ṣāliḥan innā mūqinūn.

This resembles the *law* clause of (123) above. The true sense is emphatic rather than conditional, as conveyed in the translations, as Arberry's, for instance:

(258) Ah, if thou couldst see the guilty hanging their heads before their Lord! 'Our Lord, we have seen and heard; now return us, that we may do righteousness, for we have sure faith.'

Pickthall elides the "if" that represents the Arabic *law*, reduces Arberry's "righteousness" to "right" and includes a parenthetical transition to the quoted speech of the ingrates, but otherwise is very similar:

(259) Couldst thou but see when the guilty hang their heads before their Lord, (and say): Our Lord! We have now seen and heard, so send us back; we will do right, now we are sure.

The plaintive pleading of the guilty coupled with the horror of a fate only hinted at, retains some of the effect of the original. Both (258) and (259) make sense in English, despite the lack of a transitional "saying" leading into the former of these.

A somewhat more difficult problem is posed by verses 36:45–46:[9]

(260) wa-idhā qīla lahum ittaqū mā bayna aydīkum wa-mā khalfakum laʿallakum turḥamūn.
wa-mā ta'tīhim min āyatin min āyāti rabbihim illā kānū ʿanhā muʿriḍīn.

8 Cited by Qazwīnī, 220; Zarkashī, III, 183; Bībānī, 96.

9 Cited in Ibn al-Athīr, *Mathal*, II, 326; Ibn al-Athīr, *Jāmiʿ*, 136–137; Ibn an-Naqīb, 158; Ṭūfī, 193; Qazwīnī, 219; Zarkashī, III, 188; Bībānī, 95.

Here the apodosis is entirely omitted, the answer of the ingrates to the statement missing. But as az-Zamakhsharī points out, their rejection of the warning actually can be deduced from the words *illā kānū ʿanhā muʿriḍīn*.[10] It appears (260) causes more difficulty for the translator than any of (232), (238), (254), and (257), as evidenced by the variance of the versions we are examining from each other in dealing with it.

First, Pickthall translates directly but provides us with a parenthetical insertion to represent the missing apodosis, completing the meaning according to his custom of often adding to the text for clarity. That he inserts this shows that this example is more difficult than the previous examples we have given, because he evidently feels the text would be unclear without it:

(261) When it is said unto them: Beware of that which is before you and that which is behind you, that haply ye may find mercy (they are heedless). Never came a token of the tokens of their Lord to them, but they did turn away from it!

The parenthetical expression adequately completes the meaning, but not according to the Arabic rhetorical pattern in which the insertion is superfluous with the presence of *illā kānū ʿanhā muʿriḍīn* at the end of (262), as noted in the sources cited above. Yūsuf ʿAlī and Muhammad Asad use similar parenthetical insertions to Pickthall's to complete the meaning of the text.

Also following Pickthall, Dawood (1990) also completes the apodosis, but now without parentheses, blatantly adding to the original text something which is not actually there:

(262) When it is said to them: 'Have fear of that which is before you and behind you, that you may be shown mercy,' they give no heed. Indeed, they turn away from every sign that comes to them from their Lord.

So Pickthall's parenthetical "(they are heedless)," clearly marked as an interpolation not found in the original text, now becomes an integral part of the text as "they give no heed". The Arabic figure is lost, and also, just as the Arabic rhetoricians warned in describing the apodosis here as superfluous, there is a certain repetition of meaning in "Indeed, they turn away …" not relieved by the separation of *wa-mā taʾtīhim min āyatin min āyāti rabbihim*.

10 Zamakhsharī, IV, 19; Ibn al-Athīr, *Mathal*, II, 326; Ibn al-Athīr, *Jāmiʿ*, 136–137; Qurṭubī, XV, 36; Ṭūfī, 193; Qazwīnī, 219.

Tellingly, Dawood was evidently dissatisfied with his translation here, for by 2014, he had significantly revised it:

(263) When they are told: 'Have fear of that which is before you and behind you, that you may be shown mercy,' they turn away from every sign that comes to them from their Lord.

Replacing his interpolation of his 1990 version, Dawood here rather daringly reconstructs the final sentence in order to produce a normal-sounding English sentence by erasing the Arabic rhetorical feature of *ījāz al-ḥadhf*. This conveniently coincides with Dawood's propensity for combining the short, pithy verses of the Qur'ān into longer English sentences. Yet, the bare meaning is preserved, but it does not so much resemble its Arabic form anymore. Thus, this is clearly a domesticating translation: straightforward, smooth, and easy to understand, using only short, common words, every one of them found in colloquial spoken as well as written English.

On the other hand, striving to keep to the literal form of the text without additions, Arberry gives us:

(264) And when it is said to them, 'Fear what is before you
and what is behind you; haply you will find mercy'—
yet never any sign of the signs of their Lord
comes to them, but they are turning away from it.

Closely following the Arabic, the words following the protasis of the incomplete conditional, though they do not constitute a true apodosis, do in fact complete the meaning by implication. But the clause of the protasis nevertheless constitutes a grammatically incomplete sentence in English, which Arberry has perhaps tried to ameliorate by inserting a dash, suggesting a pause, or an omission. Like Arberry, Muhammad Ali simply leaves the protasis clause hanging incomplete, in his case separated from the following verse by a period rather than a dash. In either case, the hanging clause in the form of this unconnected protasis is probably sufficient to cause the English-speaking reader hesitation or confusion.

But the way Bell treats the two verses is truly unique:

(265) 45. When one says to them:
"Fear what is before you, and
what is behind you, mayhap ye
will obtain mercy" ...

[Then on the next page, in a different column alongside other text, he has:]

Perversity of unbelievers;
Medinan.

46. But not a sign comes to
them of (all) the signs of their
Lord, but from it they have
been averting themselves.

First, in seeking like Arberry a literal representation of the Arabic text free of additions, Bell has not only separated the first of the two verses from the second, using a series of dots, but has also separated the verses in different columns to indicate his contention that the Qur'ān was composed of fragmentary scraps.[11] It seems clear here that Bell has failed to take into account the Arabic usage of ellipsis, as numerous other examples exist in the Qur'ān, which are most unlikely to be random juxtapositions of verses written on scraps of paper or parchment. However, what arrests our attention here is that Bell was able to disconnect the two verses entirely from each other and suggest a reason other than rhetorical for their proximity to each other. It must be then that this arrangement violated Bell's English rhetorical expectations, or he would not have made such an assertion, as he does not usually deliberately distort the Qur'ān to this extent. Therefore, it seems apparent that this verse in translation is likely to confuse some English-speaking readers.

There are other verses where the apodosis is omitted but replaced by something more clearly substituting for it, i.e., another sentence that is not a true apodosis, as in verses 3:184 and 35:4, 25, with 35:4 reading:[12]

(266) wa-in yukadhdhibūka fa-qad kudhdhibat rusulun min qablaka …

Az-Zamakhsharī explains this verse as lacking for the protasis *in kadhdhabūka* an apodosis such as *ta'sa* = "you might feel sad."[13]

This verse, unlike (262), presents little problem in English, as demonstrated by Bell:

11 Bell, II, 434, 437–438.
12 Cited by Qazwīnī, 225; Zarkashī, III, 209; Bībānī, 96.
13 Zamakhsharī, III, 598; Bayḍāwī, IV, 254.

(267) If they count them false, messengers have been counted false before thee, …

Arberry interprets:

(268) If they cry lies to thee, Messengers before thee
were cried lies to; …

The word order here (268) does not satisfy. The final position is potentially one of emphasis in the sentence,[14] but (268) winds down to a dangling preposition unclear in meaning, while (267) retains something of the Arabic word order as well as more nearly the proper emphasis of the original. If we were to make any comment on the better of these rhetorically (267), it would perhaps be to suggest that the English speaking reader still might prefer a real apodosis, perhaps "don't fear" or "don't mind;" however, the line is quite comprehensible as it stands.

Certain other verses displaying this kind of ellipsis may not be so readily accepted or tolerated in English, however, such as 13:31.[15]

(269) wa-law anna qurʾānan suyyirat bihi l-jibālu aw quṭṭiʿat bihi l-arḍu aw kullima bihi l-mawtā bal li-llāhi l-amru jamīʿan a-fa-lam yayʾasi lladhīna āmanū an law yashāʾu llāhu la-hadā n-nāsa jamīʿan …

This striking verse elicited various comments in the *tafsīr* literature. According to the view which later predominated, it is necessary to supply an understood meaning *la-kāna huwa hādhā l-Qurʾān* = "it would have been this Qurʾān" after *al-mawtā* as the apodosis of the conditional sentence beginning with *wa-law*. A different interpretation that may have been more popular earlier holds that rather the apodosis should be "they would not have believed," which seems better to fit the context.

The interpretation of this verse is further complicated by a dispute about the meaning of the verb *yayʾas* farther along in it. While its usual meaning is "to despair," later orthodox consensus averred that it meant "to know," and the somewhat convoluted explanations of how the latter view can be illustrate

14 Brooks & Warren, 390; Willis, 233.

15 Cited by ʿAskarī, 182; Bāqillānī, 262; Ibn al-Athīr, *Mathal*, II, 323; Ibn al-Athīr, *Jāmiʿ*, 136; Ibn an-Naqīb, 157; Ṭūfī, 192; Qazwīnī, 219; al-Muʾayyad bi-llāh, II, 62, III, 176; Zarkashī, III, 183–184, IV, 372.

that the exegetes had a problem with this, despite its orthodoxy.[16] As-Suyūṭī, for example, suggests that *yay'as* meant "to know" in two different Arabic dialects, which is a plausible but unprovable explanation.[17] A more radical suggestion as-Suyūṭī cites from Ibn ʿAbbās, however, suggests that the text originally instead must have read *yatabayyan*, meaning "to seek to clarify" or "to investigate," which, though quite a different word, is close to having the same consonantal outline in Arabic as *yay'as*.[18] This emendation of the text is supported by Devin Stewart, who views it as more reasonable.[19] However, while this emendation may seem superior to the meaning "to despair," it does not seem really to fit all that well either, and it could never be proven that it was the original wording. Thus, we are left with the *textus receptus* followed by our translators. All the translators except Bell render *yay'as* as "to know" or some variant thereof, while Bell has "despair."

This background may help to explain the English translations of the verse. For his part, Bell again has cleft the verse in two, claiming that the latter part was added to the original protasis later, and that the whole is a reflection of the despair of the Prophet's followers:[20]

> Though
> (270) 30. if only by a qur'ān the mountains had been moved, or the earth been cleft, or the dead been spoken to .... Nay, but the
> affair is entirely in Allah's hands; have not then those who have believed fallen into despair that if Allah were so to will He would guide the people in a body?

His interpretation of *yay'as*, rendered according to the most common use of the word as "fallen into despair," means that the believers have despaired that Allah has not guided the people altogether to accept Islam, in which case the context of the revelation might be a period of stagnation in the

16 Ṭabarī, XIII, 101–104; Zamakhsharī, II, 530; Bayḍāwī, III, 188; Jalāl ad-Dīn ʿAbd ar-Raḥmān b. Abī Bakr as-Suyūṭī, (849–911/1445–1505), *al-Itqān fī ʿulūm al-Qur'ān*, ed. by Muḥammad Abū al-Faḍl Ibrāhīm, Cairo: al-Hay'ah al-Miṣriyyah al-ʿĀmmah li-l-Kitāb, 1394/1974, Vol. II, p. 22.

17 Suyūṭī, *Itqān*, II, 70, 107.

18 Suyūṭī, *Itqān*, II, 327. The consonantal outline is not really the same either, however, as the Qur'ān has an additional alif which is not explained by the proposed emendation either.

19 Devin J. Stewart, "Notes on Medieval and Modern Emendations of the Qur'ān," in *The Qur'ān in Its Historical Context*, ed. by Gabriel Said Reynolds, London: Routledge, 2008, p. 231.

20 Bell, I, 232–233.

movement during the Makkan period. While this could explain the final part of the verse, the connection of the first "if" clause with the rest is certainly unclear, which also apparently reflects Bell's actual opinion that the text contains a jarring conflation of different pieces here, as indicated by his four dots. Thus Bell abandons the possibility that there is any coherent discourse here.

Arberry, on the other hand, shows us what results from trying to stick to the Arabic text literally according to the usual interpretation:

(271) If only a Koran whereby the mountains were set in motion, or the earth were cleft, or the dead were spoken to—nay, but God's is the affair altogether. Did not the believers know that, if God had willed, He would have guided men all together? …

Arberry thus maintains the "If only …" interpretation that Bell has, which appears at least to be grammatical because "If only …" with no apodosis is sometimes allowed as a complete sentence in English to express a wish, while omitting the "only" would make it sound incomplete. However, the classical Muslim interpretation of this verse as expressed by the exegetes cited above is contrary to interpreting the first clause as meaning "If only …," so that the translation does not convey the main Muslim understanding of this verse. Furthermore, Arberry's translation of the clause is also not acceptable even as an "If only …" clause expressing a wish because the word "Koran" is not provided with a verb. That is, it is still just a dangling protasis whose meaning remains unclear, as it is grammatically garbled, and hence there is no clear connection with what follows. Unlike Bell, Arberry follows the canonical interpretation of *yay'as* as meaning "know," but this does not really help, as it offers no clear guidance as to what the protasis is doing, nor is its own intent or implication discernable.

Muhammad Ali, like Arberry, uses a dash to separate the protasis from the rest of the verse:

(272) 31. And if there could be a Qur'ān with which mountains were made to pass away, or the earth were cloven asunder, or the dead were made to speak—nay, the commandment is wholly Allāh's. Do not those who believe know that, if Allāh please, He would certainly guide all the people?

Muhammad Ali's translation is somewhat similar to Arberry's, but he avoids the "If only …" interpretation. To render the dash more comprehensible to the reader, Muhammad Ali has provided a footnote in which he mentions the exegetes claiming that *la-kāna huwa hādhā l-Qur'ān* should be understood as an apodosis is unnecessary and wrong, because the following text contains the answer already, so that there is no omission in the text.[21]

Pickthall, on the other hand, with Yūsuf 'Alī doing similarly, completes the idea with a parenthetical gloss:

(273) 31. Had it been possible for a Lecture to cause the mountains to move, or the earth to be torn asunder, or the dead to speak, (this Qur'ān would have done so). Nay, but Allah's is the whole command. Do not those who believe know that, had Allah willed, He could have guided all mankind?

This translation, also avoiding the "If only …" interpretation, produces a comprehensible rendition of the conditional by including in parentheses the favored explanation of the classical commentators, but the effect obtained in the Arabic from omitting the apodosis is lost by including it in the translation. Pickthall also differentiates the hypothetical Qur'ān in the verse as "a Lecture," while describing the actual Qur'ān in his parenthetical insertion based on the classical exegetes as "this Qur'ān," whereas the Arabic uses *qur'ān* for both, in the first case indefinite and the second definite. Arabic usage is also lost here.

Using the other alternative for the missing apodosis, Muhammad Asad has:

(274) Yet even if [they should listen to] a [divine] discourse by which mountains could be moved, or the earth cleft asunder, or the dead made to speak—[they who are bent on denying the truth would still refuse to believe in it]!

Nay, but God alone has the power to decide what shall be. Have, then, they who have attained to faith not yet come to know that, had God so willed; He would indeed have guided all mankind aright?

Asad here has preferred the possibly earlier interpretation of the missing apodosis and has also separated the latter part of the verse by inserting an addi-

---

21 Muhammad Ali, 490–491, fn. 1280.

tional space. As usual, Asad is the wordiest and, like Muhammad Ali and Yūsuf ʿAlī, adds explanatory footnotes, which include a reference to Qurʾān 6:109–111 to back his interpretation.[22]

Dawood (1990) has striven more drastically to render the verse comprehensible in English without any parenthetical insertion:

(275) And even if there be a Koran that could move mountains, rend the earth asunder, and make the dead speak, surely all things are subject to God's will. Are the faithful unaware that, had He pleased, God could have guided all mankind?

Here, the second clause *bal li-llāhi l-amru jamīʿan* = "surely all things are subject to God's will" is made the apodosis of the *wa-law …* clause. While it still does not quite provide an expected answer to the conditional, it does show that even though the present Qurʾān has not accomplished any of the worldly miracles listed, God is nevertheless in charge of everything, and this fits nicely with the final clause as well.

Yet Dawood was unsatisfied with his work and tried in his 2014 version to follow the Arabic more closely by restoring the passives in the protasis:

(276) And even if there be a Koran whereby the mountains could be set in motion, the earth rent asunder, and the dead communed with, surely all things are subject to God's will. Are the faithful unaware that, had God pleased, He could have guided all mankind?

By replacing the active verbs with passive ones to mimic the Arabic, Dawood gets away from any implication that the Qurʾān itself would actually be doing the miracles rather than God. On the other hand, it does seem to bog down the nice flow of the 1990 version, and may detract from the reader immediately connecting the meaning of the apodosis to the protasis of the conditional.

But has Dawood, with all his smoothness, really represented the Arabic text here as well as the other translators, with their own respective distancing and flaws? His nice inclusion of the second clause as a seamless if not altogether obvious answer to the first clause is not validated by any of the Arabic exegetical tradition, all of which considers this to be a rhetorical device deviating from normal speech. The little word *bal*, which he has rendered as "surely," he has at least included in a way, but while in English "surely" functions as a smoothing

22 Asad, 408, fn. 54.

transition, in Arabic *bal* indicates a break in the flow of meaning, and is at least a more emphatic device than the almost inconspicuous "surely."

In the case of this verse, as we have seen, the translations differ a great deal from each other, some of which difference goes back to varying interpretations of the verse even in the Arabic. However, each translation of necessity represents a particular understanding of the verse which cuts off and eliminates other interpretations with quite arguable claims to validity as well. This is how translation tends inevitably to narrow the semantic ground of the original. Besides this, even with the best of intentions to produce a faithful translation and the greatest attempt to approximate an alien rhetoric, the English-language reader in the case of this verse may believe that the lacuna is caused by a predilection for a rambling, dangling style which is quite in contrast with the acclaimed Qurʾānic preference for brevity we have demonstrated above in numerous instances, included under *ījāz al-qiṣar*. And while Dawood may have addressed this particular caveat with some success, the result is nevertheless distanced from the original.

The omission of the result clause of a conditional as in 13:31 is far from rare in the Qurʾān. Examples of similar verses include 39:73, which contains a long dangling protasis without apodosis, though the parallel verse of 39:71, contains a complete conditional. Also, surah 84:1–5, may be taken as an example of this kind of *ḥadhf*, while 81:1–14, and 82:1–6 contain complete conditionals of similar form.

Omission of a different kind is demonstrated when part of a comparison is left out in verse 57:10:[23]

(277) lā yastawī minkum man anfaqa min qabli l-fatḥi wa-qātala ulāʾika aʿẓamu darajatan min alladhīna anfaqū min baʿdu wa-qātalū …

The second half of the comparison is omitted because of its obviousness.[24] However, despite the clarity of the Arabic, where no confusion between *man anfaqa min qabli l-fatḥi* and *qātala* is possible because of the lack of a repetition of *man*, in English this is not the case. Arberry gives for instance:

(278) Not equal is he among you who spent, and who fought before the victory; those are mightier in rank than they who spent and fought afterwards.

23 Cited by Ibn al-Athīr, *Mathal*, II, 287–288; Ibn al-Athīr, *Jāmiʿ*, 126; Ṭūfī, 183; Qazwīnī, 220; Bībānī, 96.

24 Zamakhsharī, IV, 474.

In Arabic, repeating "than they who spent and fought afterwards" before the semicolon would introduce a needless repetition that would also be monotonous in English. But its absence in the latter tongue leads to a possible confusion of first considering "he among you who spent" and "who fought" as being the unequal parties to the comparison. As "who spent" and "who fought" appear to form two distinct categories, while "Not equal" demands a comparison, it appears that these two are being compared, rather than both together being only one half of the comparison. Thus, it appears likely the reader will pause for a moment, especially as he continues into the next line and discovers about whom the comparison was originally made. The ambiguity might have been lessened or avoided by omitting the second "who," which is actually not found in the Arabic text.

Very much like Arberry in this case, Bell has not tried to do anything to prevent the ambiguity:

(279) Those of you who contributed and fought before the clearing-up are not on the same level: they are mightier in rank than those who have contributed and fought afterward—...

There is no reason any native speaker of English should be able to unravel this without considerable thought. First we find, "Those ... who contributed and fought ... are not on the same level." After that, "they" is ambiguous, and only by comparing the first "contributed and fought" with the second can the structure of the original be guessed at. On the other hand, Pickthall's parenthetical insertion again prevents confusion at the cost of erasing the ellipsis of the original:

(280) Those who spent and fought before the victory are not upon a level (with the rest of you). Such are greater in rank than those who spent and fought afterwards.

Dawood (2014) goes even farther, drastically altering the sentence:

(281) Those of you that gave before the victory, and took part in the fighting, shall receive greater honour than those who gave and fought thereafter.

Here Dawood abandons the Arabic negative for a direct, positive declaration. This eliminates any ambiguity in the English by radically transforming the sentence and is certainly a domesticating move toward the alleged and cherished directness of English.

So it would seem in this case that all the translations pay some price of distancing themselves from the original by various devices: leaving the ambiguity in the English with some unclarity, inserting an unmarked interpolation, using a parenthetical insertion to complete the meaning, or completely reordering the sentence.

A clearer example of this difficulty is provided by 39:22:[25]

(282) a-fa-man sharaḥa llāhu ṣadrahu li-l-islāmi fa-huwa ʿalā nūrin min rabbihi fa-waylun li-l-qāsiyati qulūbuhum min dhikri llāhi …

Again the second half of a comparison is omitted, but this time it is more difficult to convey the meaning into English in an acceptable way, as we could do somewhat in the preceding example (277) by merely omitting the second "who" in Arberry's translation. That is because the comparative word "equal" is present there; here, no words indicate the comparison, which is nevertheless inferred from the words that follow it.[26]

In this case, Arberry translates:

(283) Is he whose breast God has expanded unto Islam, so he walks in a light from his Lord …? But woe to those whose hearts are hardened against the remembrance of God!

In English, there is no reason the reader should be able to determine that the first part of this verse is the subject clause of a comparison, except perhaps by inference from the following words dealing with the other party to it. Even Arberry is perturbed enough by this to trail off into the ellipsis indicated by three points. Like Arberry, Bell adds three dots to mark the separation, while Muhammad Ali has a dash. None add any interpolations or insertions to their texts. This is another case where the reader is likely to gather an impression from the translations of the Qurʾān of rambling style, as in the translations of 13:31 (269) above, or alternatively that the text is even incomplete. While in (277) the question "Equal to whom?" may come to the reader's mind, in this case he may ask "Is he what?" about he whose breast Allah has expanded towards Islam, thus not even perceiving the comparison.

As is his wont, Pickthall fills in the lacunae with parenthetical additions, as do Yūsuf ʿAlī and Muhammad Asad. Pickthall reads:

25 Cited by Ibn al-Athīr, *Mathal*, II, 287; Ibn al-Athīr, *Jāmiʿ*, 126; Zarkashī, II, 185, III, 139.

26 Bayḍāwī, V, 40.

(284) 22. Is he whose bosom Allah hath expanded for the Surrender (unto Him), so that he followeth a light from His Lord, (as he who disbelieveth)? Then woe unto those whose hearts are hardened against remembrance of Allah.

We need only observe that the second sentence of this, with its transitional "Then," hardly follows the first sentence with the parenthetical addition any better than does Arberry's version without that aid, although the literal meaning of each separate sentence in Pickthall is clear. This may be because the second sentence in the Arabic has something to do with compensating for the ellipsis in the first. It may be that this verse is a case where either the original rhetorical pattern or a good deal of the clarity of meaning must be given up by the translator, though the one he chooses may not come across too clearly either.

Dawood (2014) stands alone again, solving the problem by a radical revision of the syntax of the verse:

(285) He whose bosom God has opened to Islām shall receive light from his Lord. But woe betide those whose hearts are hardened against the remembrance of God!

Dawood has not only dispensed with the clearly expressed if rhetorical question of the Arabic, but reduced the originally coordinate "light" clause to a mere predicate for his sentence. This means that Dawood, in this case, after so many revisions, still did not find an English-language solution of readability in any translation adhering to the Arabic form and syntax.

In other cases in the Qur'ān, whole sentences might be left out, though never in such a way as to confuse the meaning. One example of such an omission of considerable proportions occurs inverse 12:45–46:[27]

(286) wa-qāla lladhī najā minhumā wa-iddakara baʿda ummatin ana unabbi'-ukum bi-ta'wīlihi fa-arsilūn.
Yūsufu ayyuhā ṣ-ṣiddīqu aftinā …

27 Cited by ʿAlī b. al-Ḥusayn al-Mūsawī al-ʿAlawī ash-Sharīf al-Murtaḍā, *Amālī l-Murtaḍā: Ghurar al-fawā'id wa-durar al-qalā'id*, ed. by Muḥammad Abū al-Faḍl Ibrāhīm, Cairo: Dār Iḥyā' al-Kutub al-ʿArabiyyah, ʿĪsā al-Bābī al-Ḥalabī, 1373/1954, Vol. II, p. 71; Ibn al-Athīr, *Mathal*, II, 303; Ibn al-Athīr, *Jāmiʿ*, 129; Hāshimī, 200.

Again, what has been omitted may not actually be necessary to help the reader across the jump in time, but something might be brought to mind to complete the meaning, as Pickthall has parenthetically inserted:

(287) 45. And he of the two who was released, and (now) at length remembered, said: I am going to announce unto you the interpretation, therefore send me forth.
46. (And when he came to Joseph in the prison, he exclaimed): Joseph! O thou truthful one! Expound for us ...

Pickthall's additions erase any doubts about the meaning. Arberry has, however, no such interpolations:

(288) Then said the one who had been delivered,
remembering after a time, 'I will
myself tell you its interpretation;
so send me forth.'

'Joseph, thou true man, pronounce to us
...'

Here, then, we must move from Pharaoh's palace to Joseph's prison without the aid of any transitional words, although Arberry provides a gap in the text to indicate the caesura. The thinking reader will certainly find crossing this possible. It is quite apparent that the speaker remains the same and that the second speaker is not Pharaoh or another. But the frequency of omitting direct reference to indicate the speaker of quoted speech passages in the Qur'ān is quite noticeable as in 16:51–52 (40) above and many others, and, as is seen here in (288), foreign to English rhetorical practices. This particular pair of verses is obscure in translation because of the other, different necessity of making a mental transition of place. It might be likened to a sudden change of scene in a film, but not to other literary genres.

To make this argument clearer, we shall take a passage which certainly is obscure in English translation, 38:41–44, which we will quote in full:

(289) wa-dhkur ʿabdanā Ayyūba idh nādā rabbahu annī massanī sh-shayṭānu bi-nuṣbin wa-ʿadhāb.
urkuḍ bi-rijlika hādhā mughtasalun bāridun wa-sharāb.
wa-wahabnā lahu ahlahu wa-mithlahum maʿahum raḥmatan minnā wa-dhikrā li-ulā l-albāb.

wa-khudh bi-yadika ḍighthan fa-ḍrib bihi wa-lā taḥnath innā wajad-
nāhu ṣābiran niʿma l-ʿabdu innahu awwāb.

The entire passage constitutes an independent semantic unit exclusively concerned with the prophet Job, just as other units in the surah are concerned with other prophets. Verses 42 and the first half of 44, apparently representing the speech of God to Job, though that is nowhere mentioned in the text, seem to constitute a clear case of Qurʾānic brevity, requiring some explanation in the exegeses.[28] The Arabic exegeses favor explaining the first part of verse 44, for example, as an expiation of Job's vow to beat his wife as she was more faithful to God than he; thus, he was to beat her once lightly with a bunch of grass or date stalks.[29] Yūsuf ʿAlī, on the other hand, points out that in the actual Job story of the Old Testament (see Job 2:9–10), Job's wife urged him to become an ingrate and hence deserved to be beaten.[30] Whatever the case, the reader is likely to find the English very abridged if no supporting insertions are made, as Arberry has:

(290) Remember also Our servant Job;
when he called to his Lord, 'Behold,
Satan has visited me with weariness
and chastisement.'
'Stamp thy foot! This is a laving-place
cool, and a drink.'
And we gave to him his family, and
the like of them with them, as a mercy
from us, and a reminder unto men
possessed of minds;
and, 'Take in thy hand a bundle of
rushes, and strike therewith, and do not
fail in thy oath.' Surely we found him
a steadfast man.
How excellent a servant he was!
He was a penitent.

The abbreviation of this passage by omissions occurs both between sentences and in them. The first transition, from "chastisement" to "stamp," similar to

28 Zamakhsharī, IV, 97–98.
29 Ibn Kathīr, VI, 69; Qurṭubī, XV, 212–213.
30 Yūsuf ʿAlī, 1227, fn. 4202.

the one in 19:24–26, is perhaps not so difficult to comprehend. But this connection, and also the relationship between "Stamp thy foot!" and what follows, explained for instance in az-Zamakhsharī,[31] would perhaps be lost on the native English-speaking reader, who might not mentally join up the different phrases, regarding them rather as unconnected in meaning, hence jumbled. But while he might be able to discern the reply of God to Job's pleading in the bursting forth of a spring from beneath his feet to refresh and purify him after his tribulations, the reader is much less likely to connect the second command from God here, "Take in thy hand …," without some helping words which are not required by the Arabic. There are other points of *ījāz* in the passage, as indicated by the various insertions made in Pickthall's rendition of it:

(291) 41. And make mention (O Muhammad) of Our bondman Job, when he cried unto his Lord (saying): Lo! the devil doth afflict me with distress and torment.

42. (And it was said unto him): Strike the ground with thy foot. This (spring) is a cool bath and a refreshing drink.

43. And we bestowed on him (again) his household and therewith the like thereof, a mercy from Us, and a memorial for men of understanding.

44. And (it was said unto him): Take in thine hand a branch and smite therewith, and break not thine oath. Lo! We found him steadfast, how excellent a slave! Lo! he was ever turning in repentance (to his Lord).

Here the inclusion of "again" in writing or at least understood in v. 43 is necessary to complete the meaning, as "giving" done a second time in English must be "giving back" or "giving again." The total impression given by the two English translations of this passage remains one of a very abbreviated story, although (291) is clearly more likely to be comprehensible to the reader than (290). Moreover, the meaning or intent of the first half of v. 44 remains unclear.

Another case that requires that an omitted sentence be understood to complete the meaning occurs in verses 8:7–8:[32]

31 Zamakhsharī, IV, 97–98.

32 Mentioned as a case of *ḥadhf* by Zamakhsharī, II, 200; Bībānī, 96. However, most other rhetorical commentary ignored this, dwelling instead on the evident repetition, but az-

(292) ... wa-yurīdu llāhu an yuḥiqqa l-ḥaqqa bi-kalimātihi wa-yaqṭaʿa dābira l-kāfirīn.
li-yuḥiqqa l-ḥaqqa wa-yubṭila l-bāṭila wa-law kariha l-mujrimūn.

The problem here is that the words *li-yuḥiqqa l-ḥaqqa* and what follows them form a dependent clause that depends on nothing visible. Az-Zamakhsharī not only observes that we must understand an omitted *faʿala dhālika mā faʿalahu illā lahumā* but insists that the omitted clause must be placed after the dependent clause in order to convey the meaning that "he did what he did" especially for this end.[33] The effect of all this in English, however, is not too lucid without interpolation, as in Arberry:

(293) ... but God was desiring to verify the truth
by his words, and to cut off the unbelievers
to the last remnant,
and that he might verify the truth and
prove untrue the untrue, though the sinners
were averse to it.

Here it seems we may take the dependent "that" clause with "desiring," which is not the case with the Arabic, as we have seen. This does not achieve a very clear effect in English considered by itself either, as two clauses containing "verify the truth" are now in parallel in a coordinated series, a redundancy, not to mention the possible oddness of using infinitives and then joining a relative "that" clause in place of a third infinitive, which, though stylistically objectionable in English, is accepted in Arabic and very frequent in the Qur'ān.

Pickthall's translation differs little:

(294) ... And Allah willed that He should cause the Truth to triumph by His words, and cut the root of the disbelievers;
8. That He might cause the Truth to triumph and bring vanity to naught, however much the guilty might oppose;

Zamakhsharī denies there is repetition, because the purposes of the two instances of the repeated phrase *yuḥiqqa l-ḥaqqa* are different. See also Ibn al-Athīr, *Mathal*, III, 5; Ibn al-Athīr, *Jāmiʿ*, 204; al-Mu'ayyad bi-llāh, II, 95.

33 Zamakhsharī, II, 200.

One difference, however, is that Pickthall has omitted the "and" before the second "that," replacing it with a semicolon, a subtle move to make it more readable. Now, the latter "that" clause might be taken as a repetitive appositive to the first. Even so, neither (293) nor (294) renders the meaning of the verses correctly according to the exegesis of az-Zamakhsharī, nor do they seem appropriate in English.

As usual, Dawood goes even farther to achieve seamless readability, especially in his 1990 version:

(295) He sought to fulfill His promise and to rout the unbelievers, so that Truth should triumph and falsehood be discomfited, though the wrongdoers wished otherwise.

In this case, Dawood has greatly abridged the Arabic, quite rewriting the original. He has rendered the repeated phrase *an yuḥiqqa l-ḥaqqa* and *li-yuḥiqqa l-ḥaqqa* in two different ways, as "to fulfill His promise" and "so that Truth should triumph," entirely erasing the parallel repetition of the Arabic. He has also made the second, dangling clause then subordinate to the first sentence, as a result clause. Thus, there is neither a hint of any ellipsis nor any repetition. Moreover, his translation makes sense and is easily comprehensible.

However, again, Dawood seems to have been troubled by the lack of adherence of his text to the original, so that his 2014 version contains a considerable revision trying to bring it back closer to the Arabic original:

(296) God wished to vindicate the Truth by His words and to rout the unbelievers; to vindicate the Truth and to render falsehood vain, though the transgressors wished otherwise.

Now Dawood has restored more of the Arabic and produced a text with its semicolon reminiscent of Pickthall's. In doing so, he has conceded readability in the interest of closeness to the text, as now he has what appears to be a kind of redundant repetition for emphasis. In any case, achieving equivalence even approximately seems impossible here.

A final example of Qurʾānic brevity involves the omission of a predicate of at least one word from verse 31:27:

(297) wa-law annamā fī l-arḍi min shajaratin aqlāmun wa-l-baḥru yamudduhu min baʿdihi sabʿatu abḥurin mā nafidat kalimātu llāhi …

There appears first of all to be no word *midād*,[34] or equivalent, meaning "ink" following *al-baḥru* to complete the meaning of the second clause as *aqlāmun* completes that of the first. But az-Zamakhsharī says that the presence of *yamudduhu*, of the same trilateral root as *midād*, renders the latter unnecessary, and this explanation is possible, although it seems odd to us now, because we do not know exactly what rhetorical expectations the original hearers of the Qur'ān might have had.[35] Beside the elided word for ink, words to the effect that "the trees and seas would be used up first" are not included, only that the words of Allah would not be finished, so that is another elision.[36] Then, there are also the effects for emphasis created by the use of the singular *shajaratin* and the "plural of fewness" *kalimātu*[37] (compare with (169) above). No translation can be complete unless the meaning "with ink," is somehow included in *yamudduhu*, but the latter word does not necessarily include it, although, as mentioned above, the word "ink" comes from the same root as "to supply." Arberry's translation shows the result of an attempt to do without:

(298) Though all the trees in the earth were
pens, and the sea—seven seas after it
to replenish it,
yet would the Words of God not be spent.

Grammatically, this translation is defective, "the sea" being a dangling noun phrase without predicate. Semantically, "the" seems to be coordinate with "the trees," thus giving the meaning, "Though all the trees in the earth, and the sea, were pens …" which is of course incongruous. The clause beginning with "seven seas" also is dangling, like an *iʿtirāḍ* insertion in the English, although that is not its structure in the Arabic.

Bell's version avoids this latter objection:

(299) 26. If all the trees in the earth were pens, and the sea with seven seas after it to swell it, the words of Allah would not give out; …

---

34 That this is the omitted word is suggested by its occurrence in a parallel, similar verse, Qur'ān 18:109.

35 An alternative suggestion might be that the word *midād* has simply dropped from the text. That cannot be established with certainty, however, as all such scribal omissions are unprovable unless some evidence exists to prove them, and one is still left to explain the historical reality of the *textus receptus* which Muslims have always used and revered and which is our concern here.

36 Zamakhsharī, III, 501.

37 Zamakhsharī, III, 501.

We must note that Bell has added a footnote to this verse saying. "It seems necessary to supply 'were ink'."

Following Muhammad Ali, and followed as well by Yūsuf 'Alī, Pickthall includes those words, as is his usual practice, in parentheses in his text:

(300) 27. And if all the trees in the earth were pens, and the sea, with seven more seas to help it, (were ink), the words of Allah could not be exhausted.

While this is finally an adequate translation of the meaning of the text, the characteristic of abbreviation in the form of the original has had to be sacrificed to put that meaning across.

As usual, Dawood (2014, with 1990 almost the same) goes farther:

(301) If all the trees of the earth were pens, and the sea, replenished by seven other seas, were ink, the words of God could not be finished still.

This is very close to Pickthall, except that Dawood has omitted former's parentheses, thus interpolating "were ink" directly into the text with no indication that it is an addition not found in the Arabic.

Besides the problem of the ellipsis in this verse, there is also some loss in the translation of *annamā fī l-arḍi min shajaratin*, which according to az-Zamakhsharī bears an emphatic meaning conveying the consideration of each tree one by one.[38] This might rather be rendered something like "every single tree on earth," thus:

(302) And if every single tree on earth were made into pens ...

This would convey the idea of making every single tree on earth into innumerable pens, and would avoid the possible confusion implicit in (298), (299), (300), and (301) of producing a figure where each tree is considered a single pen, which would be ridiculous.[39]

---

38 Zamakhsharī, III, 501.

39 Dr. al-Nowaihi mentioned this possible misreading in 1975.

Conclusion

This concludes our examination of certain aspects of word order, *iltifāt* including apostrophe, use of indicative in place of imperative, indefinite nouns, *istithnāʾ munqaṭiʿ* or non-consequential exception, pleonasm and redundancy, repetition for emphasis, parallelism, juxtaposition of contrasting conditionals, coordination, lack of conjunctive, *iʿtirāḍ*, succinctness, and ellipsis. All these features are related more or less to the clear conveyance of the semantic meaning and as such are separate from style, although the frequency of their use may constitute an important element in an individual style. Some, perhaps most, of these features can be somewhat conveyed into English from the Arabic of the Qurʾān as we have seen, but others present difficulties.

Earlier, we indicated we would evaluate the verses we were going to consider in order to isolate those in which inherent rhetorical difficulties were at work from others which might present problems for other reasons. In our discussion above we have pointed to some of these other reasons, but now we shall enumerate them to ensure that we do not wrongly attribute every strangeness, confusion, or lack of elegance to rhetorical differences. Basically, as mentioned in the introduction, there are two factors other than the translated text itself, with its rhetorical features, that create the effect: the translator and the reader.

The effect of the translator on the translated text revolves around both his ability and attitudes, which must influence the result of his efforts and cause it to differ from the original however faithful a rendition he may wish to make. We must recognize that the translator may not have outstanding literary abilities himself, which may harm, or perhaps ruin, the result of his efforts, though he may, on the other hand, produce a work of good quality in its own right. However, it may be that the former possibility is the greater, because he must pay attention to the text he is obliged to follow, and, however much he might stray from it he will remain tied to it to a large extent. Thus, it is unlikely that he will produce something in the second language as great as, say, a poet writing in the idiom of his or her native tongue. Examples of this might be that no translated literature, perhaps other than the Bible, the Christian Holy Book, has reached the stature in reputation of Shakespeare in English or Dante in Italian, in spite of the fact that Shakespeare took the plots of many of his plays from Italian sources and Dante's idea of visiting heaven and hell evidently owed to predecessors in other languages. But both Shakespeare and Dante, not translating, took only ideas, and were hence free to express themselves as they chose in the idiom of their own language. Likewise, it must be recognized that the translator can never render a translation that will read as the original; also,

 | DOI:10.1163/9789004417441_017

it is likely to have more words because, as we have seen in the discussion of *ījāz al-qiṣar* above, the succinct locutions of one language that are most beautiful precisely because they sum up some truth or ideal briefly will probably often require exposition in the second language. Also, even if the excess verbiage can be reduced to a minimum, everything found in the original cannot be conveyed into the second language, for the translator will be forced to choose which effects to retain and which to drop, as in verses 7:131 (169) and 2:83 (189) above. It may be, as in the latter verse, that she will have to choose between the appearance of surface form, as Arberry did, and the effective conveyance of the meaning, as Pickthall did.

The translator also, we must remember, is only a human being of limited knowledge, and we must note particularly that she is not the same as the one who conceived the original. Thus, though the amount of her knowledge about it may vary, she cannot be aware of the conditions that gave rise to and witnessed the bringing into being of the original work as well as he who brought it out in the first place. This is especially true of a book as old as the Qurʾān, revealed fourteen centuries ago at a time now somewhat veiled from us by considerable controversy as to what was going on then. Be that as it may, it should still be possible for a translator to have some idea about what was occurring in the Prophet's lifetime, but if her knowledge is lacking on this point, it could have serious consequences for her translation. If she forgets that the Qurʾān is an oral text, as we have repeated above, she may err in her translation, as Bell has done in some cases of *iʿtirāḍ* (cf. 7:42 (222)), passing her error on to the reader. If she failed to understand the environment, milieu, or occasion of the original revelation, she may not convey the meaning as fully as possible, as Arberry has done in 2:222–223 (226), thus giving the reader a wrong impression. If she does not fully understand the grammar or rhetoric of the original language, as Bell has not in a number of examples, she may create unnecessary rhetorical problems in his translation. Above, we have noted that in the case of coordination, the insistence of more than one translator on rendering the coordinator *wa-* as "and" in English for the sake of literalness produces a result that is neither rhetorically beautiful in the translation nor faithful the original.

Also, we must remember that the attitude of the translator toward what he is translating is likely to produce a major effect on this work that does not come from the rhetoric of the original. Clearly, from the examples given, Bell's attitude towards the Book has caused him to give renderings that are at times quite at variance with the received Muslim understanding of the original, which, while quite possibly not the same as the Prophet Muhammad's understanding of it, nevertheless must be considered in a translation purporting to give the meaning as generally understood (see also 73:4–6, in Bell). Arberry, while perhaps not entertaining fixed preconceptions about the Qur'ān's history and composition in the way that Bell does, still does not have the vision of a believer. On the other hand, Pickthall wishes to convey the message of the Qur'ān in the best way possible in English. Yūsuf ʿAlī renders the monosyllabic word *rabb* as "Cherisher and Sustainer" in 1:2, hardly an equivalent of similar weight or semantic value. That no objective viewpoint exists is especially true with regard to the Qur'ān; one either believes it is a divine revelation or not. Furthermore, all of the translators being modern people, their work is bound to contain many modernisms, as indeed is the case.

On the other hand, despite all of these limitations that the translators' work is subject to, one has to acknowledge the general excellence of all seven translations considered here as literary products in English. Apart from Bell, all have been reprinted or republished in new editions, some numerous times, as readers have in effect acknowledged their excellence by continuously using, citing, and recommending them. And one would have to admit the excellence of Bell as well, as demonstrated frequently in the quotations from his work above.

The second major factor aside from the text is the reader himself, his or her knowledge, attitudes, and tastes. In some respects, these factors are parallel to those of the translator we have been discussing, but there are differences of emphasis. For example, while the translator may not realize that the Qur'ān is an oral text and that the feature of parenthesis or *iʿtirāḍ* is more common in the oral genre than in the literary ones, at least he will probably convey the feature in his translation in some way. But the reader, not understanding that what he is reading was first revealed and recited orally, may take the feature as evidence of confusion or rambling prose style. Likewise, not understanding the circumstances of the revelation of certain verses, like 2:222–223 (225) and 2:179 (238) may well prevent the English-speaking reader from sympathizing with their meaning, even if the translator has conveyed it into English with some accuracy. Indeed, the reader is far less likely than the translator to be acquainted with much of the cultural milieu of the original text. This is a factor in the domestication of foreign texts through translation and their assimilation into the culture of the receiving language, those distancing features emphasized by Venuti and others in translation studies. Readers will naturally prefer texts that are fluent, easy to read, and fulfilling of their own expectations, including rhetorical ones. Hence the great popularity of Dawood's translation in its various versions.

The reader's attitudes and tastes are also crucial factors determining how a given translation will affect her. If she is out of sympathy with a certain style, she may not enjoy anything resembling it. Many are the students who like cheap novels considered by critics to be "trash" but consider De Quincey, Carlyle, or Joyce boring because the style does not match their taste. It is entirely possible that a person who enjoys stories packed with action will have a pronounced distaste for a feature such as repetition, whether in the Qur'ān, the Old Testament, or classical English literature. Verses like 108:1–2 (36) in English might strike certain readers as pompous, as for the same reason, would many verses in the Old Testament like those we have quoted from Samuel (38). But this is a matter of taste rather than inequivalence of rhetorical devices, for, as we have pointed out, the same device does occur in English. This also can work the other way; the same feature and others might be very appealing to a reader with a taste for something biblical or exotic. Other Arabic rhetorical features like paired nouns at the end of verses might be appealing precisely because they are exotic in English. In such a case, rhetorical differences might help attract and hold the reader's interest rather than alienate her.

Another aspect of the reader's attitude that is important relates to his previous knowledge of what he is going to read and his feeling about it; of particular cogency to our discussion is his opinion about Islam. It is bound to make a good deal of difference in the majority of cases whether he approaches the book with the attitude of a believer, a neutral, or an opponent. The first of these probably will tend to overlook faults that he may come across, while the last may seek to discover faults that are not there, attributing them to imaginary reasons. This may explain, at least partly, why an English-speaking reader may reject certain rhetorical features in the Qur'ān, while he accepts identical or similar ones in the Bible. These may be external considerations we cannot be overly concerned with here, but we ought to keep them in mind to realize that there may be other barriers to understanding the translations besides insurmountable rhetorical differences.

Nevertheless, there remain certain weaknesses of expression in the translations which are attributable to differences of rhetorical features between the two languages, despite the best intentions of both the translator and the reader in trying to overcome them. Some influence only the effectiveness of expression; others may confuse the meaning itself. Some of the differences may be less reconcilable than others, especially those features of Arabic which entail constructions that are ungrammatical in English, though they are relatively few in number. We may now turn to the features listed in our discussions above which cause difficulty of one degree or another.

First among these are certain types of *iltifāt*, specifically those represented by verses 35:9 (49) and 10:22 (51). The first of these is strange and ambiguous in English, the latter strange and perhaps even ungrammatical. We might note that 36:22 (47), although somewhat less strange, might be a cause of difficulty to some readers and inevitably contains an ambiguity in English not found in the Arabic. The reason for the ambiguity is that *iltifāt* is of more restricted use in English, frequently connected in the examples we have seen to obligation in role relationships, whereas in Arabic it may be used for emphasis or to bring something to the immediate attention of the hearers or readers. In 10:22 (51), the verse graphically portrays what their predicament would be on such a stormy sea: by the shift from second person to third person plural, they are made to visualize what is happening to the others and could then draw their own conclusions or lessons from it. As there is no parallel feature in English in this instance, the translation becomes confusing at best. We have noted that in other cases of *iltifāt*, like 108:1–2 (36), there happens to be a correspondence with the English feature, so no problem results. But basically the concepts differ somewhat in the two languages; and difficulties arise where there is no English equivalent.

A second feature representing a real rhetorical difference appears to be that of *istithnāʾ munqaṭiʿ* or non-consequential exception. This form of emphasis may happen to agree, again, with the English exception rule, as in 74:38–39 (78), but 18:50 (87) appears to show a feature not found in English that would cause the English-speaking reader to pause, asking, "How can Iblis be of the jinn if he was one of the angels?" Indeed, the exegeses of both verses appear to indicate they may be taken in a number of ways, among them interpretations unlikely in English. We have seen, however, that verse 18:50 (87) can be rendered something like "The angels all fell prostrate, though Iblis, who was of the jinn, did not …," thus solving part of the problem. Alternatively, one might translate "however" or "nevertheless" in place of "except." Even so, we must consider this again a feature, though not frequent, which might give the English-speaking reader a feeling that there is strangeness or confusion in the text, because it still brings something portrayed as a kind of exception into juxtaposition with a general rule. As such, it is an emphatic device that is not easy to domesticate in English.

Third, we must make mention of pleonasm and repetition for emphasis of two kinds. That found in verse 2:98 (92), something like the reverse of non-consequential exception, includes the names of angels already included in the general term previously given in the same verse. This is without parallel in English, and, although easily understood, may give the reader an impression of a rambling, talky style, as though the speaker has forgotten what he just said. This, however, is relatively rare in the Qurʾān. Other cases of repetition of the same nouns, verbs, or phrases, as we have seen, are likely to produce a certain impression that may at times remind the reader of the Old Testament. Some repetition, like that of 55:7–9 (117) and 109:2–5 (126), may produce a feeling in some readers that it is overdone or monotonous. On the other hand, the kind of repetition for the subtle effect of understatement we have seen in 11:81 (106) is quite desirable in English. The overall effect of repetition in the Qurʾān including repetition of stories, may well seem to many readers to be overdone unless they remember that it is an oral text. In any event, however, unlike some aspects of *iltifāt* and *istithnāʾ munqaṭiʿ*, repetition for emphasis is at least a feature that is very present in English literature, oratory, and even conversation and therefore causes no insurmountable obstacle to understanding.

A fourth point of Arabic rhetoric in the Qurʾān that may seem strange or wordy when carried into English is the various sorts of parallelism. There are basically two kinds to consider; the first and perhaps most foreign to English is the use of paired nouns of similar but differing semantic intent, often at the end of a verse and in a place where one word would suffice. As we have seen, these may cause varying degrees of difficulty to the translator, particularly the *basmalah* of 1:1 and 27:30 (153) and at the beginning of the other surahs except Surah 9, because of the presence of two nouns of the same Arabic root for which there are no two similar words in English to translate them. The words *iktālū* and *kālū* of 83:1–3 (161) present a similar problem, where a feature giving a harmonious, pleasing effect in Arabic is lost in English. This loss also may occur in pairs in which the two nouns are of the same derivational pattern (33:72 (133)) or where they are nearly the same in meaning (16:7 (147)). But it must be granted as well that the mere pairing of two nouns without coordinator as in 83:12 (158) constitutes an alien rhetorical feature in English, though not necessarily unwelcome. Second, we may consider the general parallelism of such verses as 12:6 (166) and of even larger passages. This is a feature of like occurrence in the Old Testament, and, while it may produce the impression on the reader that what he is reading has a certain biblical flavor, it is certainly a feature known in some English, though out of fashion in contemporary works. It does not cause overwhelming difficulties to understanding and is not likely to be regarded as alien as much as the other kinds of Qurʾānic parallelism.

The fifth area of difficulty concerns coordination. An example of this is verse 2:83 (189), where Arberry's translation shows the impossibility of preserving everything in the original and the error of excessive literalness. Elsewhere the greater use of "and" in Arabic may produce a biblical effect like 12:6 (166), noted above. But we must also note two points: first, that this is a feature known, used, and accepted in English, only disliked in excess, and second, that, if too many "and's" occur in the English translations of the Qurʾān, it is more the fault of the translator for failing to find alternative means of expression than of underlying rhetorical differences between the two languages.

A sixth feature that appears to cause considerable difficulty at first is that of parenthesis or *iʿtirāḍ*. This item tends to be out of use in the English of today, but it must be remembered that it is essentially an oral, not a written feature, as evidenced by its increasing rareness as we move, say, from Shakespeare to the Old Testament to modern scientific writing, which is never meant to be presented orally, at least not for rhetorical effect. Hence, it is quite at home in the Qur'ān, and a little meditation on any particular instance of parenthesis there will show that it is usually rather connected with the thread of the passage, not an irrelevant insertion. Sometimes, the failure of the translator to understand or provide sufficient background may cause difficulty; elsewhere, as in 16:57 (211), idiomatic usage may be the source of trouble. We might also note that the feature known as *tadhyīl* can be very effective in English, as one could see in 21:34–35 (228) or 57:10, which present their meanings powerfully in some translations (see Pickthall).

Seventh, we must consider brevity or *ījāz al-qiṣar*, the short summing up of a complete thought in as few words as possible. This, the most idiomatic of the features we have discussed, may be impossible sometimes to convey in the full meaning of an instance of this feature except with glosses or footnotes that lose the original brevity, succinctness, and something of the rhetorical effectiveness. While it may be easy enough for Bell to convey the literal meaning of 15:94 (232) into English, even preserving the original image, the full meaning is not likely to be gathered by a reader not informed of the circumstances of the revelation. Others, like 55:1–4 (243) and 95:4–5 (249), surely lose much in translation or require extensive glosses as Bell and Yūsuf ʿAlī indeed give them. Yet, it is not that this feature is unknown in English; on the contrary, brevity packed with meaning is naturally admired, especially in literature, as for example in Macbeth's "sound and fury" speech, "It is a tale told by an idiot, full of sound and fury, signifying nothing," (Macbeth, Act V, Sc. 5, vv. 26–28). It is just that the idiom of one language cannot totally pass into the idiom of another, so what sounds excellent in one language may be silly, recondite or merely dull in another.

Finally, the eighth point of rhetoric most likely to cause difficulty to translators is ellipsis or *ījāz al-ḥadhf*, of which several types exist in the Qur'ān. This is perhaps the most apparent single feature of difference we have seen, as it often happens that the resulting translation in English is ungrammatical as well as incomprehensible. One typical kind of ellipsis is the omission of the apodosis of a conditional sentence. This is permissible in English with the sentences of the "if only" type expressing a wish, as in 32:12 (257), which thus causes little difficulty. But the use of the feature is much wider in the Arabic of the Qur'ān, as in 13:31 (269) or 36:45–46 (260), where there is no parallel in the English, so the result of any translation without a gloss to fill out the ellipsis is one of strangeness and confusion, not likely to appeal to the English speaking reader but rather likely to leave him with an impression of dangling, rambling style.

If, however, the lacuna is filled in with another sentence, though still not a real apodosis, as in 35:4 (266), the translation may be somewhat more acceptable. A second kind of ellipsis that may be even less acceptable in English is the omission of the second half of a comparison, as in 39:22 (282), where the reader will have to puzzle over a translation to divine the intent of the original and maybe readily excused for failing to do so. On the other hand, 57:10 (279) might be understood in English more readily, partly because the repetition of the full comparison in the second part of the verse makes it clear what is intended to be compared. Other omissions, such as the sentence of 12:45–46 (286) explaining where Pharaoh's cupbearer went, or the omission of sure mention of who is speaking in certain places, are also likely to cause difficulty in English. On the whole, it must be recognized that this feature is to achieve brevity and dramatic effect in the original and, while there are somewhat similar devices also with emphatic content in English like the "if only" protasis, they do not parallel the Arabic feature too closely. The semantic meaning may be carried or sometimes must be carried by parenthetical notes, but the original rhetorical device is lost.

In sum, we note that of the rhetorical features we have discussed, the most bizarre and foreign to English are those of less frequency in the Qur'ān. These features, certain points of *iltifāt*, non-consequential exception (*istithnāʾ munqaṭiʿ*), repetition of what has already been included in a general term, some kinds of ellipsis, and, perhaps, the idiomatic brevity of *ījāz al-qiṣar*, are those which sometimes cannot be rendered into English without creating constructions that are ungrammatical or at least unclear. Others, like paired refrain words at the end of verses, may or may not be translatable and may raise a similar problem, but, unlike those we have just mentioned, they may also produce a pleasing effect on an English-speaking reader who recognizes them as an exotic rhetorical feature. Certain features like parenthesis (*iʿtirāḍ*) represent a style of oral rhetoric, but could offend some readers, while they could also be effective. Features found in English such as repetition for emphasis, elaborate parallelism, and coordination in preference to subordination are only likely to be irritating in translations of the Qur'ān in that some readers may find them overdone, but they are not features fundamentally absent from English. It is just that the use of any of these to excess is discouraged in the kind of writing styles now in vogue.

Other features we have discussed seem to cause less difficulty, however, than these eight we have examined. Nevertheless, with the others, too, there may be some problems. Placement of prepositional phrase complements in the sentence, the parallelism of conditional sentences with differentiation for emphasis, the use of the indefinite noun, the use of the indicative for commands, negative and positive, and lack of conjunctive (*faṣl*) are all features that may be rendered into English with relatively minor rhetorical loss and whole semantic value.

Generally, we notice from these data that the points of rhetoric in the Qurʾān which we have discussed seem to exemplify the oral origin of Arabic rhetoric, while the lack of suitability of certain points in the English of the translations could indicate that modern English perhaps relies more on written, literary sources. This could account for the undesirability of features like certain kinds of ellipsis or parenthesis in contemporary written English. Also, it appears that the relative freedom of Arabic in certain respects, such as variant word order, compared to the more fixed order of English, is due to the presence of inflections according to case in the former language, which causes it to rely less on word order, for example, to determine meaning. This is certainly responsible for some of the differences in rhetorical devices between the two languages.

Finally, I hope that further research will be undertaken to make a complete classification of the different points of Arabic and English rhetoric and contrast the two systems fully. Another area requiring detailed examination by linguists and critics is the province of metaphor and simile, with a categorizing of any concrete rules for those that might be determined. Further, a classification of the system of semantic blocks of language used in the different languages would be beneficial. What are these in the Qurʾān and classical literature and how are they governed? In any case, we hope this study has contributed to an understanding of the problem of translation with some of its rhetorical aspects in however small a way.

Bibliography

ʿAbbās, Iḥsān (1339–1423/1920–2003). *Tārīkh an-naqd al-adabī ʿinda al-ʿarab: naqd ash-shiʿr min al-qarn ath-thānī ḥattā l-qarn ath-thāmin al-hijrī*. Beirut: Dār al-Amāna, 1391/1971.

ʿAbd al-Bāqī, Muḥammad Fuʾād (1299–1388/1882–1968). *al-Muʿjam al-mufahras li-alfāẓ al-Qurʾān al-karīm*. Cairo: Dār al-Ḥadīth, 1422/2001.

ʿAbd ar-Raḥmān, ʿĀʾishah, "Bint ash-Shāṭiʾ" (1331–1419/1913–1998). *at-Tafsīr al-bayānī li-l-Qurʾān al-karīm*. Cairo: Dār al-Maʿārif, 1990, 2 vols.

Abdel Haleem, Muhammad A.S. *Exploring the Qurʾan: Context and Impact*. London: I.B. Tauris, 2017.

Abdel Haleem, Muhammad A.S. "Grammatical Shift for Rhetorical Purposes: *Iltifat* and Related Features in the Qurʾan." *Bulletin of the School of Oriental and African Studies* 55, no. 3 (1992), 407–432.

Abdel Haleem, Muhammad A.S. *Understanding the Qurʾan: Themes and Style*. London: I.B. Tauris Publishers, 1999.

Abdul-Raof, Hussein. *Arabic Rhetoric: A Pragmatic Analysis*. London: Routledge, 2006.

Abdul-Raof, Hussein. *New Horizons in Qurʾanic Linguistics: A Syntactic, Semantic and Stylistic Analysis*. London: Routledge, 2018.

Abdul-Raof, Hussein. *Qurʾan Translation: Discourse, Texture and Exegesis*. Richmond, UK: Curzon Press, 2001.

Abdul-Raof, Hussein. "The Linguistic Architecture of the Qurʾan." *Journal of Qurʾanic Studies* 2 (2000), 37–51.

Abū ʿAlī al-Ḥasan b. Aḥmad al-Fārisī (288–377/900–987). *al-Īḍāḥ al-ʿAḍudī*. Ed. by Ḥasan Shādhilī Farhūd, n. p.: n. p., 1389/1969.

Abū Ḥayyān Muḥammad b. Yūsuf al-Gharnāṭī al-Andalusī (654–745/1256–1344). *at-Tadhyīl wa-t-takmīl fī sharḥ kitab at-tashīl*. Ed. by Ḥasan Hindāwī. Damascus: Dār al-Qalam, 1997–. At least 13 vols.

Abū al-Ḥusayn Isḥāq b. Ibrāhīm b. Sulaymān b. Wahb al-Kātib (d. after 335/946–947). *al-Burhān fī wujūh al-bayān*. Ed. by Aḥmad Maṭlūb and Khadījah al-Ḥadīthī. Baghdad: Maṭbaʿat al-ʿĀnī, 1387–1967.

Abū Mūsā, Muḥammad Muḥammad. *al-Balāghah al-qurʾāniyyah fī tafsīr az-Zamakhsharī wa-atharuhā fī d-dirāsāt al-balāghiyyah*. Cairo: Maktabat Wahbah, 1408/1988.

Alqurashi, Fahad. "Aljurjani Revisited: Creativity Explained through the Theory of Nazm (Construction)." *International Journal of Language and Literature*. 5 (2017), pp. 51–60.

Arberry, Arthur J. (1323–1389/1905–1969). *The Koran Interpreted*. London: George Allen & Unwin, Ltd., 1955. 2 vols. Another ed. London: Oxford University Press, 1964, rpt. 1972.

Aristotle (382–322 BCE). *On Rhetoric: A Theory of Civic Discourse*. Tr. by George A. Kennedy (b. 1928). 2nd ed. New York: Oxford University Press, 2007.

Asad, Muhammad (1318–1412/1900–1992). *The Message of the Qur'ān: The Full Account of the Revealed Arabic Text Accompanied by Parallel Translation*. Bristol, England: The Book Foundation, 2003.

al-ʿAskarī, Abū Hilāl al-Ḥasan b. ʿAbd Allāh (d. c. 400/c. 1010). *Kitāb aṣ-ṣināʿatayn: al-kitābah wa-sh-shiʿr*. Ed. by ʿAlī Muḥammad al-Bajāwī and Muḥammad Abū al-Faḍl Ibrāhīm. Cairo: Dār Iḥyāʾ al-Kutub al-ʿArabiyyah, ʿĪsā al-Bābī al-Ḥalabī, 1371/1952.

Badawī, Aḥmad Aḥmad. *ʿAbd al-Qāhir al-Jurjānī wa-juhūduhu fī l-balāghah al-ʿarabiyyah*. Cairo: al-Muʾassasah al-Miṣriyyah al-ʿĀmmah li-t-Taʾlīf wa-t-Tarjamah wa-ṭ-Ṭibāʿah wa-n-Nashr, 2nd printing, [1962].

al-Bāqillānī, Abū Bakr Muḥammad b. aṭ-Ṭayyib (c. 338–403/c. 950–1013). *Iʿjāz al-Qurʾān* (Dhakhāʾir al-ʿArab No. 12). Cairo: Dār al-Maʿārif, 1977.

al-Bayḍāwī, Nāṣir ad-Dīn Abū Saʿīd ʿAbd Allāh b. ʿUmar ash-Shīrāzī (d. 716/1316). *Anwār at-tanzīl wa-asrār at-taʾwīl*. Ed. by Muḥammad ʿAbd ar-Raḥmān al-Marʿashlī. Beirut: Dār Iḥyāʾ at-Turāth al-ʿArabī, 1418[/1997]. 5 vols.

Barnstone, Willis (b. 1346/1927). *The Poetics of Translation: History, Theory, Practice*. New Haven: Yale University Press, 1993.

Bell, Richard (1293–1371/1876–1952). *The Qurʾān Translated, with a Critical Re-arrangement of the Surahs*. Edinburgh: T. & T. Clark, 1937–1939. 2 vols.

Berman, Antoine. "Translation and the Trials of the Foreign." Tr. by Lawrence Venuti. In *The Translation Studies Reader*. Ed. by Lawrence Venuti. 2nd ed., New York: Routledge, 2004. Pp. 276–289.

al-Bībānī, Muḥammad [ʿAlī] al-Basyūnī (d. 1310/1892–1893). *Ḥusn aṣ-ṣanīʿ fī ʿilm al-maʿānī wa-l-bayān wa-l-badīʿ*. [Cairo]: Maṭbaʿat Dīwān ʿUmūm al-Maʿārif, 1301 [/1883].

Bonebakker, Seeger Adrianus (1923–2005), *Materials for the History of Arabic Rhetoric: from the Ḥilyat al-Muḥāḍara of Ḥātimī (Mss. 2934 and 590 of the Qarawiyyīn Mosque in Fez)*, Napoli: Istituto Orientale, 1975

Bonebakker, Seeger Adrianus (1923–2005). "Religious Prejudices against Poetry in Early Islam." *Medievalia et Humanistica: Studies in Medieval and Renaissance Culture* 7 (1976), 77–99.

Brooks, Cleanth (1906–1994), and Robert Penn Warren (1905–1989). *Modern Rhetoric*. 3rd ed. New York: Harcourt, Brace & World, 1970.

al-Bukhārī, Muḥammad b. Ismāʿīl (194–256/810–870). *The Translation of the Meanings of Sahīh al-Bukhārī: Arabic-English*. Translated by Muhammad Muhsin Khan (b. 1345/1927). Riyadh: Darussalam Publications, 1997. 9 vols.

Chowdhury, Safaruk Z. *Introducing Arabic Rhetoric*. New rev. & expanded [4th] ed. London: Dar al-Nicosia Publishing House, 2015.

Cuypers, Michel. "Semitic Rhetoric as a Key to the Question of the *naẓm* of the Qurʾanic Text." *Journal of Qurʾanic Studies* 13 (2011), 1–24.

Dawood, N[essim] J[oseph] (1346–1436/1927–2014). *The Koran*. 5th revised ed. London: Penguin Books, 1990. viii + 456 pp. Another ed: Extensively revised ed. [9th revised ed.]. London: Penguin Books, 2014.

Ḍayf, Shawqī (1328–1426/1910–2005). *al-Balāghah: taṭawwur wa-taʾrīkh*. Cairo: Dār al-Maʿārif, [1965].

Demetrius (fl. c. 200–50 BCE). *On Style*. In Aristotle. *Poetics*. Tr. by Doreen C. Innes, based on W. Rhys Roberts. Cambridge, MA: Harvard University Press (Loeb Classics 199), 1995. Pp. 309–525.

Dupriez, Bernard (b. 1352/1933). *A Dictionary of Literary Devices: Gradus, A–Z*. Tr. and adapted by Albert W. Halsall. Toronto: University of Toronto Press, 1991.

El-Awa, Salwa M.S. *Textual Relations in the Qurʾān: Relevance, Coherence and Structure*. London: Routledge, 2006.

Elimam, Ahmed Saleh. *Marked Word Order in the Qurān and Its English Translations: Patterns and Motivations*. Newcastle upon Tyne: Cambridge Scholars Publishing, 2013.

Encyclopaedia of Islam. 2nd ed. Edited by P.J. Bearman, Th. Bianquis, C.E. Bosworth, E. van Donzel, W.P. Heinrichs et al. Leiden: E.J. Brill, 1960–2005. 12 vols.

Encyclopaedia of Islam. 3rd ed. Edited by Kate Fleet, Gudrun Krämer, Denis Matringe, John Nawas, and Everett Rowson. Leiden: E.J. Brill, 2007–.

Enos, Theresa, ed. *The Encyclopedia of Rhetoric and Composition: Communication from Ancient Times to the Information Age*. New York: Routledge, 1996.

Everett, Caleb. *Linguistic Relativity: Evidence Across Languages and Cognitive Domains*. Berlin: De Gruyter Mouton, 2013.

Forster, E.M. (1879–1970). *A Passage to India*. London: Penguin Books, 1961. E-book 1969 rpt. of 1961 rev. ed.

Foster, Benjamin R. *Before the Muses: An Anthology of Akkadian Literature*. 3rd ed. Bethesda, MD: CDL Press, 2005.

Fremantle, Ann. *Loyal Enemy*. London: Hutchinson & Co., Ltd., 1938.

Gadamer, Hans-Georg (1318–1423/1900–2002). *Truth and Method*. 2nd rev. ed. Tr. by W. Glen-Doepel. Ed. by John Cumming and Garrett Barden. Translation rev. by Joel Weinsheimer and Donald G. Marshall. New York: Continuum, 1993.

Gould, Rebecca. "Inimitability versus Translatability: The Structure of Literary Meaning in Arabo-Persian Poetics." *The Translator*, 19 (2013), 81–104.

Hall, Edward T. (1914–2009). *The Silent Language*. Garden City, NY: Doubleday & Co., Inc., 1959.

Halldén, Philip. "What Is Arab Islamic Rhetoric? Rethinking the History of Muslim Oratory Art and Homiletics." *International Journal of Middle East Studies* 37, (2005), 19–38.

Hallo, William W. "Bilingualism and the Beginnings of Translation." in *Texts, Temples, and Traditions: A Tribute to Menahem Haran*. Ed. by Michael V. Fox et al. Winona Lake, IN: Eisenbrauns, 1996. Pp. 345–357.

Harb, Lara. "Form, Content, and the Inimitability of the Qurʾān in ʿAbd al-Qāhir al-Jurjānī's Works." *Middle Eastern Literatures* 18 (2015), 301–321.

Harb, Lara. "Poetics of Wonder: Aesthetic Experience in Classical Arabic Literary Theory," Ph.D. dissertation, New York University, 2014.

Harris, Robert A. *Writing with Clarity and Style: A Guide to Rhetorical Devices for Contemporary Writers*. 2nd ed. New York: Routledge, 2018.

al-Hāshimī, Aḥmad [b. Ibrāhīm b. Muṣṭafā] (1295–1362/1878–1943). *Jawāhir al-balāghah fī l-maʿānī wa-l-bayān wa-l-badīʿ*. Ed. by Yūsuf aṣ-Ṣumaylī. Beirut: al-Maktabah al-ʿAṣriyyah, [1999].

Hava, J.G. *al-Farāʾid ad-durriyyah ʿarabī-inklīzī: Al-Faraid Arabic-English Dictionary*, Beirut: Catholic Press, 1964.

Heinrichs, Wolfhart P. (1941–2014). "Contacts between Scriptural Hermeneutics and Literary Theory in Islam: The Case of Majaz." *Zeitschrift für Geschichte der Arabisch-Islamischen Wissenschaften* 7 (1991), 253–284.

Heinrichs, Wolfhart P. (1941–2014). "On the Figurative (*Majāz*) in Muslim Interpretation and Legal Hermeneutics." In Wolfhart P. Heinrichs, Mordechai Z. Cohen, and Adele Berlin, eds. *Interpreting Scriptures in Judaism, Christianity, and Islam: Overlapping Inquiries*, 2016. Pp. 249–265.

Al-Hilali, Muhammad Taqi-ud-Din (1311–1408/1893–1986), and Muhammad Muhsin Khan (b. 1345/1927). *Interpretation of the Meanings of the Noble Qur'an in the English Language: A Summarized Version of Al-Tabarî, Al-Qurtubî, and Ibn Kathîr with Comment from Sahîh-Al-Bukhârî, Summarized in One Volume*. 12th ed. Riyadh: Maktaba Dar-us-Salam, 1995.

Ḥusayn, Muḥammad Muḥammad (1330–1402/1912–1982). *Ittijāhāt haddāmah fī l-fikr al-ʿarabī al-muʿāṣir*. 2nd ed. Beirut: Dār al-Irshād, 1391/1971.

Ibn Abī al-Iṣbaʿ, Zakī ad-Dīn Abū Muḥammad ʿAbd al-ʿAẓīm b. ʿAbd al-Wāḥid al-ʿAdwānī (585–654/1189–1256). *Taḥrīr at-taḥbīr fī ṣināʿat ash-shiʿr wa-n-nathr wa-bayān iʿjāz al-Qurʾān*. Ed. by Ḥanafī Muḥammad Sharaf. Cairo: al-Majlis al-Aʿlā li-sh-Shuʾūn al-Islāmiyyah, Lajnat Iḥyāʾ at-Turāth al-Islāmī, [1383/1963].

Ibn al-Anbārī, Abū al-Barakāt Kamāl ad-Dīn ʿAbd ar-Raḥmān b. Muḥammad (513–577/1119–1181). *al-Inṣāf fī masāʾil al-khilāf bayn an-naḥwiyyīn al-Baṣriyyīn wa-l-Kūfiyyīn*. Beirut: al-Maktabah al-ʿAṣriyyah, 1424/2003. 2 vols.

Ibn al-Athīr, Abū al-Fatḥ Ḍiyāʾ ad-Dīn Naṣr Allāh b. Muḥammad (558–637/1163–1239). *al-Jāmiʿ al-kabīr fī ṣināʿat al-manẓūm min al-kalām wa-l-manthūr*. Ed. by Muṣṭafā Jawād (1905–1969). [Baghdad:] Maṭbaʿat al-Majmaʿ al-ʿIlmī, 1375[/1955–1956].

Ibn al-Athīr, Abū al-Fatḥ Ḍiyāʾ ad-Dīn Naṣr Allāh b. Muḥammad (558–637/1163–1239). *al-Mathal as-sāʾir fī adab al-kātib wa-sh-shāʿir*. Ed. by Aḥmad al-Ḥawfī and Badawī

Ṭabānah. Cairo: Dār Nahḍat Miṣr li-ṭ-Ṭibāʿah wa-n-Nashr wa-t-Tawzīʿ, 1379–1385/1959–1965. 4 vols.

Ibn Ḥazm, Abū Muḥammad ʿAlī b. Aḥmad (384–456/994–1064). *al-Iḥkām fī uṣūl al-aḥkām*. Ed. by Aḥmad Muḥammad Shākir. Beirut: Dār al-Āfāq al-Jadīdah, n. d., 8 vols.

Ibn Hishām al-Anṣārī, Jamāl ad-Dīn (d. 761/1360). *Mughnī al-labīb ʿan kutub al-aʿārīb*. Ed. Māzin al-Mubārak, Muḥammad ʿAlī Ḥamd Allāh, and Saʿīd al-Afghānī. Damascus: Dār al-Fikr, 1384/1964. 2 vols.

Ibn Kathīr, ʿImād ad-Dīn Abū al-Fidāʾ Ismāʿīl al-Qurashī (c. 701–774/c. 1300–1373). *Tafsir al-Qurʾān al-ʿaẓīm*. Beirut: Dār al-Fikr, 1389/1970. 7 vols.

Ibn Mālik, Badr ad-Dīn Muḥammad b. Jamāl ad-Dīn Muḥammad b. ʿAbd Allāh (c. 641–686/c. 1243–1287). *al-Miṣbāḥ fī l-maʿānī wa-l-bayān wa-l-badīʿ*. Ed. by Ḥusnī ʿAbd al-Jalīl Yūsuf. Cairo: Maktabat al-Ādāb, [1989].

Ibn al-Muʿtazz, Abū al-ʿAbbās ʿAbd Allāh b. Muḥammad (247–296/861–908). *Kitāb al-badīʿ*. Ed. by ʿIrfān Maṭrajī. Beirut: Muʾassasat al-Kutub ath-Thiqāfiyyah, 1433/2012.

Ibn an-Naqīb, Muhammad b. Sulaymān al-Balkhī al-Maqdisī (611–698/1214–1298). *Muqaddimat Tafsīr Ibn an-Naqīb fī ʿilm al-bayān wa-l-maʿānī wa-l-badīʿ wa-iʿjāz al-Qurʾān*. Ed. by Zakariyyā Saʿīd ʿAlī. Cairo: Maktabat al-Khānjī, 1415/1995.

Ibn Qutaybah, Abū Muḥammad ʿAbd Allāh b. Muslim (213–276/828–889). *Taʾwīl mushkil al-Qurʾān*. Ed. by as-Sayyid Aḥmad Ṣaqr. Cairo: Dār at-Turāth, 1393/1973. 2 vols. with single pagination. Another ed. Beirut: Dār al-Kutub al-ʿIlmiyyah, n. d.

Ibn as-Sarrāj, Abū Bakr Muḥammad b. al-Sarī (d. 316/929). *al-Uṣūl fī n-naḥw*. Ed. by ʿAbd al-Ḥusayn al-Fatlī. Beirut: Muʾassasat ar-Risālah, [1973?]. 3 vols.

Ihsanoglu, Ekmeleddin, ed. *World Bibliography of Translations of the Meanings of the Holy Qurʾan: Printed Translations, 1515–1980*. Istanbul: O.I.C. research Centre for Islamic History, Art and Culture, 1406/1986.

Jacobs, Roderick A. *Studies in Language: Introductory Readings in Transformational Linguistics*. Lexington, MA: Xerox College Publishing, 1979.

Jenssen, Herbjørn, *The Subtleties and Secrets of the Arabic Language: Preliminary Investigations into al-Qazwīnī's Talkhīṣ al-miftāḥ*. Bergen: Centre for Middle Eastern and Islamic Studies, University of Bergen, Norway, 1998.

Jerome (Eusebius Sophronius Hieronymus, 347–420). "Letter to Pammachius." Translated by Kathleen Davis. In Lawrence Venuti, ed. *The Translation Studies Reader*. 3rd ed. New York, Routledge, 2012. Pp. 21–30.

Johns, A.H. "A Humanistic Approach to *iʿjāz* in the Qurʾan: The Transfiguration of Language." *Journal of Qurʾanic Studies* 13 (2011), 79–99.

al-Jurjānī, Abū Bakr ʿAbd al-Qāhir b. ʿAbd ar-Raḥmān (d. 471/1079 or 474/1081). *Dalāʾil al-iʿjāz*. ed. by Maḥmūd Muḥammad Shākir. 3rd ed. Cairo: Maṭbaʿat al-Madanī, 1413/1992.

Kaplan, Robert B. (b. 1929), *The Anatomy of Rhetoric: Prolegomena to a Functional The-*

ory of Rhetoric: Essays for Teachers. Philadelphia, PA: The Center for Curriculum Development, Inc., 1972.

Kidwai, Abdur Raheem. *Bibliography of the Translations of the Meanings of the Glorious Qur'an into English, 1649–2002: A Critical Study*. Madinah: King Fahd Qur'an Printing Complex, 2007 (©2005).

Kidwai, Abdur Raheem. *God's Word, Man's Interpretations: A Critical Study of the 21st Century English Translations of the Quran*. New Delhi: Viva Books, 2018.

Kidwai, Abdur Raheem. "Muhammad Marmaduke Pickthall's English Translation of the Quran (1930): An Assessment." In *Marmaduke Pickthall: Islam and the Modern World*. Edited by Geoffrey P. Nash. Leiden: E.J. Brill, 2017. Pp. 231–248.

Kidwai, Abdur Raheem. *Translating the Untranslatable: A Critical Guide to 60 English Translations of the Quran*. 1st ed. New Delhi: Sarup Book Publishers Pvt., 2011.

Lane, Edward William (1216–1293/1801–1876). *Arabic-English Lexicon*. Ed. and completed by Stanley Lane-Poole. Reprint Cambridge, UK: Islamic Texts Society, 1984. 2 vols. xxxii + 3064 pp. Original London: Williams and Norgate, 1863–1893. 8 vols.

Large, Duncan, Motoko Akashi, Wanda Józwikowska, and Emily Rose, eds. *Untranslatability: Interdisciplinary Perspectives*. New York: Routledge, 2019.

Larkin, Margaret. "The Inimitability of the Qur'an: Two Perspectives" *Religion and Literature* 20, No. 1 (Spring, 1988) 31–47.

Larkin, Margaret. *The Theology of Meaning: ʿAbd al-Qāhir al-Jurjānī's Theory of Discourse* (American Oriental Series, Vol. 79). New Haven: American Oriental Society, 1995.

Lawrence, Bruce. *The Koran in English: A Biography*. Princeton: Princeton University Press, 2017.

Lester, Mark. *Introductory Transformational Grammar of English*. New York: Holt, Rinehart and Winston, Inc., 1971.

Lewis, Philip E. "The Measure of Translation Effects," in *The Translation Studies Reader*, Lawrence Venuti, ed., 3rd ed., London: Routledge, 2012, pp. 220–239.

Levine, Suzanne Jill, and Katie Lateef-Jan, eds. *Untranslatability Goes Global*. New York: Routledge, 2018.

Longinus (1st cent. CE). *On the Sublime*. In Aristotle. *Poetics*. Pp. 143–307. Ed. and tr. by W. Hamilton Fyfe. Rev. by Donald Russell. Cambridge, MA: Harvard University Press (Loeb Classics 199), 1995.

Lyons, John (b. 1351/1932). *Linguistic Semantics: An Introduction*. Cambridge, UK: Cambridge University Press, 1995.

Mack, Peter. *Rhetoric's Questions, Reading and Interpretation*. London: Palgrave Macmillan, 2017.

Malcolm, Noel. "The 1649 English Translation of the Koran: Its Origins & Significance." *Journal of the Warburg and Courtauld Institutes* 75 (2012), 261–295.

McAuliffe, Jane Dammen, ed. *Encyclopedia of the Qurʾān*. Leiden: E.J. Brill, 2001–2006. 7 vols.

McAuliffe, Jane Dammen, ed. *The Qur'ān: A Revised Translation; Origins; Interpretations and Analysis; Sounds, Sights, and Remedies; the Qur'ān in America*. New York: W.W. Norton & Co., 2017.

Mehren, August Ferdinand (1822–1907). *Die rhetorik der Araber nach den wichtigsten quellen dargestellt*. Copenhagen: Otto Schwartz, 1853.

Mir, Mustansir (b. 1368/1949). "Between Grammar and Rhetoric (*Balaghah*): A Look at Qur'an 2:217," *Islamic Studies* 29 (1990), 277–285.

Mir, Mustansir (b. 1368/1949). *Coherence in the Qur'ān: A Study of Islāhī's Concept of Nazm in Tadabbur-i Qur'ān*. Indianapolis: American Trust Publications, 1406/1986.

Mir, Mustansir (b. 1368/1949). "Irony in the Qur'an: A Study of the Story of Joseph." In Issa J. Boullata, ed. *Literary Structures of Religious Meaning in the Qur'an*. Richmond, Surrey, England: Curzon, 2000. Pp. 173–187.

Mir, Mustansir (b. 1368/1949). "Some Figures of Speech in the Qur'an," Religion & Literature, 40 (2008), 31–48.

Mir, Mustansir (b. 1368/1949). *Understanding Islamic Scripture: A Study of Selected Passages from the Qur'ān*. New York: Longman, 2008.

al-Mu'ayyad bi-llāh, Yaḥyā b. Ḥamzah al-Ḥusaynī al-ʿAlawī aṭ-Ṭālibī (d. 745/1344–1345). *aṭ-Ṭirāz li-asrār al-balāghah wa-ʿulūm ḥaqā'iq al-iʿjāz*. Beirut: al-Maktabah al-ʿAṣriyyah, 1425[/2004]. 3 vols.

Muhammad Ali (1293–1370/1876–1951). *The Holy Qur'ān: Arabic Text, English Translation and Commentary*. 7th ed. Chicago: Specialty Promotions Co., Inc., 1985.

Muslim b. al-Ḥajjāj al-Qushayrī an-Naysabūrī, Abū al-Ḥusayn (c. 206–261/c. 821–875). *al-Musnad aṣ-ṣaḥīḥ al-mukhtaṣar bi-naql al-ʿadl ʿan al-ʿadl ilā rasūl Allāh* (SAAS). Ed by Muḥammad Fu'ād ʿAbd al-Bāqī. Beirut: Dār Iḥyā' at-Turāth al-ʿArabī, 1970 (originally 1955–1956). 5 vols.

an-Nābulsī, ʿAbd al-Ghanī (1050–1143/1641–1731). *The Arch Rhetorician: or The Schemer's Skimmer: A Handbook of Late Arabic Badīʿ Drawn from ʿAbd al-Ghanī an-Nābulsī's Nafaḥāt al-azhār ʿala nasamāt al-asḥār*. Tr. by Pierre Cachia. Wiesbaden: Harrassowitz, 1998.

an-Naysābūrī, Niẓām ad-Dīn al-Ḥasan b. Muḥammad. *Tafsīr gharā'ib al-Qur'ān wa-raghā'ib al-furqān*. On the margin of Abū Jaʿfar Muḥammad b. Jarīr aṭ-Ṭabarī. *Jāmiʿ al-bayān fī tafsīr al-Qur'ān*. Būlāq: al-Maṭbaʿah al-Kubrā al-Amīriyyah, 1323–1329. 30 volumes.

Noy, Avigail. "The Emergence of ʿIlm al-Bayān: Classical Arabic Literary Theory in the Arabic East in the 7th/13th Century." Ph.D. dissertation. Harvard University, 2016.

an-Nuwayrī, Shihāb ad-Dīn Aḥmad b. ʿAbd al-Wahhāb (677–733/1279–1333). *Nihāyat al-arab fī funūn al-adab*. Cairo: Dār al-Kutub wa-l-Wathā'iq al-Qawmiyyah, 1423[/2002]. 33 vols.

Pickthall, Mohammed Marmaduke (1292–1355/1875–1936). *The Meaning of the Glorious Koran*. London: George Allen & Unwin, 2nd impression, 1948.

al-Qazwīnī, Jalāl ad-Dīn Muḥammad b. ʿAbd ar-Raḥmān al-Khaṭīb (666–739/1268–1338). *al-Īḍāḥ fī ʿulūm al-balāghah: al-maʿānī wa-l-bayān wa-l-badīʿ*. Ed. ʿAbd al-Qādir Ḥusayn. 1st ed. Cairo: Maktabat al-Ādāb. 1416/1996.

Quintilian (c. 35–c. 95 CE). *The Orator's Education*. Ed. and tr. by Donald A. Russell. Cambridge, MA: Harvard University Press (Loeb Classics), 2001. 5 vols.

al-Qurṭubī, Abū ʿAbd Allāh Muḥammad b. Aḥmad al-Anṣārī (d. 671/1273). *al-Jāmiʿ li-aḥkām al-Qurʾān*. Cairo: Dār al-Kitāb al-ʿArabī li-ṭ-Ṭibāʿah wa-n-Nashr, 1387/1967. 20 vols.

Quṭb, Sayyid (1324–1386/1906–1966). *Fī ẓilāl al-Qurʾān*. Beirut: Dār ash-Shurūq, 1394/1974. 6 vols.

Quṭb, Sayyid (1324–1386/1906–1966). *at-Taṣwīr al-fannī fī l-Qurʾān*, Cairo: Dār al-Shurūq, 1993.

ar-Rāfiʿī, Muṣṭafā Ṣādiq (1298–1356/1880–1937). *Iʿjāz al-Qurʾān wa-l-balāghah an-nabawiyyah*. Beirut: al-Maktabah al-ʿAṣriyyah, 1424/2003 (originally published in 1926).

Reuschel, Wolfgang (1924–1991). 'Wa-kāna llāhu ʿalīman raḥīman', *Studia Orientalia in Memoriam Caroli Brockelmann* (Sonderausgabe der Wissenschaftlichen Zeitschrift der Martin-Luther-Universität Halle-Wittenberg, Gesellschafts- und sprachwissenschaftliche Reihe), Heft 2/3, Jahrgang XVII, 1968, pp. 147–153.

Rhetorica ad Herrenium: Ad C. Herrenium: De Ratione Dicendi (written c. 86–82 BCE). Ed. and tr. by Harry Caplan. Cambridge, MA: Harvard University Press (Loeb Classics), 1954.

Robinson, Douglas (b. 1954). *The Translator's Turn*. Baltimore: The Johns Hopkins University Press, 1991.

Robinson, Neal. *Discovering the Qur'an: A Contemporary Approach to a Veiled Text*. 2nd ed. Washington, DC: Georgetown University Press, 2003.

ar-Rummānī, Abū al-Ḥasan ʿAlī b. ʿĪsā (296–386/909–996). "an-Nukat fī iʿjāz al-Qurʾān." In *Thalāth rasāʾil fī iʿjāz al-Qurʾān li-r-Rummānī wa-l-Khattābī wa-ʿAbd al-Qāhir al-Jurjānī, fī d-dirāsāt al-qurʾāniyyah wa-n-naqd al-adabī*. Ed. by Muhammad Khalaf Allāh and Muhammad Zaghlūl Salām. 3rd ed. Cairo: Dār al-Maʿārif, [1976]. Pp. 73–113.

ar-Rummānī, Abū al-Ḥasan ʿAlī b. ʿĪsā, (296–386/909–996), Abū Sulaymān Ḥamd b. Muḥammad al-Khaṭṭābī, (319–388/931–998), and Abū Bakr ʿAbd al-Qāhir b. ʿAbd ar-Raḥmān al-Jurjānī (d. 471/1079 or 474/1081). *Three Treatises on the Iʿjāz of the Qurʾān: Qurʾanic Studies and Literary Criticism*. Ed. by Muḥammad Khalaf-Allāh Aḥmad and Muḥammad Zaghlūl Sallām. Tr. by Issa J. Boullata. Reviewed by Terri L. DeYoung. Reading, England: Garnet Publishing, 2014.

aṣ-Ṣaffār, Ibtisām Marhūn. *at-Taʿābīr al-qurʾāniyyah wa-l-bīʾah al-ʿarabiyyah fī mashāhid al-qiyāmah*. an-Najaf: Maṭbaʿat al-Adab, 1387/1967.

Al-Sahli, Abdullah S. "Non-canonical Word Order: Its Types and Rhetorical Purposes with Reference to Five English Translations of the Meanings of the Holy Qur'an." Ph.D. dissertation. Durham University, 1996.

as-Sakkākī, Abū Yaʿqūb Yūsuf b. Abī Bakr Muḥammad b. ʿAlī (555–626/1160–1229). *Miftāḥ al-ʿulūm*. 2nd ed. Ed. by Naʿīm Zarzūr. Beirut: Dār al-Kutub al-ʿIlmiyyah, 1407/1987.

Salama, Mohammad. *The Qurʾān and Modern Arabic Literary Criticism from Ṭāhā to Naṣr*. London, Bloomsbury Academic, 2018.

as-Samarrāʾī, Fāḍil Ṣāliḥ. *Maʿānī n-naḥw*. Amman: Dār al-Fikr li-ṭ-Ṭibāʿah wa-n-Nashr wa-t-Tawzīʿ, 1420/2000. 4 vols.

ash-Sharīf al-Murtaḍā, ʿAlī b. al-Ḥusayn al-Mūsawī al-ʿAlawī (355–436/966–1044). *Amālī l-Murtaḍā: Ghurar al-fawāʾid wa-durar al-qalāʾid*. Ed. by Muḥammad Abū al-Faḍl Ibrāhīm. Cairo: Dār Iḥyāʾ al-Kutub al-ʿArabiyyah, ʿĪsā al-Bābī al-Ḥalabī, 1373/1954. 2 vols.

ash-Shāṭibī, Abū Isḥāq Ibrāhīm b. Mūsā al-Lakhmī (c. 730–790/c. 1330–1388). *al-Muwāfaqāt fī uṣūl al-aḥkām*. Ed. Muḥammad al-Khiḍr Ḥusayn at-Tūnisī. Cairo: Dār Iḥyāʾ al-Kutub al-ʿArabiyyah (Fayṣal ʿIsā al-Bābī al-Ḥalabī), [1969–1970]. 4 vols. in 2.

Sībawayh, Abū Bishr ʿAmr b. ʿUthmān b. Qanbar (c. 143–c. 180/c. 760–c. 796). *Kitāb Sībawayh*. Ed. by ʿAbd as-Salām Muḥammad Hārūn. Cairo: Maktabat al-Khānjī, 1408/1988. 4 vols.

as-Sīrāfī, Abū Saʿīd al-Ḥasan b. ʿAbd Allāh b. al-Marzubān (294–368/897–979). *Sharḥ kitab Sībawayh*. Ed. by Aḥmad Ḥasan Mahdalī and ʿAlī Sayyid ʿAlī. Beirut: Dār al-Kutub al-ʿIlmiyyah, 2008. 5 vols.

as-Sīrāfī, Yūsuf b. Abī Saʿīd al-Ḥasan (330–385/c. 942–995). *Sharḥ abyāt Sībawayh*. Ed. by Muḥammad ʿAlī ar-Rīḥ Hāshim. Cairo: Maktabat al-Kulliyāt al-Azhariyyah, 1394/1974. 2 vols.

Skreslet, Paula Youngman, and Rebecca Skreslet. *The Literature of Islam: A Guide to the Primary Sources in English Translation*. Lanham, MD: The Scarecrow Press, Inc. and American Theological Library Association, 2006.

Smyth, William. "Criticism in the Post-Classical Period: A Survey." In *Arabic Literature in the Post-Classical Period*. Ed. by Roger Allen and D.S. Richards. Cambridge: Cambridge University Press, 2008. Pp. 387–417.

Steiner, George (b. 1348/1929). *After Babel: Aspects of Language and Translation*. 3nd ed. Oxford: Oxford University Press, 1998.

Stewart, Devin J. "Divine Epithets and the *Dibacchius*: *Clausulae* and Qurʾanic Rhythm." *Journal of Qurʾanic Studies* 15.2 (2013), 22–64.

Stewart, Devin J. "Notes on Medieval and Modern Emendations of the Qurʾān." In *The Qurʾān in Its Historical Context*. Ed. by Gabriel Said Reynolds. London: Routledge, 2008. Pp. 225–248.

Stewart, Devin J. "Poetic License in the Qurʾan: Ibn al-Saʾigh al-Ḥanafi's *Ihkam al-Ray fi Ahkam al-Ay*." *Journal of Qurʾanic Studies* 11.1 (2009), 1–54.

Stewart, Devin J. "*Sajʿ* in the Qurʾan: Prosody and Structure." *Journal of Arabic Literature* 21 (1990), 101–139.

Stewart, Devin J. "The Cognate Curse in the Qur'an." *Journal of the International Qur'anic Studies Association* 2 (2017), 47–87, here pp. 74–75.

Stewart, Devin J. "Understanding the Koran in English: Notes on Translation, Form, and Prophetic Typology." In Zeinab Ibrahim, Nagwa Kasabgy, and Sabiha Aydelott, eds. *Diversity in Language: Contrastive Studies in English and Arabic Theoretical and Applied Linguistics*. Cairo: American University in Cairo Press, 2000. Pp. 31–48.

Strunk, William Jr. (1869–1946), and E.B. White (1899–1985). *The Elements of Style*. 4th ed. New York: Pearson Education, Inc., 2009.

Sulaymān, Muḥammad. *Ḥadath al-aḥdāth fī l-Islām: al-iqdām ʿalā tarjamat al-Qurʾān*. Cairo: al-Maṭbaʿah as-Salafiyyah, 1355/1936.

Suleiman, Yasir. *Arabic in the Fray: Language Ideology and Cultural Politics*. Edinburgh: Edinburgh University Press, 2013.

as-Suyūṭī, Jalāl ad-Dīn ʿAbd ar-Raḥmān b. Abī Bakr, (849–911/1445–1505). *al-Itqān fī ʿulūm al-Qurʾān*. Ed. by Muḥammad Abū al-Faḍl Ibrāhīm. Cairo: al-Hayʾah al-Miṣriyyah al-ʿĀmmah li-l-Kitāb, 1394/1974. 4 vols.

Ṭabānah, Badawī [Aḥmad] (1332–at least 1418/1914–at least 1997). *al-Bayān al-ʿarabī: dirāsah fī taṭawwur al-fikrah al-balāghiyyah ʿind al-ʾArab wa-manāhijuhā wa-maṣādiruhā l-kubrā*. 4th ed. Cairo: Maktabat al-Anjlū al-Miṣriyyah, 1388/1968.

Ṭabānah, Badawī [Aḥmad] (1332–at least 1418/1914–at least 1997). *Muʿjam al-balāghah*. 3rd rev. ed. Jiddah: Dār al-Manārah, 1408/1988.

aṭ-Ṭabarī, Abū Jaʿfar Muḥammad b. Jarīr (224–310/839–923). *Jāmiʿ al-bayān fī tafsīr al-Qurʾān*. Būlāq: al-Maṭbaʿah al-Kubrā al-Amīriyyah, 1323–1329. 30 volumes.

Tibawi, Abdul Latif (1910–1981). "Is the Qurʾān Translatable? Early Muslim Opinion." *The Muslim World* 52 (1962), 4–16.

aṭ-Ṭūfī, Najm ad-Dīn Sulaymān b. ʿAbd al-Qawī (675–716/1276–1316). *al-Iksīr fī ʿilm al-tafsīr*. Ed. by ʿAbd al-Qādir Ḥusayn. Cairo: Maktabat al-Ādāb, 1397/1977.

ʿUmar, Aḥmad Mukhtār, and ʿAbd al-ʿĀl Sālim Makram. *Muʿjam al-qirāʾāt al-qurʾāniyyah, maʿa muqaddimah fī l-qirāʾāt wa-ashhar al-qurrāʾ*. 2nd ed. Kuwait: Maṭbūʿāt Jāmiʿat al-Kuwayt, 1408/1988. 8 vols.

[Umm Muhammad Aminah Assami (b. 1940).] *The Qurʾān: Arabic Text with Corresponding English Meanings*, revised and edited by Saheeh International, Jeddah: Abul-Qasim Publishing House, 1997.

Venuti, Lawrence. *The Translator's Invisibility: A History of Translation*. 2nd ed. reissued with a new introduction. Abingdon, UK: Routledge, 2018.

Venuti, Lawrence, ed. *The Translation Studies Reader*. 3rd ed. London: Routledge, 2012.

Voltaire (1696–1778), *Oeuvres complètes*, Vol. VII, *Dictionnaire philosophique*, Paris: L'Imprimerie de Fain, 1817.

Welch, Alford T. "The Translatability of the Qurʾān: Literary and Theological Implications of What the Qurʾān Says about Itself." In David M. Goldenberg, ed. *Translation of Scripture: Proceedings of a Conference at the Annenberg Research Institute, May 15–16, 1989*. Philadelphia: Annenberg Research Institute, 1990. Pp. 249–285.

Williams, Joseph M. (1933–2008) and Gregory G. Colomb (1951–2011). *Style: Lessons in Clarity and Grace*. 10th ed. New York: Longman, 2010.

Willis, Hulon. *A Brief Handbook of English*. New York: Harcourt, Brace, Jovanovich, Inc., 1975.

Wilson, M. Brett. "The First Translations of the Qur'an in Modern Turkey (1924–1938)." *The International Journal of Middle Eastern Studies* 41 (2009), 419–435.

Yūsuf ʿAlī, ʿAbd Allāh (1289–1373/1872–1953). *The Holy Qurʾān: Text, Translation, and Commentary*. 3rd ed. 1938. Reprint Beirut: Dār al-ʿArabiyyah, 1968.

az-Zamakhsharī, Abū al-Qāsim Jār Allāh Maḥmūd b. ʿUmar (467–538/1075–1144). *al-Kashshāf ʿan ḥaqāʾiq ghawāmiḍ at-tanzīl wa ʿuyūn al-aqāwīl fī wujūh at-taʾwīl*. 3rd ed. Beirut: Dār al-Kitāb al-ʿArabī, 1407[/1986–1987]. 4 vols.

az-Zarkashī, Abū ʿAbd Allāh Badr ad-Dīn Muḥammad b. ʿAbd Allāh b. Bahādur (745–794/1344–1392). *al-Burhān fī ʿulūm al-Qurʾān*. Ed. Muḥammad Abū al-Faḍl Ibrāhīm. 1st ed. Cairo: Dār at-Turāth (ʿĪsā al-Bābī al-Ḥalabī), 1376/1957. 4 vols.

az-Zuḥaylī, Wahbah (1350 or 1351–1436/1932–2015). *al-Fiqh al-islāmī wa-adillatuhu: al-shāmil li-l-adillah ash-sharʿiyyah wa-l-ārāʾ al-madhhabiyyah wa-ahamm an-naẓariyyāt al-fiqhiyyah wa-taḥqīq al-aḥādīth an-nabawiyyah wa-takhrījihā*, 3rd ed., Damascus: Dār al-Fikr, 1409/1989.

az-Zuḥaylī, Wahbah (1350 or 1351–1436/1932–2015). *al-Tafsīr al-munīr fī l-ʿaqīdah wa-sh-sharīʿah wa-l-manhaj*. 1st ed. Beirut: Dār al-Fikr al-Muʿāṣir, 1411/1991. 30 vols. in 15.

Index of Qur'ānic Surahs and Verses

1:1 179
1:2 176
2:2 67–68
2:5–6 130–131
2:14–15 124–127
2:23–24 9
2:83 120–122, 175, 179
2:84 62–63
2:98 79–80, 178
2:179 145–147, 176
2:222–223 139–140, 175–176
2:256 35–36
3:36 135–136
3:110 63–66
3:139 66
3:184 157
4:11 65
4:56 100–101
4:71 80
4:81 87
4:132 87
4:158 100–101
4:165 100–101
5:15 8
7:12 77
7:42 137–139, 175
7:131 106, 111, 175
7:169 117–118
8:7–8 169–171
9 (surah) 103
9:128 103
10:22 58–59, 177
10:38 9
10:64 101
11:13–14 9
11:54 116–117
11:55 116
11:81 85–86, 178
12:1 8
12:6 108–109, 179
12:45–46 166–167, 181
12:53 136–137
13:31 158–163, 165, 180
15:1 8
15:27 77
15:30 80
15:94 144–145, 180
16:7 101, 179
16:49–50 77
16:51–52 52–53, 167
16:57 134–135, 180
16:103 8
17:1 81
17:77 101
17:86–87 74–76
17:88 9
18:50 76–78, 178
18:79 153
18:109 172n34
19:24–26 169
19:88–89 55–56
21:34–35 140–142, 180
23:81–82 127–128
26 (surah) 93
26:2 8
26:131–134 128–130
26:195 8
27 (surah) 93
27:1 8
27:30 103–104, 179
28:2 8
30:30 101
31:27 171–172
32:12 154, 180
33:3 87
33:38 101
33:48 87
33:72 97–99, 101, 105, 179
34:40–41 77
35:4 157–158, 181
35:9 57–58, 177
35:43 101
36:20–21 86
36:22 56–57, 177
36:45–46 154–157, 180
36:69 8
37:64 36–38
38:41–44 167–168
38:76 77
39:22 165–166, 181
39:71 163
39:73 163

40:85	101
48:7	100–101
48:19	100–101
48:23	101
48:29	103
52:34	9
53:11–13	118–120
53:23	68–69
54 (surah)	93
55 (surah)	93
55:1–4	147–149, 180
55:7–9	88–90, 106, 178
55:15	77
55:68	80
57:10	163–164, 180–181
69:1–3	90
72:2	43–46
72:11	77
72:22	47
73:4–6	175
74:38–39	73, 178
77 (surah)	93, 104
78 (surah)	104
80 (surah)	104
81:1–4	38–39, 69
81:1–14	163
81:14	69–70
82 (surah)	104
82:1–6	163
82:13–14	115–116
83 (surah)	104–105
83:1–3	106–108
83:7–28	108
83:12	105–106, 179
83:29	127n11
83:34	127n11
84 (surah)	104
84:1–5	163
85 (surah)	104
87 (surah)	104
88 (surah)	104
91 (surah)	104
92 (surah)	104
95:4–5	149–150, 180
101:1–3	90
102:3–7	90–92
108:1–2	51, 177–178
109:2–5	92, 178
109:6	42–43
114:1–3, 5–6	90

Index of Proper Names

ʿAbbāsids 28
ʿAbd al-Qādir ad-Dihlawī, Shāh xii n14
Abdel Haleem, Muhammad A.S. ix, 32, 48n1, 50n12, 62n1
Abdul Hakim Khan, Mohammad, of Patiala 17
Abdul-Raof, Hussein 32, 34, 42n7, 49, 95
Abu'l-Fadl, Mirza 17
Abū l-Ḥusayn Isḥāq b. Ibrāhīm al-Kātib 65
Abū Mūsā, Muḥammad Muḥammad 14, 32
Abu Ẓabyān (hadith transmitter) 73
Ahmadis 17–18
Akkadian 1n1
Aleppo 7
Ali, Muhammad, of Lahore ix, 14, 16–20, 24, 26
  verses translated by 64, 68–69, 82, 99–100, 103, 112–113, 117, 119, 135–136, 156, 160–162, 165, 173
ʿAlī, Zakariyyā Saʿīd 95
Americans 8
American University in Cairo viii, xiii
Anglicans 18
Arabic language 7–8, 27
Arabic literature 11, 28
Arabs 7, 95
Arberry, Arthur J. ix, 14, 19–20, 22–26
  verses translated by 35–37, 39–40, 42–44, 46–47, 58–59, 62, 64, 67–70, 75, 79–82, 86–89, 91–93, 98–103, 106–107, 109, 112–113, 115–117, 119–122, 125–132, 134–137, 139–141, 144–148, 150, 153–154, 156–158, 160, 163–168, 170, 172, 175
Aristotle 83, 143
Asad, Muhammad ix, 14, 17, 24, 26
  verses translated by 64, 68–69, 78, 82, 99–100, 103, 112–113, 119, 129–130, 135–136, 155, 161–162, 165
ʿAskarī, Abū Hilāl al- 28, 32
Azhar, al- 18

Badawī, Aḥmad Aḥmad 32
Bayḍāwī, Nāṣir ad-Dīn Abū Saʿīd ʿAbd Allāh b. ʿUmar al- 13–14
Bell, Richard ix, 14, 19–22, 24, 26
  verses translated by 38–39, 42–44, 46–47, 51, 53–54, 56, 59, 61, 62, 64, 68, 82, 85, 88–89, 91, 98–99, 101–103, 105, 107, 109, 112–113, 116–117, 119–120, 126–128, 132, 135–136, 138–140, 145–146, 148–150, 153, 156–160, 164–165, 172–173, 175–176, 180
Berman, Antoine 2, 40n109
Bībānī, Muḥammad ʿAlī al-Basyūnī al- 30, 42n7
Bible vii, xi, 2, 15, 17, 25–26, 55, 93, 111, 120, 123, 151, 174, 177
  Amos 96
  Chronicles 123
  David 52
  Ecclesiastes 96
  Ezekiel 15
  Isaiah 15, 54–55, 95–96
  Jeremiah 15
  Jerusalem 123
  New Testament 15
  Old Testament 15, 51, 55, 63, 84, 87, 95–96, 168, 177–180
  Psalms 96
  Samuel 51, 177
  Saul 52
  Septuagint 2
  Solomon 123
  Zechariah 84, 89
Bint ash-Shāṭiʾ, ʿĀʾishah ʿAbd ar-Raḥmān 13–14, 32
Bonebakker, Seeger A. 31
Book of Mormon 15n
Boullata, Issa J. 30
British 18–19
British Empire 20
Bryn Mawr College xiii
Bukhārī, Muḥammad b. Ismāʿīl al- 63

Cachia, Pierre 31
Carlyle, Thomas 176
Chowdhury, S.Z. 49
Christians vii, xi, 2, 17, 19
Cleary, Thomas ix
Companions of the Prophet 64, 159
Cooper, James Fenimore 8

Dante Alighieri 174
Darwish, Manar xiii
Daryābādī, ʿAbdul Mājid 17
Dawood, N.J. ix, 14, 23–24, 26, 176
verses translated by 42–43, 64, 68–69, 75–77, 82, 86, 89–90, 98, 101–103, 107–108, 110, 112–113, 117–118, 122–123, 128, 134–137, 141–142, 145, 147, 149–151, 155–156, 162–164, 166, 171, 173
Ḍayf, Shawqī 32
Demetrius 44n9, 83, 143, 152
De Quincey, Thomas 176
Dihlawi, Mirza Hairat 17
Dihlawī, Shāh Walī Allāh al- xii n14
Dupriez, Bernard 79

Ebla & Eblaite 1n1
English language 8, 22–23
Europeans 21
Ezabi, Yehia al- xiii

First World War 18
Forster, E.M. 4–5

Gadamer, Hans-Georg 3
German romantics 5
Ghamrāwī, Muḥammad Aḥmad al- 18
God 9, 15, 51, 85, 97, 125
Greek xiv, 2, 11, 14, 48–49, 83, 94, 143

Ḥafṣ ʿan ʿĀṣim 12n32
Hammad, Ahmad Zaki ix
Harb, Lara 31
Hāshimī, Aḥmad b. Ibrāhīm b. Muṣṭafā al- 30, 42n7
Hebrew scriptures 2, 15, 111
Heinrichs, Wolfhart P. 31
Herder, Johann Gottfried 5
Hilali, Muhammad Taqi-ud-Din Al- 12–13
Homer 11
Ḥudhayfah b. al-Yamān 86n9

Ibn ʿAbbās, ʿAbd Allāh 73, 159
Ibn al-Athīr, Abū al-Fatḥ Ḍiyāʾ ad-Dīn Naṣr Allāh b. Muḥammad viii, 29, 31–32, 41, 42n7, 48, 54n20, 94–95, 152
Ibn al-Muʿtazz, Abū al-ʿAbbās ʿAbd Allāh b. Muḥammad 28, 32
Ibn an-Naqīb, Muhammad b. Sulaymān al-Maqdisī 29, 32, 94–95
Ibn Ḥazm, Abū Muḥammad ʿAlī b. Aḥmad 2
Ibn Kathīr, ʿImād ad-Dīn Abū al-Fidāʾ Ismāʿīl 13–14, 77n15, 138
Ibn Mālik, Badr ad-Dīn Muḥammad b. Muḥammad 29
Ibn Qutaybah, Abū Muḥammad ʿAbd Allāh b. Muslim 10, 91n14
Iliad 11
India 18
Indians 4–5
Iṣlāḥī, Amīn Aḥsan vii n2
Islam 9, 11, 24, 28

Jacobs, Roderick 9
Jāhiliyyah 16
Jenssen, Herbjørn 33, 35
Jews vii
Johns, A.H. 32
Joyce, James 176
Jurjānī, Abū Bakr ʿAbd al-Qāhir b. ʿAbd ar-Raḥmān al- xii–xiii, 16, 28–31, 35n100, 41, 118, 124–125, 130

Kamāl, Muṣṭafā "Ataturk" xii
Kaplan, Robert xii, 7, 95–96
Khalidi, Tarif ix
Khan, Muhammad Muhsin 12–13
Khaṭṭābī, Abū Sulaymān Ḥamd b. Muḥammad al- 30

Large, Duncan 2
Latin 83
Lewis, Philip E. 53n19
Longinus 48–49, 50n12, 143

Makkah 143
Makkan period 160
Maktabah al-Shāmilah, al- 127n13, 129n16
Marāghī, Muḥammad Muṣṭafā al- 18–19
Marracci, Luigi 13
Maṭlūb, Aḥmad 32
Mehren, August Ferdinand 30
Middle Ages 10
Middle East 24, 39
Mir, Mustansir 32, 49n6

Muhammad (Prophet) 52, 63, 74, 80, 81n9, 82, 93, 119, 126, 144–145, 175
Mujāhid b. Jabr 10, 66
Muslims vii, ix, xi–xii, 9–14, 17–19, 21–22, 63, 65–66, 73, 86, 101, 172n35, 175
Muʿtazilīs 10, 13, 137

an-Nābulsī, ʿAbd al-Ghanī 31
Nasr, Seyyed Hossein ix
Nizam of Hyderabad 18
North Africa 12n32
Nowaihi, Mohammed al- ix, xiii, 70n8, 72n1 & 5, 143n4, 173n39
Noy, Avigail 8n23, 31–32

Odyssey 11
Orwell, George 8
Oxford World's Classics 22, 25

Pakistan 24
Palmer, E.H. 19
Penguin Classics 23, 26, 90
Persian xii, 50n13
Pickthall, Muhammad Marmaduke ix, 13–14, 17–22, 24–26
  verses translated by 35, 37, 44, 46–47, 54–57, 63–65, 68–71, 73, 75–78, 80–82, 86–89, 92–93, 98–103, 105, 107, 109–110, 112–113, 115, 117–122, 125–127, 131–132, 135–138, 141, 145–146, 148, 154–155, 161, 164–167, 169–171, 173, 175–176
Protestants 2

Qatādah b. Diʿāmah as-Sadūsī 10, 86n9
Qazwīnī, Jalāl ad-Dīn Muḥammad b. ʿAbd ar-Raḥmān al-Khaṭīb al- viii, 30–34, 67, 83n6, 94–95, 133n1
Quintilian 44n9, 83, 133, 152
Qurʾānic characters and features
  Abraham 109
  angels 73, 77–80, 85–86, 178
  Gabriel 79–80
  God 162, 168–169
  Heaven 23
  Hell 23, 38, 91, 150
  Hūd 117
  Iblīs 77–78, 178
  Isaac 109
  Jacob, family of 108–109
  jaḥīm 38
  Jews 117
  jinn 44, 76–78, 178
  Job 168–169
  Joseph 109, 136, 167
  Joseph's brothers 108–109
  Judgement Day and Resurrection Day 23, 39, 69, 73, 93
  Khiḍr, al- 153
  Lot 85–86
  Mary and her mother 136
  Michael 79–80
  Moses 112
  Pharaoh 112, 167, 181
  Satan 77
  Sodom 85
  Zaqqūm 36
  Zulaykhā 136
Qurṭubī, Abū ʿAbd Allāh Muḥammad b. Aḥmad al- 13–14, 63, 66, 73
Quṭb, Sayyid vii n2, 32

Rafīʿ ad-Dīn ad-Dihlawī, Shāh xii n14
al-Rāfiʿī, Muṣṭafā Ṣādiq 32
Reinart, Benedikt 29
Rhetorica ad Herrenium 83, 152
Rimush of Akkad 1n1
Riyadh 12
Rodwell, J.M. 19, 21
Romans xiv, 14, 84, 94
Ross, Alexander 16
Rummānī, Abū al-Ḥasan ʿAlī b. ʿĪsā al- 28, 30, 143

Sakkākī, Abū Yaʿqūb Yūsuf b. Muḥammad as- viii, 29–31, 42n7, 67, 83n6, 127n13, 129n16, 133n1
Salama, Mohammad 31
Sale, George 13, 16
Sargon of Akkad 1n1
Saudi Arabia 12–13, 24
Schmidt, Richard xiii
Semitic languages 94
Shakespeare 46, 52, 61, 84, 93, 115–116, 126, 174, 180
Shakespearean personages
    Anthony (Mark Antony) 84
    Brutus 84
    Caesar, Julius 84

Macbeth 180
Ophelia 52
Polonius 52
Sībawayh 28
Smyth, William 31
Stewart, Devin J. 32, 125, 159
South Asia 24
South Asians 19
Steiner, George xi
Stewart, Devin J. 125, 159
Suddī, Ismāʿīl b. ʿAbd ar-Raḥmān as- 86n9
Sulaymān, Muḥammad xi n11
Sumerian 1n1
Sunnis 13, 18
Suyūṭī, Jalāl ad-Dīn ʿAbd ar-Raḥmān b. Abī Bakr as- 159
Syrians 7

Ṭabānah, Badawī 32
Ṭabarī, Abū Jaʿfar Muḥammad b. Jarīr aṭ- 10, 13, 66, 85–86
Temple University ix, xiii
Tirmidhī, Abū ʿĪsā Muḥammad ibn ʿĪsā al- 63
Ṭūfī, Najm ad-Dīn Sulaymān b. ʿAbd al-Qawī aṭ- viii, 29, 32, 41, 42n7
Turkey xii

ʿUmar b. al-Khaṭṭāb 66
Umm Muhammad Aminah Assami x n7
United Nations 24
Urdu xii

Venuti, Lawrence ix, x n6, xiii, 2, 6n13, 23, 176
Virgil 44n9
Voltaire 21
von Humboldt, Wilhelm 5

Warsh ʿan Nāfiʿ 12n32
West Africa 12n32
Willis, Hulon 133

Yūsuf ʿAlī, ʿAbd Allāh ix, 13–14, 19–20, 24–26
verses translated by 42, 46–47, 59–60, 64, 74–76, 82, 99, 104, 112–113, 135–136, 144, 146–147, 149–150, 155, 161–162, 165, 168, 173, 176, 180

Zamakhsharī, Abū al-Qāsim Jār Allāh Maḥmūd b. ʿUmar az- 13–14, 29, 53, 54n20, 55, 59–60, 65, 67, 70, 76, 77n15, 81, 85, 88, 92, 97n16, 112, 116, 131, 137–139, 147–149, 157, 169–170, 172–173
Zarkashī, Abū ʿAbd Allāh Badr ad-Dīn Muḥammad b. ʿAbd Allāh az- viii, 30, 32, 51, 55, 56n24, 94

Index of Subjects

ambiguity, textual 44–45, 57, 116, 145, 164–165, 177
antithesis 94–95, 111, 147
apostrophe 49, 174, see also *iltifāt*
appositive (*badal*) 120–121, 127–130, 171
asyndeton (lack of conjunctive, *faṣl*)) 28, 40, 114, 124–132, 141, 174, 182

balāghah 13, 27, 124
biblical language 15, 18–19, 22, 26, 52, 55, 84, 111, 123, 177, 179
brevity 8, 39–40, 79, 92, 118, 122, 143–148, 150–153, 163, 168, 171, 180–181

canonization 1–2, 29
clarity 8, 50–51, 79, 90, 109, 149, 155, 163, 166
coherence 133
colloquializing 122
concision 8, 79, 143, 152
contrasting conditional sentences 111–113, 174
coordination (*waṣl*) 28, 40, 58, 95, 110–111, 114–125, 127, 130, 132, 149, 174–175, 179, 181

directness 8, 141, 164

ellipsis (*ījāz al-ḥadhf*) 28, 40, 42, 143, 152–174, 180–182
emphasis, rhetorical (*tawkīd*) 37, 40, 44, 49, 51, 54, 58–59, 62, 67–69, 72, 78, 80–85, 87, 90–92, 96, 99–100, 104, 113, 115–116, 118, 122, 126–127, 131, 133, 141, 158, 171–174, 176, 178–179, 181
extra-rhetorical features 35–40

Hadith 10, 28, 63, 73, 77n15, 81n9
ḥaṣr 42–43, 113
ḥurūf al-muqaṭṭaʿāt, al- 2n6
hyperbaton 41, see also inversion of word order
hysteron proteron 41, 54, see also inversion of word order

ījāz (see also succinctness, ellipsis) 143, 152, 169

iʿjāz xii, 10, 30
ikhrāj al-kalāmi ʿalā khilāfi muqtaḍā ẓ-ẓāhir 62, 70
ʿilm al-badīʿ 29, 33–34, 94, 133n1
ʿilm al-bayān x, 28–29, 31, 33–34
ʿilm al-maʿānī ix–x, 28–29, 33–35, 38–39, 133n1
iltifāt 48–62, 67, 72, 124, 133–134, 140, 152, 174, 177–179, 181
indefinite nouns see *tankīr* (lack of article)
indicative in place of imperative or jussive 62–66, 121–122, 174, 181–182
inversion of word order (*taqdīm wa-taʾkhīr*) 41–47, 174
iʾtilāf 95

jinās 49
jinās ṣarfī 95

kamāl al-ittiṣāl (total semantic identity) 123

literalism 3–4, 6, 13, 19–20, 37, 42, 53, 62, 68, 74, 76, 86, 89, 100, 110, 116, 127n11, 131–132, 137, 156–157, 160, 175, 179

majāz 10, 31
muʾākhāh 95
mumāthalah 95
munāsabah 94–95
muqābalah 94–95, 111
murāʿāt an-naẓīr 95, 97
muṭābaqah (antithetical juxtaposition, also called *ṭibāq*) 94–95, 146
muwāzanah 95

naḥw 33
naẓm 28
non-consequential exception (*istithnāʾ munqaṭiʿ*) 72–79, 174, 178–179, 181

orality 15–16, 50, 52, 59, 81, 83, 85, 91, 93, 124, 133, 175–176, 179–182
oratory 79, 81, 84, 179
orientalism 5, 22

parallelism xii, 7, 34, 40, 87, 94–111, 114, 121, 129n16, 148, 174, 179, 181
parenthesis (*iʿtirāḍ*) 40, 75, 79, 87, 124, 130, 133–142, 172, 174–176, 179–182
pleonasm and redundancy (*iṭnāb*) 28, 40, 79–83, 90, 143, 174, 178–179
polyptôton 48–49
polysyndeton 120
postmodernism vii, x–xi

qirāʾāt 12n32

repetition for emphasis (*tikrār*) 81, 83–93, 171, 174, 178–179, 181

sajʿ mutawāz 95
salaf 63
ṣarfah 9
second language teaching & learning 6
subordination 58, 87, 181
succinctness (*ījāz al-qiṣar*) 28, 40, 99, 143–152, 163, 174–175, 180–181

tadhyīl 140, 143, 180
tanāsub 94–95
tankīr (lack of article) 67–71, 174, 181
tarṣīʿ 95
tashābuh 94–95
tatmīm bi-l-ityān bi-faḍlah, at- 82
tawfīq 95
textualist-literalism 3
translation
  domesticating ix, 7, 20–23, 78, 89–90, 110, 123, 131, 149–150, 156, 164, 176, 178
  English Qurʾān translation tradition 16–17
  foreignizing 22, 89–90, 134, 137, 149
  free x
  interlinear xii
  literalist 20
  literary xi
  transparent 2

ʿulamāʾ 12
ultraliteralism 2–3
understatement 52, 70, 85, 178
untranslatability 2

Western influence 9
Whorf hypothesis 5